David —

for

your

way

July '94

For Mother Meera
and Shams-i-Tabriz

The Sun of the face of Shams-ud-Din, the Glory of Tabriz,
has never shone on anything mortal without making it eternal.

—Rumi

Many divine persons are here. We are showing man a way out.
We are offering him the Divine Light, the Divine Knowledge.
We are bringing down into the consciousness of the earth the
Divine Consciousness. Now man must choose.

—Mother Meera, *Answers*

Acknowledgements

My deepest thanks to:

Chief Editor Muriel Maufroy and Assistant Editors Marianne Dresser, Kathy Glass, and Jeannie Trizzino.

The California Institute of Integral Studies and especially President Robert McDermott, for his generosity and wisdom.

Anne Teich for all her patience.

Rina Sircar for the quiet flame of her truth.

All my pupils who gave me permission.

Bokara Legendre whose kindness, vision, and hospitality made all of this possible.

Richard Grossinger who believed.

My deepest gratitude to Faustin Bray and Brian Wallace for having the courage to tape the original talks and make them available.

Contents

Preface

"Love's Glory," Rumi wrote, "is not a small thing." The lectures I gave in San Francisco at the California Institute of Integral Studies in April, May, and June 1993 were intended as a Sufi celebration in and for this time of Love's Glory, and of the wonder of the supreme mystic poet and prophet that Rumi was and is. Each lecture was a dance, a dance of mirrors, in which essential spiritual themes returned to be reflected in different constellations and harmonies, a dance around Rumi and that mystery of Love he lived and expressed so completely. Before I left my home in Paris to give the lectures in San Francisco, I had a dream in which I found myself asking an old man, sitting in a sunlit empty mosque, "How should I talk of Rumi in modern America?" He smiled and said, "Be passionate and precise, drunken and perfectly sober." I tried as hard as I knew how to honor his advice.

This book arises as its own dance out of the dance of those lectures. Naturally I have honed and shaped and added here and there, but I have fought hard to preserve the flow, the passion, the wildness, the sudden naked truth that happened last spring in Rumi's Presence and, I believe, with his blessing. Each chapter mirrors the others but dances in its own way. Read slowly, dance wildly.

May the blessing and the Presence of the Eternal Beloved inspire always all who come to this book with Love.

Love's Apocalypse, Love's Glory

One breath from the breath of the lover would be enough to
    burn away the world,
To scatter this insignificant universe like grains of sand.
The whole of the cosmos would become a Sea,
And sacred terror rubble this Sea to nothing.
No human being would remain, and no creature:
A smoke would come from heaven: there would be no more
    man or angel:
Out of this smoke, flame would suddenly flash-out across
    heaven.
That second, the sky would split apart and neither space nor
    existence remain.
Vast groans would rise up out of the breast of the universe,
    groans mingled with desolate moaning,
And fire eat up water, and water eat up fire:
The waves of the Sea of the Void would drown in their flood
    the horseman of day and night:
The sun itself fades, vanishes, before this flaming-out of the
    soul of man.
Do not ask anyone who is not intimate with the secrets
When the intimate of the secret himself cannot answer you.
Mars will lose its swagger, Jupiter burn the book of the world,
The moon will not hold its empire, its joy will be smirched
    with agony,
Mercury will shipwreck in mud, Saturn burn itself to death;
Venus, singer of heaven, play no longer her songs of joy.
The rainbow will flee, and the cup, and the wine,
There will be no more happiness or rapture, no more wound
    or cure,
Water will no longer dance with light, wind no longer sweep
    the ground,
Gardens no longer abandon themselves to laughter, April's
    clouds no longer scatter their dew.

There will be no more grief, no more consolation, no more
    "enemy" or "witness,"
No more flute or song, or lute or mode, no more high or
    low pitch.
Causes will faint away: the cupbearer will serve himself,
The soul will recite, "O my Lord most high": the heart will
    cry it out, "My Lord knows best."
Rise up! The painter of Eternity has set to work one more time
To trace miraculous figures on the crazy curtain of the world.
God has lit a fire to burn the heart of the universe,
The Sun of God has the East for a heart: the splendor of
    that East
Irradiates at all moments the son of Adam, Jesus, son of Mary.

Chapter One

The Journey to Love

WHEN THE GREAT Sufi mystic Master and poet, Jalal-ud-Din Rumi, died at sunset in Konya, southern Turkey, on December 17th, 1273, at the age of sixty-six, he had lived for almost thirty years in the radiance of enlightenment. He had composed 3,500 odes, 2,000 quatrains, a massive spiritual epic called the *Mathnawi,* and founded the Mevlevi order that, under his son Sultan Walad and his successors, was to spread the glory of his work and sacred vision throughout the whole vast extent of the Islamic world, from Tangiers to Cairo, Lahore, and Sarajevo, into the humblest, most remote villages of Afghanistan, Turkey, Iran, and India. Through all the centuries since his death and all the vicissitudes and tragedies of Moslem history, his odes have been chanted by crowds on pilgrimages and sung with the highest reverence in religious assemblies. Orientalists acknowledge Rumi as the greatest of all mystic poets, and Easterners worship his work as second in grandeur, depth, mystery, and holiness only to the *Koran.* Before World War II, there were almost 1,00,000 disciples of the Mevlevi order throughout the Balkans, Africa, and Asia. No other poet in history—not even Shakespeare or Dante—has had so exalted and comprehensive an impact on the civilization he adorned, and no other poet has aroused such ecstatic and intimate adoration.

But this vast influence is just a beginning of Rumi's gift to humankind. Not long before he left his body, Rumi wrote of his passion for his Master, Shams, and its significance:

Those tender words we said to one another
Are stored in the secret heart of heaven.
One day, like the rain they will fall and spread
And their mystery will grow green over the world.

That day has come and this greening of the world by the mystery of Rumi's love for Shams and its revelations is beginning. In the last thirty years news of Rumi's greatness has spread, not only through Islam, but through the rest of the world in scholarly works and translations, and in artistic representations of all kinds. Rumi is increasingly seen for what I believe he is—not only our supreme poet—but also an essential guide to the new mystical Renaissance that is struggling to be born against terrible odds in the rubble of our dying civilization. Rumi is a stern, gentle awakener and doctor of souls trying to help us recover the vision of the enlightened heart before it is too late and we destroy ourselves and our planet.

"My death is my wedding with eternity," Rumi wrote. From that Light he lives in beyond space and time, he is radiating to a darkened world the fire of his infinite love and hope, urging us all onward, whatever our belief or unbelief, into the miracle of our real divine nature and the feast of the divine life on earth.

I am, as many of you know, a disciple of Mother Meera. Mother Meera, as many of you also know, is an incarnation of the Divine Mother on earth working with all religions and all mystical traditions with simplicity and unconditional Love to transform humanity at this moment and to give humanity a chance in this time to find its spiritual truth again and transform the terrifying conditions that threaten us all. I am teaching Rumi because in my journey with, in, for, through, and by Mother Meera, by, through, with, and in the Divine Mother, I have found that my noblest guide and most precise inspiration has been Jalal-ud-Din Rumi. Rumi says, and it is something the Divine Mother is now saying to us all in the despair and confusion of this apocalyptic age:

"If you have lost heart in the path of love, flee to me without delay. I am a fortress invincible."

Rumi also said:

"Love's creed is separate from all religions. The creed and denomination of lovers is God."

He also said:

"My religion is to live through love."

He also said:

"If you have not been a lover, count not your life as lived; On the day of reckoning, it will not be counted."

He also said:

"Never be without love, or you will be dead. Die with love and remain alive."

He also said:

"Wherever you are and in every circumstance, try always to be a lover and a passionate lover. Once you have possessed love, you will remain a lover in the tomb, on the day of resurrection, in paradise and forever."

In Rumi we have, with Ramakrishna, Aurobindo, and Kabir, one of the very few universal beings that the world religions have produced who has possessed and lived Love in its splendor. He is someone whose realization was so complete, so multifaceted, so infinite in its depth and intensity that he goes beyond all religious denominations and definitions to show humankind the fullness of what a human being in love with and empowered by God can become.

André Malraux said that if the twenty-first century is to be, it will have to be religious. And Teilhard de Chardin, just before he died, said, "Humankind is being brought to a moment where it will have to decide between suicide and adoration."

Rumi is one of the greatest mystic poets in the world. He is also, I believe, of all the great poets and religious masters that we have, the supreme master of adoration. So, at this time, when we need to be inspired to love the world that we are in the midst of destroying, when we have forgotten our divine identity and its ecstasies and responsibilities, a guide and witness like Rumi to the glory of God and the soul and to the necessity of a religion of love that transcends all dogmas to embrace the entire creation, is beyond price.

Rumi was a Sufi, and a Sufi is something that many commentators have tried to define, but cannot. Instead, I am going to tell you three Sufi stories and follow them with extracts from Rumi's prose works and poems. Experience, feel, respond to, vibrate with what a Sufi is, the intensity, the absoluteness, the passion, the urgency, the wildness, the nakedness, the violent sweetness. You will hear the accents of a broken heart, you will hear cries for transformation, you will hear hunger for a world renewed by the Divine Light.

The first story is about a lion. There was a lion cub frolicking in the long grass when suddenly he discovered that all the lions had left. He was a small cub who didn't know much and when a flock of sheep came along, he tagged after them. And the sheep brought him up and taught him to walk, talk, snore, and *baa* like them, to chat about real estate, and pour derisive scorn on all things holy, like all the best educated sheep.

One day, another lion happened to be striding through the mountains and saw this ludicrous sight: a lion cub walking, talking, *baa*ing, sniveling like a sheep. With a great roar, the lion ran down the hillside, scattered the flock of sheep, grabbed the lion cub, dragged it to a pond, and forced it to look into the pond, saying, "Look, you are not a sheep, you are like me, you are a lion. You are a lion and you have the truth, the sincerity, the passion, and the majesty of a lion." Then the lion gave an immense, glorious roar. This terrified and excited the cub. The lion turned to the cub and said: "Now you roar." The cub's first attempts were pathetic rumblings, halfway between a *baa* and a shriek. But slowly, under the tutelage of the lion, the lion cub grew into claiming his lionhood and began over many years to learn how to roar.

Rumi is a lion of passion trying to teach a humanity of depressed sheep how to roar. To roar with freedom, with majesty, with divine tenderness, to roar with the full naked power of divine Love.

Now for the second Sufi story.

An emperor had a slave whom he loved immensely and he wanted to know if the slave really loved him. So, into a room heaped with treasures of all kinds, with jewels and deeds to vast estates, he summoned all of his slaves and said to them, "You are free. Whatever you want in this room, you can take." The slaves could hardly believe their luck. They ran about trying to cram as much of what was in the room into their pockets, and then scampered out of the room, yowling, hollering, and clapping their hands. But the slave whom the emperor loved did not move from where he was standing. When the room was empty, the slave walked quietly over to the emperor and stood by him, his eyes full of love. The emperor said to him, "What do you want?" And the slave said, "I want you. Just you." And the emperor said to the slave, "Because all you want is me, all that I possess is yours."

Rumi is the slave and hero of love who can help us, in 1993, at the end of our civilization, to find in our battered hearts the passion and faith to let all illusions go and reach for ultimate Reality. And Rumi is also the achieved mystic who tells us that if we do, then all of the glories and the powers of the Emperor of Reality will be ours. He wrote in the *Mathnawi:* "It is a burning of the heart that I want; it is this burning that is everything, more precious than the empire of the world, because it calls God secretly in the night."

The last story is told all over the world by many different traditions. Here it is in the Sufi tradition. It is really the story of all our lives.

There was a man who lived in Istanbul, a poor man. One night he dreamed vividly of a very great treasure. In a courtyard, through a door, he saw a pile of blazing jewels heaped by the side of an old man with a beard. In the dream, a voice told him an address, 3 Stassanopoulis Street, Cairo. Because he had learned enough to trust his dream visions, he went on a long, arduous journey to 3 Stassanopoulis Street in Cairo. One day, many years later, he came to that doorway, entered through it into a courtyard full of light, saw the old man from his dream sitting on the bench, went up to him, and said, "I had a dream many years ago, and in the dream I saw you sitting exactly where you are sitting now, and I saw this great heap of treasure by you. I have come to tell you my dream and to claim my treasure." The old man smiled, embraced him, and said, "How strange, I had a dream last night that under a bed in a poor house in Istanbul there was the greatest treasure I have ever seen." At that moment, the poor man saw that what he had been looking for all those years was really under his own bed, in his own heart, at the core of his own life.

Aflaki, Rumi's biographer, tells us that one day a man came to Rumi and said: "Please God that I could go to the other-world: I would at least be at peace there because the creator is there." "What do you know about where He is?" answered Rumi. "Everything in this or that world is in you: whatever you desire, work for it by yourself, for you are the microcosm."

Those three Sufi stories will give you a glimpse of what Sufism and Rumi are about. Sufism is a religion of direct love, direct inner experience. It is the mystic core of Islam, but it transcends all dogma, all hierarchy, all intellectual concepts. It is a direct way to the Heart. In Rumi's poetry we have the most glorious explosion of Sufi passion, Sufi love, and Sufi knowledge that the world has been given. Because the Divine Mother in Mother Meera is bringing down into the world a great Light of unconditional love, I have turned to Rumi to try to give to you what I have found in him, which is the inspiration to love this world unconditionally with passion and fearlessness. That fearless passion all of us need now more than ever in order to have the strength, vision, and radical confidence to endure this terrible time and to act on every front and in every dimension with enlightened love to save the planet. Rumi believed as he said in his *Discourses* that:

There is one thing in the world which must never be forgotten. If you were to forget everything else, but did not forget that, then there would be no cause to worry. Whereas if you performed and remembered and didn't forget every single thing, but forgot that one thing, then you would have done nothing whatsoever. It is just as if a king had sent you to the country to carry out a specific task. You go and perform a hundred other tasks, but if you did not perform that particular task, on account of which you had gone to the country, it is as though you had performed nothing at all. So man has come into this world for a particular task and that is his purpose. If he does not perform it, then he will have done nothing. If you say, "Even if I do not perform that task, yet so many tasks are performed by me," you were not created for those other tasks.

Rumi goes on:

It is as though you were to procure a sword of priceless Indian steel such as is to be found only in the treasures of kings and were to convert it into a butcher's knife, for cutting up putrid meat, saying "I am not letting this sword stand idle, look I am putting it to so many useful purposes." Or it is as though you were to take a golden bowl and cook turnips in it. Whereas for a single grain of that gold you could procure a hundred pots. Or it is as though you were to take a dagger of the finest temper and make of it a nail for a broken gourd, saying, "I am making good use of it. I am hanging the gourd on it. I am not letting this dagger stand idle." How lamentable, how ridiculous that would be! When the gourd can be perfectly well served by means of a wooden or iron nail whose value is a mere farthing, how does it make sense to employ for the task a dagger valued at a hundred pounds? God most high has set an infinite price on you, for he says, in the *Koran*, "God has bought from

the believers their selves and their possessions against
the gift of Paradise."

The poet says,

> You are more precious than both
> Heaven and Earth.
> What can I say more? You know not your own worth.
> Sell not yourself a little price
> Being so precious in God's eyes.

Rumi is telling us that nothing is worth anything, except
the uncovering and enacting of our divine Self. Everything else
is evasion, frivolity, self-parody, self-destruction. To know and
love our divine Selves is the only reason we are here.

The following ten poems come from a book of re-creations
I did of Rumi, called *Love's Fire:*

> What do you hope to find
> In the soul's streets
> In the bloody streets of the heart
> That have no news, even of yourself?

> Ignorant men are the soul's enemy
> Shatter the jar of smug words
> Cling for life to those who know
> Prop a mirror in water, it rusts.

> How long will we fill our pockets
> Like children with dirt and stones?
> Let the world go. Holding it
> We never know ourselves, never are airborne.

> I lost my world, my fame, my mind—
> The Sun appeared, and all the shadows ran.
> I ran after them, but vanished as I ran—
> Light ran after me and hunted me down.

Body of earth, don't talk of earth
Tell the story of pure mirrors
The Creator has given you this splendor—
Why talk of anything else?

In love with him, my soul
Lives the subtlest of passions
Lives like a gypsy—
Each day a different house
Each night under the stars.

I was once like you, 'enlightened,' 'rational,'
I too scoffed at lovers.
Now I am drunk, crazed, thin with misery—
No one's safe! Watch out!

Reason, leave now! You'll not find wisdom here!
Were you thin as a hair, there'd be no room.
The Sun is risen! In its vast dazzle
Every lamp is drowned.

Desperation, let me always know
How to welcome you—
And put in your hands the torch
To burn down the house.

You only need smell the wine
For vision to flame from each void—
Such flames from wine's aroma!
Imagine if you were the wine.

To all of those who find it hard to imagine this splendor of
awakening, the glory of the wine, Rumi writes in a letter,

And if you don't believe these words, think for a moment,
how could a drop of semen believe you if you told it

that God has created a world outside its world of darkness. A world where there is a sky, a sun, moonlight, provinces, towns, villages, gardens; where there exist creatures like kings, rich men, people in good health, bad health, blind men. No imagination or intelligence could believe this story, that there exists outside this darkness and this food of blood another world and another kind of marvelous food. Although this drop ignored and denied such a possibility, it could not help arriving at it, for it was forced outside.

And Rumi adds,

One day, you will find yourself outside this world which is similar to the maternal womb. You will leave this earth to enter, while you are yet in the body, a vast expanse, knowing that the words, "God's earth is vast," designate this region from which the saints have come.

We are all, before we begin on the mystic path, like the drop of sperm in the darkness: refusing to believe in a world of "sky and sun" simply because all we know is darkness. But the world of Rumi, of Kabir, of Ramakrishna, of St. Francis—that "vast region from which the saints have come"—that and only that is worthy of being called the real world, the world of reality. For it is the world as seen by the eyes of awakened love, by the eyes of the heart purified, impassioned, and illumined by adoration. To be born into that real world while in a body is the goal of human incarnation.

Rumi's son, Sultan Walad, wrote:

A human being must be born twice. Once from his mother, and again from his own body and his own existence. The body is like an egg, and the essence of man must become a bird in that egg through the warmth of love, and then he can escape from his body and fly in the eternal world of the soul beyond time and space.

To learn to fly in the eternal world beyond time and space and to act with the passion, joy, and wisdom of its love in this world is why we are here.

The man far from love's snare is a bird without wings. What does he know of the universe? For he knows nothing of those who know.

As long as Mary did not feel the pain of childbirth, she did not go toward the tree of blessing. "The pangs of childbirth drew her to the trunk of the palm tree." Pain took her to the tree, and the barren tree bore fruit. This body is like Mary, and each of us has a Jesus inside him. If the pain appears, our Jesus will be born. If no pain arrives, Jesus will return to Origin by the same secret way he came and we will be deprived of him and reap no joy.

Generations have passed and this is a new generation. The moon is the same, the water different. Justice is the same justice, learning the same learning, but people and nations have changed. Generation upon generation has passed, my friend, but these meanings are constant and everlasting. The water in the stream may have changed many times, but the reflection of the moon and the stars remains the same.

There are many ways to search but the object of the search is always the same. Don't you see that the roads to Mecca are all different, one coming from Byzantium, the other from Syria, others running through land or sea? The roads are different, the goal's one.... When people come there, all quarrels or differences or disputes that happened along the road are resolved. Those who shouted at each other along the road "you are wrong" or "you are an infidel" forget their differences when they come there because there, all hearts are in unison.

I have come to understand that every complete mystical life—which is really to say every complete human life—has four essential stages. Like any schema, this one has limitations but it is helpful. Rumi lived through all four stages, but before we enter Rumi's life and attempt to follow him on his journey into love, I would like to go into these stages in some detail. Having some sense of what is at stake in the full journey into love and of what has inevitably to be given and endured helps us to appreciate the depth, courage, and urgency of the inspiration Rumi continues to send us.

The first stage is childhood where each of us has an experience of clear ecstasy, a sustained, often luminous, and sometimes directly disturbing experience of union with reality. I believe if we all rediscovered our childhood, we would be aware of moments of divine grace, moments when we were aware of being the substratum of the universe, and of the universe being a magical field for our delights and our energies.

But childhood is also the source of wounds, of humiliation, of abandonment, the source of the first terrors. And around those wounds, terrors, and abandonment, and around the conventions of the culture and the expectations of our parents and of our world, stage two arises.

Stage two can be thought of as the creation of the false self, the creation of the unreal self, the self that identifies itself with biography, with duties and conventions, with the desire to succeed, with the hunger to dominate experience and dominate the world. This false self is invariably erected around the wounds of childhood as a kind of scaffold to protect them, and is also a response to the conventions of the world, to the expectations of everyone around us. So it is a hybrid, rickety, jittery, unsatisfactory structure which ignorance of any alternative keeps us wanting to prolong. Most people, unfortunately, live their entire lives in stage two as victims of this creation of their own panic and of the communal hallucination that we call society. If you are very lucky or desperate, you will be driven in stage two to search, to quest, to long for something other than the anxiety, panic, despair, and unsatisfactory joys that seem to fulfill the life and expectations of the false self. The tragedy is if you think you are happy in stage two. The tragedy of our culture is that it is a stage-two culture designed to keep people trapped there and designed to keep them exactly at the pitch of panic and desperation at which they will go on fulfilling all the false needs of the false self and dancing its death-dance of ignorance.

When you really see what our culture is, how unprecedented it is in its brutality, how unprecedented, too, in the brilliance of the weapons that it has placed in the hands of this brutality and its will to deny and destroy all possibilities of transcendence, then you realize how profound are the obstacles that prevent us from ever getting out of stage two. Nervous breakdowns, schizophrenia, outbursts of paranoia, drug addiction, and desperate love affairs are all symptoms of a hunger to escape stage two. All of these desperations and hungers are symptoms of an unacknowledged and hidden need to escape from the prison the modern world has become, this godless worldwide high-tech concentration camp of reason that we are in.

What happens, then, to take somebody from stage two into stage three? Often, a breakdown occurs. If you are lucky, that breakdown will happen early because the pain of childhood or the painful contrast between your inner self and the outer world will become so great that you'll be haunted by fears of suicide or driven to really look at all the facts of your life. The tragedy is when that does not happen, when people drift into middle age and suddenly have a midlife crisis in which they realize that they have done nothing in their lives, have written nothing meaningful, nor spoken one authentic word out of what they imagine to be their minds. This is terrifying but it is what this culture prepares for almost everybody: a good nervous breakdown when it is too late to be of use. So my best wish for you is to have your breakdown when young. It is best, I think, to squeeze it into the last days of your twenties and make it prolonged. So prolonged, in fact, that you will have to begin the search for another reality, seriously and passionately. And this will take you into stage three of this journey.

Sometimes stage three begins with a series of visions, or a series of dreams which you cannot deny because of their intensity and strangeness. It can also begin by an extraordinary meeting. If you are lucky, it is with somebody like Shams or Mother Meera or Ramana Maharshi. This is a moment of terror, shock, and ecstasy, when you know, because another human being is incarnating it in front of you, that everything you have understood about the world, about identity, about the nature of reality, is a stupid fiction of your false self. The world absolutely falls and fades away and you are shocked to the core of your being by a possibility so outrageous that no words have ever been able to describe it adequately. Even the greatest mystic poets fail to describe this possibility, which is nothing less than being a part of the Godhead itself radiating in experience. You see truth enacted in front of you in a human being who, through many signs and many powers, shows you that he or she is in a Reality which you did not even imagine. Then you enter the whirlwind of divine transformation. The agonies of the false self are small compared with the agonies of the spirit. The agonies of the false self are paltry, suburban melodramas; the agonies of the spirit are played out in the immense theater of the Divine and they mirror the struggle between good and evil in the universe, the struggle for the victory of Light in this dimension and in matter. So they have a terror, a range, a splendor, and a goal greater than anything that can be imagined until you are being whirled about in their fire.

What happens in stage three is that the false self is burnt alive. The false self is mocked, derided, lacerated, opened up by visionary ecstasy, by dreams, by unmistakable moments of shattering insight, by immense joy and immense griefs, by the sudden penetration into the heart of all the pains of the world and all the joys of the world, by becoming as you walk down the street the flower on the curb or the old woman in front of you, or the windshield of the passing car, without any mediation, without any veil. Stage three is also marked by the collapse of all the games that kept stage two going. If you are a writer, you probably fall silent. If you are an actor, you see the obscenity and the idiocy of what you are doing. If you are a professor, every dreary word which comes out of your mouth will literally look like a dead butterfly. The exposure is total. In this stage everything is taken away from the false self so that it dies. All its hiding places are unnervingly opened up and dissolved.

But while this savage and often hilarious destruction is going on, and simultaneously with it, the Divine Light comes up in the mind and knowledge is born of an unmistakable, irreducible identity with that Light that is bliss, peace, and awareness. This does not and cannot happen quickly. It happens in bursts, in swells, in trials, in spirals, and is often accompanied by other forms of breakdown, temptation, or desolation, which the searcher has to experience for himself or herself within the terms of his or her own self which is being transformed, of his or her own personality. Very few people ever get to the end of stage three. This is because stage three requires—and the word is *requires*—total surrender to the higher Path. It requires total abandon to the Beloved. It requires total faith in the divine power of the divine Master, because nothing can get you through the ordeals of stage three but that faith. You are in a completely new field about which you know nothing. It is vaster, more immense, more majestic, more terrible than anything the ego-mind can even begin to imagine. In this field of total novelty— abrasive, wild, completely foreign—you have only one recourse and that is to grasp the hand of the divine Master for absolute dear life. Unless you are holding the hand of the Beloved in abandonment and humility, you can only fall over the cliff of the mind and be shattered on the rocks below. That shattering can take dramatic forms: it can be madness, it can be real schizophrenia, it can be extreme inflation of the self, because the experiences in stage three can lead you to imagine that you have completed the entire experience, and so can identify yourself with Christ and the Buddha. The West is now full of people identifying the spiritual experiences that happen in stage three with the completion of the Path, with enlightenment. This is nonsense; these experiences in the whirling fire of stage three are just the beginning.

Very few people get to the end of stage three because very few people are prepared to suffer enough. That is the truth. Who is prepared to give up everything for the Beloved? Who is prepared to give up every area of their life including the most secret, the most deliciously pornographic, the most elaborate, the most cherished, to the unspeakably searching eye of the Divine Light? Who is prepared to try and wed every moment of their daily life, every breath they take, every thought they have to the Light? Transformation is a huge task, hugely beautiful and hugely difficult.

Stage three ends—and the mystical traditions agree on this—with the direct vision of the divine nature of Reality and the divine nature of the Self. And this is a direct vision of the Divine Light, seen normally, ordinarily, permanently, as a state of grace and nature. You know that you and the Light are one, and at any moment in which you focus or still yourself, the divine Light appears, literally. It is a white Light, it is colorless, manifesting everything. It is the Light of the Divine Mind. It is the Light of the Self, and at the end of stage three, that Light comes up forever. Nothing can ever eclipse it. This most extraordinary moment is not dramatic. It happens in a blink and suddenly you realize that you are not looking out, but looking in, and all the barriers between you and the world, you and the world and others, you and the world and others and the Light, are dissolved. This is an enlightenment experience. But it is not the end of the journey. I think it is important, at this moment in our culture, to make it clear that this illumination is not enlightenment. Stage three ends with this illumination, the coming up of the divine Light, and with it the coming up of the certainty of the divine world. But this is just the beginning of the most important stage of all. Stage four has its own subtle agonies, but fortunately at stage four something else has entered the picture and it can only be described as a massive sense of humor.

By stage four you know beyond any doubt that the person suffering is an illusion, that the false self is constantly tempting you to dance into new shapes. You know that. You can be trapped and caught and humiliated again and again by shadows and desires, but the game is so obvious, the illusion so transparent, that you start laughing even as you fall. There is a tremendous sense of humor that helps you through the various ordeals of stage four. Stage four is the integration of the divine Self with the human self, of the absolute with the relative, and that work of integration has to go down eventually into each cell of the body. So it is a work of bringing the entire human experience up to the level of the divine Light, of letting the Light come down and soak all the way through the body, heart, and mind and then letting the heart, mind, and body flower endlessly in that Light.

So the point of stage four is this huge work of integration which is generally the work of several lifetimes. We talk of the Buddha's enlightenment at thirty-six and people then imagine that the Buddha just walked around for fifty years giving extraordinary teachings. I do not believe that the enlightenment the Buddha knew at thirty-six was as complete as the enlightenment he had right at the end of his life when he entered *parinirvana*. I believe that his enlightenment experience at Bodhgaya was integrated into every form of life as he went around, and that in him a massive polyphony of enlightenment grew and gathered strength. Right until the last moment, the Buddha was traveling in enlightenment fields. A Tibetan Master once said to me, "An enlightened Master can travel more in a minute than other people can travel in 144,000 lifetimes." This is because the state of enlightenment is a state of infinite expansion, of infinite receptivity to the Light; the mind that is in the enlightenment field is exploding ceaselessly, endlessly opening up and up. The bird of gnosis, free from the prison of the false self, is free to fly on and on into the Light, into vision after vision, metamorphosis after metamorphosis.

Why I have gone into these stages in some detail is because

Rumi lived them right to the end. He lived, I believe, everything you can live and was able, within the inevitable limitations of language—limitations he knew intimately—to express, with precision and glory, all the experiences of all the stages, and gesture, again and again, into the unknowable splendor beyond them. For the last thirty years of his life, Rumi lived as an enlightened being, a constantly self-transforming divinized Master. And the work he left has the sacred power to initiate directly that can only come from someone who has not only burnt away in the fire of divine Love but become that Fire.

Rumi wrote:

"At the time of Spring, all the earth's secrets become manifest: when my spring comes my spiritual mysteries blossom forth."

This is Rumi's springtime. We are living in it—an age of apocalypse that is also an age of rebirth. And who could speak to us more inspiringly of ourselves than this poet who, more than any other, lived out apocalypse and rebirth in his own being? What the human race needs now is not more religions or dogmas, but witnesses to divine Reality and Glory, lovers of God and the world who can speak out of their love clearly and guide us into our own Fire. Rumi is a supreme witness of the Fire, and anyone who comes to his words with awe and an open longing heart will be drawn by them into the heart of Reality. As Rumi said:

> If you are seeking, seek Us with joy for we live in the
>   kingdom of joy.
> Do not give your heart to anything else
> But to the love of those who are clear joy.
> Do not stray into the neighborhood of despair
> For there are hopes: they are real, they exist
> Do not go in the direction of darkness—
> I tell you: suns exist.

Rumi was born into a distinguished family of jurists and religious scholars on September 30, 1207 in Balkh, a town in

Khorassan (now Afghanistan). His father, Baha-ud-Din Walad, called by his contemporaries the "Sultan of scholars," was a famous theologian, Sufi, and mystic whose courage, integrity, grandeur of heart, and passion for a directly spiritual rather than philosophical or dogmatic approach to God profoundly moved and inspired his son.

The epoch Rumi was born into was one of terrifying turmoil, not unlike our own. The Ottoman Empire was menaced from within and without: from within by religious decadence and rampant political corruption; from without, by the Christian Crusaders on the one hand and the savage Mongol armies of Genghis Khan on the other. This turmoil seared Rumi's life with fear and chaos very early on. At the age of twelve, in 1219, he fled Balkh with his father, who was being attacked by religious enemies and foresaw the destruction of the city by the Mongols. Baha-ud-Din was right: a year later Balkh lay in ruins.

A decade of wandering over Asia Minor and Arabia followed. Rumi and his family went on a pilgrimage to Mecca and stopped on the way at Nishapur, where the young Jalal-ud-Din met the great Persian Sufi poet Attar, who predicted "this boy will open a gate in the heart of Love." Rumi, in turn, never forgot his meeting with the author of "The Conference of the Birds" and used to say of him, "Attar has travelled through all the seven cities of Love, while I live still in the corner of a narrow street." Later in his travels Rumi went with his father to Damascus, where he met the greatest Sufi metaphysician of the age, Ibn-Arabi. It is said that when Ibn-Arabi saw Rumi walking behind his father he exclaimed, "Glory be to God, an ocean is walking behind a lake." At eighteen, Rumi married Gauher-Khatoun, the daughter of a grandee of Samarkand, and quickly fathered two children with her—Sultan Walad and Ala-ud-Din Tchelebi. After stays in Laranda and Arzanjan in Armenia, Rumi's father was invited by the Sultan of Konya, Ala-ud-Din Kaykobad, to go and live there in 1229. A college was created in Konya especially for him, and Baha-ud-Din taught there until his death two years later in 1231. Rumi found himself his father's successor at the astonishingly precocious age of twenty-four.

His spiritual and intellectual education continued smoothly, as did his rise to preeminence over his contemporaries. Tirmidhi, a pupil of his father, came to teach Rumi for nine years the essentials of Sufi philosophy and sent him again on his travels to Aleppo and Damascus, where his already formidable skills in all the various disciplines—mathematics, physics, law, astronomy, Arabic and Persian language and grammar, prosody, Koranic commentary, jurisprudence—were honed and ripened. At thirty-one Rumi returned to Konya, a brilliantly articulate, accomplished, pious, ascetic young scholar with his famous father's spiritual blessings on his head. He quickly acquired a reputation and followers. By 1244, wrote his son Sultan Walad, Rumi had "ten thousand disciples."

Everything could have conspired to keep Rumi content in this frozen, limited, but flattering role of his "false self"—the dominant example of his father, orthodox and intellectual for all his mysticism, the fear of instability that so unstable a childhood had undoubtedly bred, the rewards of easy adulation, unthreatened by radical inner hunger or external controversy. Rumi had studied Sufi philosophy, met some of the great mystic masters of his time, could lecture alluringly on the mystical path (as well as jurisprudence and Koranic studies), had accomplished several retreats, but by his later admission, he had made no fundamental spiritual breakthrough. He was in fact, at thirty-six, in the most dangerous part of stage two, the moment when he could have been so dazzled by his own gifts and fame that he would have been trapped for life by the glamour of his own reflection and by all the subtle forms of intellectual and spiritual pride that so astonishing an early success engendered. The spiritual greatness that was undoubtedly latent in him—his father, Attar, and Ibn-Arabi had all recognized it—could well have been diverted or even perverted by his own brilliance and the seduction of celebrity. The ferocity and precision of Rumi's later attacks on mental pride and the hunger of fame show how intimately he knew and understood the dangers of both.

But the great burning and shattering by Love that saved, destroyed, and transfigured Rumi was at hand. Sometime in early December 1244, Rumi met Shams-i-Tabriz, who was to change his life—and the spiritual history of the human race—by plunging Rumi into the fire of divine transformation and initiating him into the secrets of divine Love. "I was raw," Rumi wrote later, "then I was burnt: then I was cooked." Sultan Walad wrote in his *Walad-Nama* about his father: "His supreme guide on the mystical path was Shams-i-Tabriz. God consented that Shams should manifest himself to him particularly and that it should be for him alone.... Nobody else would have been worthy of such a vision.... He saw him, who cannot be seen, he heard what nobody had heard from anyone before.... He fell in love with him and was annihilated."

Rumi wrote:

> I have seen the noble king with a face of glory
> He who is the eye and the sun of heaven
> He who is the companion and healer of all beings
> He who is the soul and the universe that births souls
> He who bestows wisdom on wisdom, purity on purity
> He who is the prayer-mat of the soul of saints
> Each atom of my body cries out separately:
> "Glory be to God."

Who was this mysterious, terrifying, majestic dervish in his sixties "wrapped in coarse black felt" that Rumi met that December in 1244 and came to love as the equal of Jesus and Mohammed, inseparable from God Himself? Who was Shams, whose name means "Sun," who came from Tabriz in Iran, whose violent and vocal contempt for most of the famous living or dead Sufi masters had made him notorious all over Asia Minor, and whose presence and mystic power were so vast, so shattering, so resplendent that the greatest poet of the world spent a lifetime dazedly lost for words trying to describe both him and them? And why did this aging, lonely, scornful man, the Sun of Tabriz, known as "Parindah" (the flier) because he had spent a lifetime traveling everywhere in search of truth, come on November 29, 1244 to Konya, staying in the *caravanserai* of the sugar merchants in a miserable room, giving himself up to extreme mortifications?

Aflaki tells us, "Shams prayed to God that it might be revealed to him who the most occult of the favorites of the divine Will was, so that he might go to him and learn still more of the mysteries of Divine Love. The son of Baha-ud-Din of Balkh was designated to him as the man most in favor with God. So Shams went to Konya." Another chronicler, Daulat Shah, takes us deeper: "Shams-i-Tabriz was in search of a man. A man who could share his spiritual confidence. A man who could bear the brunt of his dynamic personality, a man who was capable of receiving and imbibing his emotional experience, a man whom he could shape, destroy, build, regenerate, and elevate. It was in search of such a man that he flitted from land to land like a bird. His master, Rukn-ud-Din Sanjabi, pointed him at last in the right direction and told him to go to Konya."

But there is a vaster truth waiting to be found in an earlier story told about Shams by Aflaki. In this story, Aflaki shows us a Shams alone and anguished, but aware too that most people find his scalding presence unbearable, and aware that he has an immense power of vision to communicate. Shams begs God, "Give me one person who can bear me, one person who is brave, strong, clear, wild enough for me to shatter and remake in such a way that through him I can give everything that I have to give to the world." "What will you give me in return?" God asks Shams, and Shams replies: "My life."

This wonderful and terrible story of Aflaki's brings us to the threshold of the mystery that was and is Shams. I have meditated on Shams' and Rumi's relationship for twenty years and I'd like to give you what I believe to have happened. It is an astonishing story if you think deeply about it. I believe Shams-i-Tabriz was a man who became divinized, who achieved total realization. When you attain that summit of realization you are beyond all normal forms of communication, all words, all concepts, all ideas are far beneath you, and what you then need is someone who can be your mouthpiece. Someone who is still human, still evolving, still developing, who you can "destroy, burn, regenerate, and elevate" by degrees and stages into the immensity that you are. Someone who you can initiate into the fire of the revelation that you are, and so, through him or her, initiate the world. Christ, the Buddha, Socrates, Ramakrishna, all wrote nothing; but they all had disciples who they drew deeply into their inmost heart and illuminated and made able by an extraordinary alchemy of divine Love to communicate their message to the world in forms in which some saving flashes of its splendor could be reflected.

For Shams, Rumi was that disciple. Shams knew how essential his vision and realization were, not only to Islam but to the world and to the survival of the world. So he was prepared—had, in fact, to be prepared (knowing, as he must have known, how much depended on his fire being transmitted)—to pay the final price, as Christ too had been prepared. "What will you give me in return?" God asked Shams. And Shams answered, "My life."

Shams' bargain with God and his final sacrifice power all the events that follow his meeting with Rumi and are the Sun that irradiates not only all of Rumi's poetry but the entire transmission through Rumi's being, work, and sacred order to the world. Shams knew that when he came to Konya he was to meet in Rumi the man who could be the heart and the mouthpiece through which the revelation that he had been graced with could blaze out not only to Islam and his own epoch but to the whole world and for the rest of human history. He knew too that when he met Rumi he would have only a brief time left to live: he had offered God his life in return for the glory and wonder of giving everything God had given him to Rumi

and through Rumi to all of humanity. God, he knew, would
enforce the bargain, because its extreme devotion and passion
were the very condition in which so transfiguring a gift could
be given.

Rumi gave up everything for Shams, but Shams had already
given up everything for Rumi, had already made the final sacrifice so that their supreme mystical love affair could be possible, so that the transmission of ecstasy and gnosis from his heart
to Rumi's heart could be as pure, lucid, and complete as possible, so the world, through the uncompromising incandescence
of that transmission could be given its deepest testimony of all
of the divine power of Love, and so that we, now, facing the
end—or the possibility of the end—of the planet could have
his and Rumi's love and its passionate ecstatic knowledge to
turn to, to help save ourselves and the world. Rumi wrote:

> From Tabriz has shone the face of Shams of Tabriz.
> Shams is the one through whom the Light enters the
> world.

Only now can we begin to see the prophetic depth of Shams'
realization and begin to comprehend the grandeur of what was
at stake in his sacrifice and the transmission it made possible.

According to one of the versions of their meeting, Rumi in
early December, 1244, was leaving his college situated in the
coffee trader market, on his way to the bazaar riding a mule.
His students were following him on foot. Suddenly Shams ran
after him, grasped the mule's bridle, and asked Rumi who was
the greatest, Bayazid (a great Sufi mystic in the tradition of Al-
Hallaj), or Mohammed? Maulana (Rumi) answered that it was
a strange question, Mohammed being the seal of the prophets.
"What is the meaning then of this," answered Shams. "The
Prophet said to God, 'I have not known Thee as I should have,'
and Bayazid said, 'Glory be to me. How high is my dignity.'"
At this moment Rumi fainted. When he recovered, he took
Shams by the hand and led him to the college on foot, where
they kept to themselves in a cell for forty days.

There are two other versions and they each represent a facet of the devastating effect Shams had on Rumi, and had to have if he were to communicate his essence to him in time. One day Maulana was sitting at home surrounded by his students and his books when Shams-ud-Din entered, saluted him, and pointing to the books, asked, "What are these?" Rumi answered, "You cannot know." He had hardly pronounced these words when fire fell on the books and they were burned. Rumi gasped, "What is that?" Shams answered, "You cannot know," and left.

Another version of the meeting says that when Shams arrived in Konya, Rumi was sitting by a fountain and had deposited his books near him. Shams asked, "What are these?" Maulana answered, "These are words. Why should you care about them?" Shams threw all the books into the water. Maulana exclaimed, "How dare you! In some of these books were important manuscripts by my father that cannot be found anywhere else." Shams plunged his hand into the water and took the books out one by one, and none of them were wet. Rumi asked, "What is your secret?" Shams answered, "*dhawq* [desire for God] and *hal* [spiritual state]. Why should you care about these?" and they embraced and left, and went into seclusion.

I believe the first version is the real one because it is the most concrete. Everything is contained in it. It has a marvelous theatrical truth. Rumi is on his mule and he is being led by his students. He is the Prince on his horse in his ego's magnificence, learning, splendor, and power. And right in the middle of the market place of Konya, an old man wrapped in coarse black felt comes up to him and asks him a question which seems crazy, a question on which the whole of the rest of his life would depend. And when Rumi answers it conventionally, Shams replies in such a way that Rumi falls off his mule. He falls off the mule of his fame, his reputation, his glamour, his power. It is as if Shams takes the great sword of mystical passion and knowledge and cuts Rumi down. To Shams' question, "Who is greater, Mohammed or Bayazid?", Rumi gave the conventional answer. What else could he do? Faced with

this madman, in the middle of the bazaar, the leading young
intellectual of Konya gives the accepted and conventional
answer: "Obviously Mohammed is the greatest of the prophets.
It is to him that the glory belongs." Then Shams fixes him with
his gaze and says, "But why did the Prophet say, 'I have not
known Thee as I should have,' and why did Bayazid say, 'Glory
be to me. How high is my dignity.'" Rumi did not answer. He
fainted. Actually he did not faint, he went into *samadhi*, he
went into wordless ecstasy. He was given a vision of truth at
that moment, of the truth that Bayazid knew of the unspeakably great dignity and glory of the soul. Everything that he
thought, everything that he had been, everything he thought
he understood was entirely and forever obliterated in that
moment of shattering power and love that Shams gave him,
which destroyed and remade him.

> The image of the Beloved suddenly lifted its head
>   from the heart
> Like the moon from the horizon, like a flower from a
>   branch
> All the world's images ran before his image, scraps of
>   iron in a magnet's grip.

And Rumi got up and wordlessly went towards Shams and
took him by the hand and held on to his hand despite the en-
mity and incomprehension of his whole world, and despite all
the extreme suffering that fidelity to his master would bring
him. He let Shams' hand lead him through all the horrors and
ordeals of the false self's death-by-fire and through labyrinths
of loss, mourning, desolation, and near madness, until the Fire
of Love had done its work, Rumi was "cooked" and complete,
and he and Shams were one in the eternal Light—one Love,
one Fire, one Force, one Sun.

Let us meditate again on Sultan Walad's description of the
meeting of Shams' triumph, this time in its complete form:

The seeker is the one who finds, for the beloved becomes the lover. My father's supreme guide on the mystical path was Shams-i-Tabriz. And God consented that Shams should manifest himself to him particularly and that it should be for him alone. Nobody else would have been worthy of such a vision. After such a long wait, Maulana saw Shams' face and the secrets became as clear to him as daylight. He saw Him who cannot be seen, he heard what nobody had ever heard from anyone before. He fell in love with him and was annihilated.

In those forty days that Shams and Rumi spent together, a massive transmission took place, a transmission from Shams' heart to Rumi's heart of the divine secrets of which Shams was master. But there are two essential stages that Rumi still had to go through. When you contemplate the next three years of Rumi's mystical education, it is almost impossible to imagine how he survived it, so great, so immense, and so painful is its intensity! But the terrifying speed, wildness, violence, and ferocity of Rumi's transformation were essential. Shams knew he had very little time and that Rumi had to be utterly and completely remade for the revelation he was destined to transmit to be potent in him.

What happened was this: Rumi's disciples got jealous of the passion that sprang up between their revered, handsome, and proud young master and this wild dervish from nowhere that he took deep into his life and with whom he spent so much time. They became jealous, and mocked and hated Shams. They treated Shams so badly that he suddenly left for the first time. Rumi went out of his mind with grief because he knew by now just how great Shams was and that Shams' mind and heart contained the secrets of the universe. He had fallen irremediably and spiritually in love. So with that first separation, Rumi nearly lost his mind. He was so beside himself with grief that he used to go down to where the camels and the caravans came in and beg everyone who came to Konya, "Have you seen Shams?

Have you seen Shams-i-Tabriz?" After months of agony, he
heard that Shams was in Damascus and he sent his second son,
Sultan Walad, to Damascus to bring Shams back.

Sultan Walad went to Damascus. He persuaded Shams to
come back and himself escorted him to Konya, walking in
front of Shams' horse for three months. Sultan Walad tells us
that when Shams and Rumi met after that long agony of separation, they ran into each other's arms and "you could not
tell the lover from the beloved."

Again Shams and Rumi went into the deepest mystical
union. They went into long ecstatic communion, they danced,
they sang, and they exchanged divine secrets, and the transmission continued with furious power. Again, the jealousy of
the disciples grew, wilder and wilder, until the moment, that
terrible moment in December 1247, when there was a knock
at the door of Rumi's house. Shams got up calmly and said,
"It is time. I am going. I am called to my death." And he went
out into the night and was never seen again.

Why did Rumi have to undergo such complex and relent-
less agony? Rumi wrote himself:

> The grapes of my body can only become wine
> After the winemaker tramples me.
> I surrender my spirit like grapes to his trampling
> So my inmost heart can blaze and dance with joy.
> Although the grapes go on weeping blood and sobbing
> "I cannot bear any more anguish, any more cruelty"
> The trampler stuffs cotton in his ears: "I am not
>   working in ignorance
> You can deny me if you want, you have every excuse,
> But it is I who am the Master of this Work.
> And when through my Passion you reach Perfection,
> You will never be done praising my name."

Rumi had to be shattered by Love to become Love itself,
emptied and broken to be filled and remade, burnt away for
the Fire to come and live in him *as* him and use his being as Its

mask in time. There was a divine purpose to each stage of Rumi's suffering. The first separation from Shams, at a time when their ecstatic union seemed unbreakable, plunged Rumi into the most extreme imaginable longing for Shams, in which every cell of his heart, mind, and soul became a dark wound and womb of absence that yearned for the glory of Shams' presence of Light. So when Shams returned, an even deeper, wilder, more total transmission of his Light-Being could be poured into a Rumi hollowed and seared clean by savage longing.

But even this was not the final stage of the "winemaker's trampling." One last stripping, one last death, one last baptism in dereliction was necessary before Rumi could achieve complete union with Shams and the eternal Beloved wearing Shams' face and streaming through Shams' eyes Its Light of revelation. There was a great danger that had still to be overcome—the danger that Shams, while he remained in the body, would be for Rumi a veil, even if a blazing and almost completely transparent one, between him and the Light itself. Shams' love and the majesty of his realization had taken Rumi stage by stage, vision by vision, empowerment by empowerment, to the final threshold of enlightenment. Now all that remained between Rumi and the total divine vision, the Glory, was Shams himself, or rather Rumi's holy passion for Shams. That final veil had to be burnt away. Shams himself had to disappear in the body, the physical presence of Shams had to be withdrawn from Rumi so that Shams in his essence could be reborn in final splendor in the heart of Rumi's heart and Divine Love announce its victory over space and time.

When Shams disappeared that last time, probably murdered and likely by Rumi's own eldest son, Rumi lost his mind again. He was inconsolable for months. Weeping, singing, and dancing in the streets, he went mad with grief. The last traces of his false self, of any self-concern, of any hunger for some unconscious corner of separation from Shams, were dissolved in the acid of atrocious pain. But then, very slowly, very subtly, the miracle became clear to him that Shams had only died

to be reborn in the depth of his own being, and that the fire
of his agony had finally fused him with his Beloved, beyond
space and time, and transformed all of him into the glory of
divine gold. With that ecstatic certainty, Rumi dissolved into
the Deathless.

Sultan Walad reports his father saying at this time of Shams:

> Although we are far from him in the flesh—without
> body or soul, we are both one and the same Light. You
> can see him, if you want, or you can see me. I am him,
> he is me, O seeker! Why do I say me or him when he is
> myself and I am he? All is him and I am contained in
> him.... As I am he, what am I looking for? I am him
> now and I am speaking of myself.

Let us now share a few of the extraordinary poems that
came from that triumphant fusion, beyond space and time,
that soul-lovemaking into final divine truth.

No poetry that the world has been given has this range of
passion, agony, and radiance. Rumi lived the entire terrible
and glorious story of the human journey into divine Being,
and every word he gave us has the scar of the divine Fire on
it. Every poem is that Fire speaking to us of Itself with the
fiercest possible urgency, clarity, and wild vision.

> Seizing my life in your hands, you thrashed me clean
> On the savage rocks of eternal mind.
> How its colors bled, until they grew white!
> You smile and sit back: I dry in your sun.

> The Sea boils with passion for you
> The clouds pour pearls at your feet
> A lightning from your love has pierced the earth
> This smoke curling to heaven is its child.

> We were green: we ripened and grew golden
> The Sea terrified us: we learned how to drown.
> Squat and earthbound, we unfolded huge wings.
> We started sober: are love's startled drunkards.

You hide in your cloak of nothingness
Reflect ghost in your glass of being
I am nothing, yet appear: transparent dream
Where your eternity briefly trembles.

This love sacrifices all souls, however wise, however
    "awakened"
Cuts off their heads without a sword, hangs them
    without a scaffold.
We are the guests of the one who devours his guests
The friends of the one who slaughters his friends....
Although by his gaze he brings death to so many lovers
Let yourself be killed by him: is he not the water of life?
Never, ever, grow bitter: he is the friend and kills gently.
Keep your heart noble, for this most noble love
Kills only kings near God and men free from passion.
We are like the night, earth's shadow.
He is the Sun: He splits open the night with a sword
    soaked in dawn....

The man to whom is unveiled the mystery of Love
Exists no longer, but vanishes into love.
Place before the Sun a burning candle
And watch its brilliance disappear before that blaze,
The candle exists no longer, it is transformed into Light,
There are no more signs of it, it itself becomes sign....

You are my soul, my universe: what do I have to do
    with the soul and the universe?
For me you are ever-flowing treasure: what do I have
    to do with profit or loss?
One minute, I am the friend of the wine, another the
    friend of him who burns me.
I have come to this age of ruins, so what do I have to
    do with time's melodrama?
I am terrified by the whole world, I am sprung free of
    the whole world,

I am neither "hidden" nor "apparent." What do I
   have to do with existence or space?
I am drunk on union with you, I need and want and
   care about no one else.
Since I am your prey, what do I care about fate's bow
   and its arrows?
I live at the bottom of the stream, why would I go
   looking for water?
What could or would I say about this stream that
   flows and flows?
I have given up existence, why go on staggering under
   the burden of this mountain?
Since the wolf is my shepherd, why put up with the
   pretensions of the shepherd?
What abandon! What drunkenness! You hold the cup
   in your hand
Blessed is the place you are, and glorious to the eye of
   the heart.
Each atom, by your grace, is a universe, each drop of
   water a soul.
No one who has ever had a sign from you need worry
   again about "name" or "sign"
To find the place of splendor, at the bottom of the Sea
   of truths
You have to dive, dive head first: what do I have to do
   with feet that scurry?
With the sword of the One God you have hacked a
   Path for us:
You have stolen all my clothes: What will I give to the
   toll-man?
From your beauty ablaze like the sun, from the curls
   of your hair,
My heart has become ecstatic: O my soul, hand me
   this brimming cup,
Do not weigh pain and misery, contemplate love,
   contemplate friendship:

Do not mull over tyranny and neglect: think of all
    those who have their eyes fixed on you.
Surname all grief "grace": transmute pain and
    anguish into joy
And ask from joy all happiness, all security, all peace.
Demand that security, that peace, demand them,
Choose the company of those withdrawn in love
Listen to those who open a path to you: listen, and
    don't say a word.

Glorious is the moment we sit in the palace, you and I
Two forms, two faces, but a single soul, you and I
The flowers will blaze and bird cries shower us with
    immortality
The moment we enter the garden, you and I
All the stars of heaven will run out to gaze at us
As we burn as the full moon itself, you and I
The fire-winged birds of heaven will rage with envy
In that place we laugh ecstatically, you and I
What a miracle, you and I, entwined in the same nest
While I am here in Konya, and you are in Khorassan
What a miracle, you and I, one love, one lover, one Fire
In this world and the next, in an ecstasy without end.

Let us look finally at perhaps the most beautiful of all poems
that Rumi wrote to Shams:

Suddenly, in the sky at dawn, a moon appeared,
Descended from the sky
Turned its burning gaze on me,
Like a hawk during the hunt seizing a bird,
Grabbed me and flew with me high into heaven.
When I looked at myself, I could not see myself
For in this moon, my body, by grace, had become soul.
And when I traveled in this soul, I saw nothing but moon,
Until the mystery of eternal theophany lay open to me.
All the nine heavenly spheres were drowned in this moon.

The skiff of my being drowned, dissolved, entirely, in
    that Sea.
Then, that Sea broke up into waves, Intelligence
    danced back,
And launched its song,
And the Sea covered over with foam,
And from each bubble of foam something sprang,
    clothed in form.
Something sprang from each light-bubble, clothed in a
    body.
Then each bubble of body-foam received a sign from
    the Sea,
Melted immediately and followed the flow of its waves.
Without the saving, redeeming help of my Lord,
Shams-ul-Haqq of Tabriz,
No one can contemplate the moon, no one can
    become the Sea.

The moon, the Light of gnosis, of direct ecstatic vision,
descended at dawn like a hawk, seized Rumi, and flew with
him into the highest reaches of consciousness. There Rumi
became one with the soul and was initiated into its ultimate
secret, for when he traveled in soul, beyond all concepts, beyond
time and space, he saw nothing but moon, the Divine Light
Itself. Everything—he, Shams, the entire creation, the soul—
were all One. And so Rumi experienced, as he tells us, the mystery which can never be expressed but which can be lived, the
mystery of the eternal theophany, the endless Fire-dance of
God in and as creation.

Rumi saw and knew that everything that happens and all
things that exist are nothing but the Divine blazing in its own
Beauty and Love for Itself. And as he knew and saw this, his
own being dissolved in bliss into the Sea of Light. Annihilation prepared another even more more profound revelation;
Rumi then saw the Sea break up into waves and all creation
arise magically from an ecstatic foaming of the divine Light-

Sea. So the full vision of what the cosmos is, and of how, at all moments, all manifested and separate things are secretly one with their source of Light—and so with each other—was given to Rumi. Through the saving and redeeming grace of his divine Master, Shams-i-Tabriz, Rumi had become, at last, the eye of Love itself, looking out in Love, at Love growing, dancing, and flowing in the Light of Love in all things.

> Love is an infinite Sea whose skies are a bubble of foam.
> Know that it is the waves of Love that turn the wheels
> of Heaven:
> Without Love, nothing in the world would have life.
> How is an inorganic thing transformed into a plant?
> How are plants sacrificed to become rich with spirit?
> How is spirit sacrificed to become Breath,
> One scent of which is potent enough to make Mary
> pregnant?
> Every single atom is drunk on this Perfection and runs
> towards It
> And what does this running secretly say but "Glory
> be to God."

Chapter Two

The Price of Adoration

AT THE CENTER of the Western mind, at this moment, the birth
is taking place of an extraordinary new openness, an extraordinary new curiosity, a willingness to take the great mystics
on their own terms, to see them as the true geniuses, the true
heroes, and the real guides of mankind. This moment is also
a sacred moment in the history of Rumi's mission to the human
race, a moment of insemination, a moment when he and the
Light that he is are entering the human consciousness to make
it pregnant with love. It is extremely important that we all realize in exactly what moment we are listening to Rumi, at what
time of history and with what responsibility.

Just recently, I opened the paper and saw that the United
Nations had put out a report about the situation of the rainforest. The report mourns the fact that for over ten years the
human race has had at its disposal information that reveals
quite clearly the devastation being done to the forest and the
consequences of that devastation. The horror goes on; this
year an area greater than the size of Oklahoma will be destroyed. In thirty-six years there will be no rainforests at all.
No one has any real idea what such an incalculable loss might
mean, but the consequence of it can only be devastating and
perhaps lethal. So I think that if you are really to listen to
what is being attempted to be given to you, both through me
and beyond me by Rumi, you must come to a savage moment
of recognition and an extreme moment of understanding: you

must see and know that the world, as we know it, is ending, that the whole of our civilization is crumbling around us, and that humanity has very little time to make up its communal mind about whether it wants to survive or not. What more indications do we need of a massive and unprecedented crisis than the ones which have been given to us in the last seventy years? The creation of a bomb designed to destroy human beings in unprecedented numbers. The rape and exploitation of the environment even after the facts of that rape and exploitation have come through. The horrible rubbling of the psyche by a mass media pledged to triviality, obscenity, and pornography. The destruction is triple: it is going on in the natural world, in the emotional world, and in the spiritual world. All these worlds that make up our human identity are being threatened with annihilation and we are conspiring with that annihilation.

A deadly cocktail of apathy, fear, paralysis, and self-loathing drugs nearly all of us. How powerful this cocktail is, how easily it makes us ignore the facts, how easily it lulls us into a completely illusory sense of security, and how easily it gives us the sense that we understand and are doing something, when in fact what we need to understand is that we are in an unprecedented crisis, have very little time and are doing fantastically little about it, are in fact being suicidally passive. Why then teach Rumi? Why then listen to Rumi? The core of our problem as human beings is that we are in a massive psychic depression. This depression is everywhere and it eats away at every resolve we take, at every passion, and every attempt at health. It is a massive worldwide depression and its cause is a fundamental loss of our identity, our memory of our Divine origin. That depression is the cause of the killing all around us of all those sources of wisdom that give us the truth about our nature and our place in the world. It is not by chance that a civilization that has done what we have done to the earth has also tried to extinguish all the native voices, all the wise voices of the world, the voices of the Amerindians, the Aborigines, the great Tibetan Masters, all those voices that had kept alive in their wonder a sense of our Divine origin. What would a psychotic do but try and kill all of those people in the room that remind him or her of his true nature and his true origin? That is what we as a species are doing and that is what we have been doing quite systematically and with appalling brutality for many decades.

So I ask the question: Why listen to Rumi? I suggest that it is to hear news about your real Self. I suggest that your heart is hungry to hear news about your true identity, about your Divine origin, about the splendor and glory of that origin, and about the splendor and glory of the world as revealed in the eye of the heart, in the sight of the true and awakened heart. And I suggest that behind that hunger is a desperate need to be filled with a food that our culture has been denying us and to come to spiritual recognition and understanding, at a moment where that recognition and that understanding are crucial for the survival of the world.

Crucial for the survival of the world: because the only way to cure this horrific psychic agony that is freezing, paralyzing, and destroying everyone in various ways on the earth is to awaken everyone, to give everyone this sense of what he or she really is, to bring back into the heart of the human race the glory of our Divine origin and the glory of the visionary truth that those who have lived in that origin, and who have become that origin, know to be real. And this is not a question of curiosity, a case of being delighted and enraptured by a great mystic or extraordinary poetry. It is a question of life and death, of survival. If we don't open to this testimony of our Divine origin and of the divinity of the earth, and of our secret interconnectedness with all things now, if we don't go on a journey to transform ourselves in the light of that knowledge, and if we don't succeed in transforming ourselves to an unprecedented extent to allow the Divine to act through us, there will be no human race, no habitable world. So on listening to Rumi and witnesses like him depends the future.

How long will you move backward? Come forward; do
not stray in unbelief, come dancing to religion. Look,
the elixir is hidden in the poison, come to the poison and
come, return to the root of the root of your own self.

You may think that you are earthly beings but you have
been kneaded from the substance of certainty. You are
the guardians of God's Light, so come, return to the root
of the root of your own self.

Once you have tied yourself to selflessness, you will be
delivered from selfhood and released from the ties of a
hundred snares. So come, return to the root of the root
of your own self.

You were born vice regent of the children of God but
you have lowered your eyes to this sad world, alas, how
can you be happy with these scraps? So come, return to
the root of the root of your own self.

Though you are the talisman protecting the world's treasure, within yourself you are the mine. Open your hidden eyes and come, return to the root of the root of your
own self.

You were born of the rays of God's majesty and have
gained the good fortune of your auspicious star, so how
long will you suffer at the hands of non-existent things?
Come, return to the root of the root of your own self.

You are a ruby in the heart of granite, how long will
you try to deceive us? We can see the truth in your eyes,
so come, come, return to the root of the root of your
own self . . .

The King is here, Shams-i-Tabriz has placed before you
the cup of eternity. Glory, glory be to God! What marvelous pure wine! So come, drink with me, drink now,
return to the root of the root of your own self.

—Rumi, from the *Diwan*

These words spoken by Rumi in the middle of the thirteenth century were words that he knew would carry down the centuries and keep alive their eternally fresh message of our eternal identity, to be spoken at a time in history when they could be heard and in which their necessity was clearer than ever. Don't think it is in any way strange that these poets, and this man in particular, are coming back into our hearts now, because they are the supreme guides to the transformation by love which we must all go through now if we are to save the planet.

How will we save the planet? Only by awakening to who we are. And how will we act when we awaken to who we are? We shall act with Divine love, with Divine passion, with Divine power, with Divine truth, and that Action, because it will have upon it the seal of the Beloved, because it will be springing out of the will of the Beloved, will give us the solutions that cannot be obtained in ordinary consciousness, that cannot be even understood, glimpsed, aimed at, or even sketched, while we remain in the prison house of the ego.

So this journey that gives Rumi the right to speak with that ecstasy, authenticity, and knowledge is not a journey taken by a mystic in the thirteenth century; it is the central human journey that we, now, at this particular terrifying historical moment, are called upon to take. We are all of us at this moment in history called upon to give up everything we think we are, everything we think we know, all our pitiful, small, vain games and identities, to take the journey in the presence of the Divine to the presence of the Divine so that the Divine can act through us, help us to help ourselves and save the planet.

> You are the guardians of God's light ...
> You are the talisman
> You were born of the rays of God's majesty.

Rumi is an initiatory poet. He is initiating anyone who can hear to the deepest truth of their own being, he is hungry to fill you with *shakti,* the Divine force, the wildness and ecstasy and madness of the Divine passion. He can fling before us his rubies and pearls and diamonds, he can speak of the highest truth, he can fashion works of consummate, outrageous beauty, but nothing can happen if we are not receptive. Nothing can happen; the words cannot engender the Divine children that they are meant to if we do not allow ourselves, all of ourselves, to be a womb. Every cell in the body, mind, and heart must become a womb to receive the Divine Light of the truth so that the truth can start its wild sweet work of change. And every cell must be open now, this moment, for as Rumi says of his own poetry, "My poetry is like Egyptian bread. Night passes and you cannot eat it"—for come tomorrow, come the next moment, it will be stale. You have to enter into the nakedness of the instant where it is born and you have to meet it like a child runs to his mother with ecstasy. You have to meet it now, in the core of the moment, in the core of the transmission. Otherwise, nothing can happen.

> My poetry is like Egyptian bread.
> Night passes and you cannot eat it.
> Eat it, eat it while it is fresh, before the dust settles.

Rumi knows how easily the dust settles. We hear these words, but we know that as soon as we go out into the darkness, grief, fear, and anxiety of our false selves and our world, the dust settles again. So it is even more important when the truths of the Divine Love are uttered to remain in a state of total receptivity so that we can be penetrated right to a core which can never, ever, close again, that we can be wounded by the Divine Beauty with such a deep gash that nothing can ever heal that gash except the hand of the Beloved.

This is what Rumi is saying: "Lay yourself on the slab of openness and wait for the knife of my beauty to gash you so deep with the Beloved's radiance that you can never recover. Because if you recover, you are in danger. If you recover, you are part of the disaster that is destroying the world. If you recover, you, yourself, might as well be running into those rainforests and sawing them down."

In every poem, every story, every line of every poem and story, Rumi is saying to us, tenderly or majestically, quietly or railingly or wittily: "Never, ever recover or even want to from the wound of Divine Love, of Divine Longing, so you will come to long with your whole being to participate now in the vast transformation that destiny is demanding of the human race." Rumi is a madman, and he is trying to do nothing less than send the human race mad with Divine Love.

> My poetry is like Egyptian bread.
> Night passes and you cannot eat it.
> Eat it while it is fresh, before the dust settles.
> Its place is in the tropics of awareness.
> It dies in this world because of the cold.

Rumi wants to destroy and annihilate the ego so that you can all be placed in the Divine Light and in the Divine experience, and he is saying, "Its place, the place of my work, is in the tropics, the tropics of awareness, the heat of love, the heat of ecstasy, the heat of passion, somewhere wildly fertile and fecund, the depth of the heart, the open heart." How will we understand a word of what this man is attempting to give to us if we do not, all of us, open the tropics of awareness within us? That is, open our entire being to everything that we have ever known of ecstasy and of joy. Coalesce, condense, transmute everything, every ecstasy that you have ever had, sexual, emotional, musical, looking at a sunset, looking at the sea. Condense them, meditate on them, draw them deep into your heart, and at that moment, when the heart is filled with bliss, then read Rumi's poetry. Read it by the light of that bliss. And then his poetry will take us even further into that bliss, even deeper into that joy, even more insanely and purely into the heart of our own pure sanity.

> Eat is while it is fresh, before the dust settles.
> Its place is in the tropics of awareness.
> It dies in this world because of the cold.

This world is cold, our hearts are cold, our minds are cold, and what Rumi is attempting to do, what he is doing in language, is bringing down the subtlety, the flash and the fire, the heat and the ecstasy of the Divine consciousness that surrounds us, that bubbles up underneath everything, but which the coldness of our ego, the coldness of our mind, the coldness of our heart, prevents us from reaching or tasting at every moment. So he is saying, "Don't grow cold, you can't hear me if you grow cold, I am trying to give you everything, I can give you everything, but you have to open, you have to become a womb."

Poetry like Rumi's demands of us what listening to Maria Callas, for example, demands. Rumi is absolutely awake, and awakening has a very fierce edge, the edge of the sword of discrimination, the sword of ecstasy; it has a fire in it, and you have to consent when you listen to and read Rumi to be sliced by that sword and invaded by that fire. You have to know where the sword is coming from, who is speaking to you, and you have to consent to the lovemaking with his spirit that his spirit is really demanding of you, just as Callas' voice is really demanding that you listen because the truths that she is burning her voice away to tell are truths that can save an entire civilization. What Callas is doing when she sings is pleading for love against patriarchal madness. That voice is always there, burning away, begging love to win in a world which is being ruined by a crazy, masculine hardness and deadness of heart. Every time Callas was on stage she wanted what can happen in a Rumi poem to happen, she wanted incineration to happen; she did not mind burning herself away if you could catch flame also. She knew that if you could catch flame in just a part of your heart when you listened to her, your whole being would be shifted, just as Rumi knows that if you can listen in your life to one half of one verse that he has written, your entire life can change. When Rumi is asking you to listen "in the tropics of awareness," he is asking you to let him give you, from within yourself, an experience of illumination. He knows he can give it, he knows that you can receive it, and he knows that his poetry is a vehicle for transformation. But for that transformation to happen, there has to be nakedness and freshness, and to be naked and fresh is always hard. We think we want the experience of a Rumi poem but half-unconsciously we know that if we do expose ourselves to it, to him, we will be burnt by passion, seared by awareness, and have to change everything. And so we all find ourselves constantly and subtly tempted to "admire" this poetry, keep it at a safe psychic distance by "marveling" at it, or "explaining" or even "adoring" it. Rumi knew this fear of illumination in himself and so in us and this is why he wrote: "Like a fish my poetry flops on the ground, a moment later it is lifeless. If you can eat it, imagining it to be flesh, you have to paint many fantastic images: You will, O man, devour your own imagination, not these ancient words." This is subtle, angry, and brilliant: Rumi is telling us that unless we are totally exposed, "naked and fresh" to the truth he is trying to transmit, we will just be trapped in "imagination," a delicious but vapid labyrinth of "fantastic images." What Rumi is trying to do, as Callas is trying to do, is to destroy us with love and passion so another, far nobler self can rise phoenix-like from the ashes. And for this to be possible, he knows we have to be willing to die in that way, or what is real in what he is saying is being betrayed.

In the *Discourses*, Rumi says of the disciples of a certain sheik, "These were not concerned with the other world at all, they had fixed their heart upon this world entirely; some had come for the sake of eating bread and some to inspect the bread." This very harsh statement of Rumi's forces us to ask ourselves: Why do we go to teachers? Why do we go to something which is inspiring? Sometimes it is because we want to appropriate what is being held out for our own fantasy of mastery, for our own fantasy of spiritual domination, and Rumi is saying that this is one of the subtlest and most extreme dangers. Rumi is implying: If you want to understand my poetry, stay in the position of a lover, stay in the position of a humble person seeking the truth. Don't claim this poetry as your

own, because it may take you many years of profound anguish
and searching really to understand what this poetry is and
really to be able to quote it as your own. Be humble before the
majesty of illumination. "These words are like a beautiful
bride." He is saying the words that I am speaking to you are
like the most beautiful of women; and he adds, "If a beautiful woman is purchased to sell again, how can that woman
love her purchaser or fix her heart on him? Since the pleasure
of that merchant is in selling, he is as good as impotent. He
buys the girl to sell her, not having the manhood and virility
to purchase her for himself." That again is a very harsh, very
powerful statement. Rumi is saying, if you hear something that
inspires you in what I am saying, realize that it comes from a
state of passion and surrender, and realize that to understand
it completely, you will have to enter into that passion and that
surrender. You will have to purchase the bride for yourself,
you will have to win her as I won her—with tears, with suffering, and pride in my Divine Self, with endless prayer, joy,
and continual surrender. Because if you are taking these perceptions and using them as your own before they are really
yours, you are damning yourself, you are locking yourself in
an egocentric prison, and you are preventing the alchemical
magic from taking place. And he goes on, and this is directed
really to the heart of the modern fascination with mysticism
which can so easily turn into an aping of mystic awareness
rather than a surrender to the process that makes mysticism
possible. He says,

> If a fine Indian sword falls into the hand of a hermaph-
> rodite, he takes it in order to sell it. If a pahlavi bow
> falls into his hands, that is also in order to sell it since
> he has not the strength of arm to draw it himself. He
> desires the bow for the string's sake and he has not the
> aptitude for the string, and when the hermaphrodite
> sells the bow, he gives the price of that for rouge and
> indigo. What else would he do?

Rumi is savagely scornful of the way in which people misappropriate the high spiritual truths that he is trying to partake, use them for their own advancement, sell them to be counted masters or whatever, so they can be praised. This is the very worst thing that you can do with spiritual revelation and he is really warning us all against that.

And then Rumi gives a further warning, the most difficult warning that we are ever given, and it is suitably stated in terms of a paradox. "Beware, do not say I have understood. The more you have understood and grasped them, the further you will be from understanding them." The understanding of this is not an understanding, not a mental or emotional game, nor a game even of the highest spiritual intelligence. It is a game played out for the Beloved by the entire being in absolute, fiery, naked simplicity and sincerity. Anything less is trivial. Rumi is saying, "Don't think you understand, there is no understanding, there is jumping into the fire, there is stripping for the Beloved, there is a cry of joy, a wild act of lovemaking with the Divine Spirit, but don't call that understanding, don't try to wrap it around into a formula; that won't help you, that will prevent you from being helped." He is saying, if anything is happening, it is happening outside anything that you could now call your understanding, and if you think that you are understanding, you are missing the point, you are not submitting to the experience. He is saying: "Don't understand. Be led from joy to joy to joy. Allow yourself to be filled by the ecstasy and glory of the Presence again and again. And never claim what little perception comes to you when you are filled with the glory of the Presence because those perceptions turn into prisons that keep you a slave."

Do you begin to see how serious these injunctions are and why he is giving them? What Rumi is trying to do is to prepare us for the moment where we could receive what he has spent an entire lifetime, many lifetimes probably, suffering and working to give the human race. "All your trouble," he is saying, "all your misfortunes and disappointments arise from that

understanding." He is saying, "If you want the transformation
in God, surrender and you will be given all the information
necessary and all the insights in their right time, but there can
never be complete understanding. That desire to understand
is the ego's desire to control; to imperialize the highest kind of
knowledge for its own ends. That desire to understand is the
ego's desperate attempt to pretend that it is doing the initiation, that it is initiating itself, and if it succeeds in making you
believe that, you are trapped—far more trapped, in fact, thinking that you *know* than knowing that you don't know." Many
seekers on the Path really think they know the Divine Truth
and it is just this concept that traps them and stifles their
growth. That is the danger of the Western mind approaching
these truths. It is a danger we all go through and suffer from.
Rumi is begging us not to pretend to understand.

I have been reading and re-reading the *Koran*. What has
struck me most profoundly is how grand and majestic the
Koranic view of God is. God is always transcending any concept that we can have of him, God always goes beyond anything that Mohammed can say of him, God is always talked
about in terms of the most total respect, of the most total
beauty and splendor. And this is behind the vision of the Divine
Majesty and the Divine Glory that permeates and saturates
Rumi's poetry, as it permeates and saturates the glorious music
that has come out of Islam, the vision of Ibn-Arabi, the genius
of the architecture of Edirne, Granada, Agra, and Medina.
This sense of the ineffable majesty, unknowable glory, infinite
intensity, and splendor of the Divine blazes in every phrase of
the *Koran*. And the word that the Sufis give to this infinite
splendor, this glory, is a word that comes up thousands of times
in Rumi's poetry. It is the clue to his experience, to his abject
and rapturous humility before the experience. It is the clue to
his transmission to us, and the clue to the power of the transmission. The word is *Kibriya*. This word means Divine Glory,
Divine Grandeur. As Gerard Manley Hopkins wrote: "God's
grandeur will flame out like shining from shook foil." Rumi is

not teaching you that you, too, can be God. Rumi is not saying that the final state can be attained without much difficulty. He is saying that the ultimate knowledge is a knowledge of *Kibriya*, of the Divine Glory manifesting in everything as everything. And before that knowledge, one is just heart-struck, washed away with wonder, with awe, with rapture, with mad joy. You see all sorts of people claiming that they have had an enlightenment experience. They all look so depressed. If they had the experience of *Kibriya*, they would be leaping out of their skin, they would be howling with joy, embracing, sobbing, dancing. It is a very extreme experience and it destroys the ego's fantasies of its own identity. One experience of *Kibriya* is an experience that reaches down to the very source of one's own pride, because once you have, even for a second, glimpsed what Rumi and the Sufi mystics are talking to us about, the Divine Glory, how could you even imagine that you exist in the face of the glory of that eternal existence? You know that you don't exist, you are wiped out, only That is. I want to stress how essential this vision of the Divine Glory and adoration of the Divine Glory are for us at this point in time. We have to learn how to adore God, adore God in ourselves, in the rapture that rises in the heart when we think of the Divine, when we experience the Divine. We have to adore God in everything that surrounds us, in the beings with whom we are privileged to share this astonishing theater of enlightenment, to adore God in the dew in the grass, the birds, the forests, the smell of the sea, in everything that is arriving to us because everything that is arriving to us is nothing other than the scent of *Kibriya*, the perfume of *Kibriya*. Only adoration can open us up sufficiently to the kind of ecstatic love that we need now to be able to surrender as much as we will need to surrender, to have this transformation as fast as it needs to happen, to work as hard as we will have to work for this transformation to happen, and to suffer as much as we will all have to suffer, privately and publicly, for this transformation to do its work in the world. Only adoration can give us the strength.

What is adoration? Adoration is letting the hand of the Divine reach out to us with a cup of mystic wine, and say drink, and be drunk, so that you won't mind that you are bleeding, you won't mind that you are sobbing, you won't mind that you are dying. Adoration is letting the wine make you drunk with the lucid bliss of mystic knowledge, and with that lucid bliss you will work tirelessly, you will suffer tirelessly, you will open again and again to the power that is trying to save the world through you, through all of us at this very late moment.

Rumi is the supreme Master of this adoration. He is the supreme guide on the Path of Love for the human race. He has traveled every stage of its desolation, its suffering, and its stripping. He knows the cost, and he knows that the cost does not matter because the glory, the *Kibriya,* is so great. What does it matter if you have fifty-two nervous breakdowns, lose your right leg, die of cancer? It does not matter. It does not matter if you have used those experiences to enter into the *Kibriya* and to be a transmitter, as far as you can be, of the Divine Love at this moment. It is much too late to care whether we are going to suffer or not, whether it is going to be painful or not. It is clearly going to be appallingly painful to watch the world fall apart. It is clearly going to involve suffering on all of our parts, in all of our hearts. What does it matter? Be drunk with adoration. Open your hearts endlessly to the love of God and never close them. Allow the Light to burn you and transform you, so that you can stand with Rumi and the friends of Rumi, the mystics of the earth, and play your part in the transformation of the world that is our responsibility historically, at this moment.

> How long will you move backwards? Come forward. Enter not into unbelief, come to religion. Look, the elixir is hidden in the poison. Come to the poison, accept it, take it and come, return to the root of the root of your own self.

Although in form you are earthly, you have been kneaded from the substance of certainty, you guard the treasury of God's Light, so come, return to the root of the root of your own self.

Once you have tied yourself to selflessness, you will be delivered from selfhood, and released from the ties of a hundred snares, so come, return to the root of the root of your own self.

You were born of the children of God vice-regent but you have turned your eyes to this low world. How can you be happy with just this? So come, return to the root of the root of your own self.

Though you are the talisman protecting the world's treasure, within yourself you are the mine. Open your hidden eyes and come, return to the root of the root of your own self.

You were born of the rays of God's majesty and again the good fortune of your auspicious star, so how long will you suffer at the hands of non-existent things? Come, return to the root of the root of your own self.

Your are a ruby in the midst of granite. How long will you try to deceive us? We can see the truth in your eyes. So come, return to the root of the root of your own self.

The King, Shams of Tabriz, has placed before you the cup of eternity. Drink and be drunk forever. Glory be to God. What marvelous, pure wine. So come, return to the root of the root of your own self.

Let us return to *Kibriya*, the glory. In the Christian mass, God is approached in adoration in the following order: *Laudamus te, Benedicimus te, Adoramus te, Glorificamus te.* "*Laudamus te*": we praise you. The first movement of adoration is praise, to praise these gifts, this glorious place, this nature, this body that can experience so much, the soul which can experience so much, this heart that can suffer and love so much. Then *"benedicimus te,"* out of the praise comes blessing, we bless you, my God, we bless you because once we have praised you, we are open to the source of joy, we are open to the glory of where we are. Then we bless God, *"benedicimus te."* Hear Bach's setting of this in the *B minor Mass* when Bach dances out of his mind with joy. When he sets these words, you feel the whole heart opening to bless the Divine Mother and the Divine Father for having given us these bodies, this heart, this soul, this transcendent opportunity. And out of that act of praising and then blessing—it is very subtle—then comes *"adoramus te,"* we adore you, we lay our entire being before you, we worship you, we love you with every fiber of our being, with every cell in our body, because we have learned how to praise, we have learned how to bless this experience, and out of this great fountain of blessing, this great fountain of praise, comes the secret movement of adoration. Then finally, as a consummation of the pieces, out of that adoration is born *"Glorificamus te,"* we glorify You, because You are *Kibriya,* You are glorious, You in us are glorious. We glorify You and we glorify You in all the different aspects of our life: we glorify You when we make love, we offer our lovemaking to You because You have given us this joy. We glorify You when we eat because You have given us this food. We glorify You when we read Rumi because You have given us your Divine messenger, with all his sweetness, passion, and fiery wildness. We glorify You when we sit and watch the sunset because You are burning in all the colors and splendors before us. We glorify You and we make our lives a theater of Your glorification, and in that act is transformation and enlightenment. This passing from praising to blessing, to adoration, and finally to this continual and incessant act of glorification that arises out of the heart of adoration, brings the transformation of every perception, every act, every moment, and is the Divine life on earth. To live that Divine life on earth is our destiny and our origin; and to help prepare that Divine life on earth is why we are here now, to help humanity make a transition so dangerous and difficult that it will require everything of us. And that transition is to an understanding, a total opening to the nature of the glory of God. There is this phrase in the *Koran* which with *Kibriya* is the source of all of mystical insight in Islam. It is the most amazing promise that God makes in the *Koran* and it is the promise of transformation through adoration:

> My slave does not cease to draw near to me with devotions of his own free will.

One of the very beautiful things about Islam is that there are no illusions in it about what being human is. If you are very lucky, you become God's slave. None of this New Age business about being on a par with God or being immortal— *you are God's slave.* To be the slave of God is the ultimate dignity. To be the servant is the ultimate honor.

> My slave does not cease to draw near to me with devotions of his own free will.

"Of his own, her own free will." What God asks of man is adoration from free love, free rejoicing, free blessing of this astonishing experience. "My slave does not cease to draw near to me with devotions of his own free will, until I love him." "Until I love him": in that moment when God loves the soul— God in a certain divine sense always loves the soul—but what is really being said here, mystically, is when the soul feels the presence of this Divine Love and this Divine Love becomes consciously active in the mind and the heart of the lover. "When I love him or her," God says, "I am the hearing with which he hears, the sight with which he sees, the hand he smites with, and the foot he walks on." That is not a poem, that is a literal statement about what happens to the divinized human being. The Divine becomes the person and the person hears with the ears of God, sees with the eyes of God, listens with the love of God, strokes with the hand of God, and walks on the feet of

God. It is, in other words, the complete Divine experience in
a body. And that is what God is promising to humankind as
the reward for adoration, as the result of adoration. It is the
ultimate promise underlying all mystical traditions. When your
heart has been purified, the Sufis say, the eye of the heart opens
and that eye sees the Beloved in every person, in every blade
of grass, the shining of the shining in every event and every
action. The Christians would say that when you have been
Christed, you will experience reality as Christ and you will
love reality with Christ's heart, you will taste reality with
Christ's mouth, and suffer with Christ's love, and long with
Christ's longing. But Christ is not out there, Christ is *here* waiting to be unfolded and waiting to be lived completely in you!
Through adoration of His cosmic Glory you enter and unite
with It. All the mystical traditions meet on this promise:

> My slave does not cease to draw near to me with devo-
> tions of his own free will until I love him or her. And
> when I love her, I am the hearing with which she hears,
> the sight with which she sees, the hand with which she
> smites, the foot she walks on.

Then the transmutation is complete and you are living consciously as a part of the Divine in a totally Divine world, radiating Divine Love, Divine Knowledge, Divine Compassion.
That was Rumi's destiny, that is our destiny, and these poems
blaze out of that awareness.

I want to read to you again from the beginning of *Love's
Fire,* which is a collection of Rumi's *Rubaiyat,* the four-line
telegrams from the Absolute that he wrote toward the end of
his life. By then, I think, he was tired of the meditative flow of
the *Mathnawi,* and he wanted to go right to the heart of the
question and explode insight in the core of the mind. So these
poems are violent, ecstatic, fierce, and short.

Love's Fire begins as the quest really begins, with us asking some very demanding questions of ourselves:

What do you hope to find
In the soul's streets
In the bloody streets of the heart
That have no news even of yourself?

That is the first question; I put that as the first poem.
That is the question that we really are asking the human
race at the moment. What are you going to find in the soul's
streets or in the bloody streets of Bosnia, if you don't have any
news and the only news that means anything is the news that
the mystics of every tradition have been giving us—who we
are and where we are. If you have no news even of yourself,
what are you going to find in human life? What are you going
to find in this experience? What will it mean to you? You are
wandering in the dark. *Samsara* is a nightmare of ignorance.
And then the second poem, another blow.

Anywhere you find a lullaby,
Leave; safety is final danger.
When you come across a storyteller
Know a house is being destroyed.

Rumi is saying that anything that consoles you, any place
where you find rest, is likely to be a place where your ego is
basking in a false sun, so leave. "Safety is final danger." That
should be written in every mall in America. It is when you are
safe, when you think you are happy, when you get your life
sorted out, when you feel that all these goods will make you
happy, that you are in total danger because your heart has
closed and you are, in fact, in that state of coma to which
everyone in this society seems to aspire.

Anywhere you find a lullaby,
Leave; safety is final danger.
When you come across a storyteller
Know a house is being destroyed.

The storytellers will give you all sorts of fancy recipes for
transformation, they will give you all sorts of guides, but if

you follow them, your house will be destroyed. Because there is one path and one path only, really; and that is the Path of passion, abandon, surrender, opening, and burning. Whether you are Buddhist, Hindu, or Sufi, that is the eternal Path. And then Rumi says,

> Never think the earth void or dead.
> It's a hare awake with shut eyes:
> It's a saucepan, simmering with broth,
> One clear look and you will see it's in ferment.

If you are dead, you see the universe as dead. If your soul is closed, you have no sense of the immense aliveness of everything. When you are in trance and when you see the Divine world and look at a blade of grass, you see the swarming in light of millions of atoms, you see the atoms dancing, you experience the ecstatic connection between you and the blade of grass, and you see that the entire universe is dancing inside the blade of grass. There is nothing that is not totally alive. The rocks are dancing, everything is dancing. "Never think the earth void or dead" because that is the fatal illusion, that is what enables us to exploit and rape nature. To be able to commit atrocities on the Jews, the Germans had to imagine that the Jews were *untermenschen,* that they were vermin. To imagine that the earth is dead is to conspire in its destruction, without any conscience. So when Rumi says, "Never think the earth void or dead; it is a hare," he is saying, "it is awake and it is quivering." Have you ever seen anything more alive than a hare? It is awake with shut eyes but suddenly its eyes will open and you will be looking directly into the eyes of the hare and seeing that the creation is boiling and dancing and simmering in the Divine Light. "It is a saucepan simmering with broth," a crucible. The universe, the creation, is a crucible, "a saucepan simmering with broth." One of the wonderful things about Rumi is that so many of his images are direct, natural, homey images. They are from the bedroom or the bathroom, the kitchen or the fields. Rumi talking to people in this way is talking with the total simplicity of someone who knows that all processes are divine. Just one clear look in the awakened mind and you will see the world is in ferment. And when you see that the world is in ferment, you will be in ferment and it will be about time. You should at least be as alive as a blade of grass. Let's aim for the state of quivering aliveness of a blade of grass. Then he says:

> Ignorant men are the soul's enemy,
> Shatter the jar of smug words.
> Cling for life to those who know.
> Prop a mirror in water, it rusts.

Rumi is not saying, "I think it would be advisable for you to go and visit a few Masters, if you have time; you have such busy lives." He says you *have* to cling to those who know, because only that clinging to the feet of the enlightened ones can give you the slightest chance of ending the tyranny of the ego, because you'll see holiness again and again being enacted in front of you. He knows the recipes, he says, "Ignorant men are the soul's enemy."

"Shatter the jar of smug words," shatter it, don't even look at it, break it. As long as you remain in your rational mind, as long as you remain in ordinary consciousness, no truth of the Divine nature can get through to you. You are just wandering in darkness. "Shatter the jar." He is full of these violent words. Rumi knows how much truth costs and hurts. "Prop a mirror in water and it rusts." You have to keep the mirror above the water. The water is desire, the water is obsession, the water is worldly activity. If you just put the mirror of your soul in all of that, it will rust and you will never see the Beloved's face clearly reflected in it.

The imagery of the mirror is crucial to Sufism. In the *Koran* it is said that Joseph was the most beautiful human being that God had ever created. In Sufi mysticism Joseph came to be a symbol of the Divine Beauty of the Beloved. He was apparently so beautiful that when Potiphar's wife assembled a group of women to look at him, they all cut their hands with the knives they were using to eat their food, because they were in such a trance at his loveliness. One of his brothers, after they had been reunited with Joseph, asked him: "What can I bring to you? You who have everything? You are the beloved of God and you have everything." And Joseph said to him, "You go and think about it; it will be revealed to you in a dream what you can bring to me." And the dream was this: the brother saw that the only thing that he could bring to Joseph was a mirror in which Joseph could see his own face.

So the only thing that the heart can bring to God is an absolutely clear mirror in which the Divine gazes down and sees the Divine reflecting back and experiences the bliss of its own beauty. And the function of polishing the heart, of going on a spiritual discipline of transformation, is to be a mirror in which the Divine can gaze with rapture on its own beauty. That is one of the most profound symbols that man has ever been given, and it is the symbol that runs through the whole of the Sufi transmission.

Rumi goes on:

> How long will we fill our pockets
> Like children, with dirt and stones?
> Let the world go. Holding it,
> We never know ourselves, never are airborne.

When he says let the world go, Rumi means our addictions, our desires, our desires for fame and power. We don't need anything; the whole world is us and we cannot even begin to suspect the majesty of that Divine Self if we are holding on to obsessions and activities, because we are defining ourselves outside ourselves and that is the source of all of our mistakes. When we drop the world, drop the definitions and concepts, then we are airborne.

Of course, this is not simply an image. It refers to a Divine experience. It refers to an experience in meditation which is simply becoming one with the space, with infinite space. This happens in the higher levels of meditation when the ego fades, dissolves, and you leave the body. At that moment you are airborne because you have let the world go into you, into your vast, Divine Self.

I mention this because Rumi's poetry manages to be scientific as well as ecstatic. All real ecstasies are scientific because they are precise, lucid information of this other dimension. So you appreciate Rumi's poetry more and more as you go higher. There is a double code going on. For those who don't know, his poetry is a tremendous inspiration to go into the mystic dimension, because it is full of an ecstatic invitation: Come here and you will know this. But to those who have been there, at least for ten or twelve seconds, for half a second, one millisecond, or ten years, there is only increased awe and rapture that this man could have been so precise as well as so ecstatic. This gives us a clue as to what true spiritual knowledge is.

True spiritual knowledge is simultaneously ecstatic and lucid. If that were known, the scientific rejection of spiritual awareness would be forever unmasked for what it is—*fear*. Scientists don't want to go into trance before reality because it would stop them from pretending that they have control. But if they went into trance before reality they would discover a kind of control rooted in the control of the Divine Itself, and that would bring real scientific breakthrough. Rumi then describes in four lines the adoration, the true cost of transformation:

> I lost my world, my fame, my mind.
> The Sun appeared and all the shadows ran
> I ran after them but vanished as I ran
> Light ran after me and hunted me down.

He is saying, I lost my world, I lost the whole of my environment, my fame, my mind, I lost everything that I thought I knew, *everything*, because the Sun appeared, the Divine Light came up, the Master appeared in Shams, and I knew that I knew nothing, and all the shadows and darkness in me, all the illusions ran away. I ran after them, but even as I ran after them, the Sun shone on me, so I vanished as I ran. Once the Sun has come up, as you run after the shadows, the Sun itself is eating away the shadows so there is nowhere to run and the you who is running vanishes, too. The runner vanishes, the runner dissolves, and the experience of the ego no longer exists even as you are desperately reaching out for it. That is one of the funniest games of the Master.

The game goes on and on and sometimes the Divine gives you what you think you want, to reveal that both you the wanter and the thing that is wanted are unreal. And then the last line really describes what happens once the pact has been sealed between the Beloved and the heart, "Light ran after me and hunted me down." The Light hunts you. Anyone who has been with a great Master knows that after a certain stage they are being hunted, there is nowhere they can go to escape. Even if they plunge into vice, the Master will be there waiting. "Even if you go to Hell," Ramana Maharshi says, "I'll come and find you." There is absolutely nowhere after a certain stage that you can hide and nothing you can do, either. You can fall down drunk and just before you fall down drunk, you see the Master smiling. After a certain stage, God is in everything and is everywhere. Light hunts you down to kill you, to end the false self forever.

And then the recipe for transformation is given. You have been through this questioning, this opening, the price, and Rumi simply says,

> Circle the Sun, you become a sun.
> Circle a Master and you become one.
> You'd be a ruby, if you danced around this mine.
> Dance around him, you'll glitter like gold.

He is saying that there is one way out and that is to love a Divine Master with all your heart, mind, and soul, and to circle the sun so that the sun and you can become one. And you become a ruby. There is a Sufi myth that rubies are made by the sun shining into the rock and building the ruby within it by an alchemy of sunlight. This is what happens in the relationship with a Divine Master. The Divine Love and Power are trained on you slowly, inexorably, and they transmute you in this alchemy of adoration. "Dance around him or her, you will glitter like gold." What makes you glitter like gold is the commitment to love, the experience of that love, and the unashamed display of that love dancing round the Master.

If you really show that love and dance around the Master, then you come to take on, even against your will, some of the shining of the beloved. You will be changed into him or her. That is the alchemy and it is real because . . .

> This body is a mirror of heaven;
> Its energy makes angels jealous.
> Our purity astounds seraphim
> Devils shiver at our nerve.

When the Divine energies in the body are awakened when the *kundalini* is released or when the *shakti* is given, whatever way you describe this alchemy, you are aware that what you have been living up to that moment has been just a tenth of what you are. Now instead of being a cup going to the ocean, and each time getting just a cup full, you are a cup living in the ocean being filled by the ocean itself, the ocean of *shakti,* the ocean of energy. That is the true state of the body and mind. "Its energies make angels jealous" because each human being has a special power, an inheritance from the Divine, which may have been neglected, but "the angels weep with jealousy" when they see an enlightened being because an enlightened being has energies that they don't have.

"Our purity astounds seraphim," is a very subtle line. To be pure in this dimension with all the temptations that we have to be impure, with all our ignorance built into our ego, is a very astonishing achievement. And when we reach this achievement, as Rumi did, as the Buddha did, as Mirabai did, that purity is one with the Divine Purity in a way that not even the angels are one with.

The last line gives us courage when we meet evil, "Devils shiver at our nerve." It has a double meaning. You could say we are so crazy that we think we can do anything and get away with it: we can burn, rape, destroy, exploit, and while even devils know that they are going to get punished, we don't because we are idiots. That is one way of reading the line, but another way is that we have a kind of nerve, a kind of clarity and capacity for action that the diabolic does not have. We have courage that even the diabolic does not, and this courage can take us beyond the angels into the heart of God.

And immediately, *Love's Fire* turns to tell you: All right, you got one picture of the body but that is not all of it. I tried to structure the book in such a way that whatever insight happens, you will never be allowed to rest in it. So after this image of what the body is, Rumi says,

> Body of earth, don't talk of earth,
> Tell the story of pure mirrors.
> The Creator has given you this splendor.
> Why talk of anything else?

We all know everything about the earth, desires, madness, and lunacy. Forget it for a second, let's tell the real story first —the story of the human race, the story of Rumi and Shams. It is the story of two mirrors, the soul and the beloved. It is the story of awakening. It is the story of pure mirrors, of becoming the mirror in which the face of infinite beauty can be reflected. At that moment, the worldly story is over. The Divine story—the only real story—has begun, and then the magic dances.

"The Creator has given you this splendor." The word is *Kibriya*. Rumi is using it in a very daring way. He is saying that the *Kibriya* has given you the *Kibriya*. You are That. You have the splendor, the supernovas are dancing in you, Betelgeuse is blazing in you, the tornado is turning in you, worlds are being born and destroyed in you. You are Shiva, you are the Divine Mother, you are That. "The Creator has given you this splendor. Why talk of anything else?" And suddenly all talk ceases at this moment, because enough has been given. If you really know what these first nine poems mean and what they have pointed you to, you don't need any more talk, you are sick to death of talk. What you need is Divine experience, rapture.

At this point, in the tenth poem of the book,

> Suddenly he is here. He is here.
> Heads touch, secrets start singing,
> Time's barn is flattened by storm wind
> We crumple on its straw like drunks.

No more talk. The Divine comes, the Divine destroys, and the Divine makes drunk. "Heads touch and secrets start singing," the singing in silence. It is not in the words. The words, I hope, are valuable, but what is entering is beyond words and the secrets are singing.

Rumi is an initiatory poet, the secrets start to sing. It is a lovely image because we are the secrets. All the secrets are in our blood, our cells, our minds, our dreams. What a Divine poet does is awaken the secret singing within ourselves, which we then listen to and never stop hearing. And then this wonderful image of time's barn: blank, bleak, and dark. We are in this barn that is flattened by the storm wind of the Divine Presence, and we are flattened with it and crumple on its straw like drunks.

Then he warns us:

> No one can wear the jewel of reality
> Except the One in whose fire it was born.
> I have a friend who wears it on his forehead;
> Our foreheads touch tonight, and mine burns.

You can't fake whether you wear the jewel of reality or not. Only the one who has become one with the One wears the jewel. Only the Divine Master wears the jewel, only the divinized being, because that jewel is the jewel of transforming power, of powerful splendor, and it can only be given to someone who has been reborn in the fire of *Kibriya,* of the Divine Presence. Then Rumi says of Shams, "I have a friend who wears it on his forehead." He knows who Shams is and he knows that Shams has been through the transformation, and he says this wonderful phrase, so tender, "Our foreheads touch tonight and mine burns." The transmission takes place. It is really transmission of the third eye to the third eye, the awakening of the eye in the fire, and when that eye wakens, it sees the Divine Light in everything, the world burning in the fire.

By this time, Rumi has been seared by Divine Love and can no longer reclaim his life. He says:

> In love with him, my soul
> Lives the subtlest of passions,
> Lives like a gypsy
> Each day a different house.
> Each night under the stars.

That is one of the supreme spiritual poems of the world. It describes the highest state of abandonment.

"In love with him my soul lives the subtlest of passions." This is a clue. Confusing any of the kinds of love that we have been describing with ordinary forms of love would be a very dangerous thing. Because the love for the Beloved is the most extreme and the subtlest of passions, and it takes you away from all concepts and all homes. You live like a gypsy. Anybody who has really had the experience of Divine Love, whether they live in a house or not, whether they travel or not, is living like a gypsy, from state to state, from hour to hour. Anything can happen. When you are in love like this, you realize that the universe is being reimagined at every second in the mind of God. Rumi says it in the *Mathnawi* and also in the odes collected in the *Diwan:* when you really see with a child's mind, you see that everything is always eternally fresh, nothing is old, nothing is stale. You see the Unborn. You see the timeless in time. When you enter that total freshness you see that the Divine Fire is giving birth to the universe every millisecond and that you are participating in this Divine birth at every millisecond. So you are by definition a gypsy, at that moment, because you are living from birth to birth. No home, no place.

> In love with him, my soul
> Lives the subtlest of passions,
> Lives like a gypsy
> Each day a different house.
> Each night under the stars.

Rumi's poetry is full of the glory, beauty, spaciousness, and vastness of the night. It is in the night that thoughts die down and the heart can open to the mystery of the Presence of the Beloved. It is in the night that the stars send us the perfume of the Beloved's Presence, and it is in the night that a Sufi prays. Rumi again and again says to his disciples: You are sleeping too much, stay up all night. What does it matter that you have a sleepless night, pray, pray, God comes to those secretly in the night who have a burning in the heart. The night for him is the place where the Beloved is met in secrecy beyond form, beyond all the shapes of the world. So "each night" is spent "under the stars" in this ecstatic communion with the Divine Presence.

Then Rumi turns and addresses the people who might be reading his words and says,

> I was once like you, enlightened and "rational"
> I, too, scoffed at lovers
> Now I am drunk, crazed, thin with misery.
> No one is safe! Watch out.

Rumi's whole message to us is very powerful because it comes from a man who had all the temptations of rational power. He was a very brilliant man. He was beautiful and famous, he could have had anything he wanted, but he gave all of those things up when he realized that *Kibriya* dissolved them all.

"I was once like you, enlightened and 'rational,'" I once wanted the power of the mind and the safety of the ego, and

"I, too, scoffed at lovers," because lovers are ridiculous. It is ridiculous to come into a room and see somebody crying and sobbing and opening. It is absurd to the rational mind. But to be in a state of love *is* absurd to the rational mind. To be in a state of love is to be naked, it is not to care a damn what the rational mind can possibly think. It is to choose the saving lucidity of Divine madness over the nihilistic rationality of human madness.

"Now I am drunk, crazed, thin with misery. No one is safe," because if I could get to this state, anybody can. I resisted it, God knows, more than anybody could possibly resist it, but "Light ran after me and hunted me down." So Rumi is playing this extraordinary game in his poetry; he is saying, don't think that I don't know how you are evading this poetry, this Light. I have evaded it in every possible way that you try to evade it. I have been a whore of reason, I have been a lover of pleasure. I know what you are up to. It does not work. You will never escape the Divine Beauty once you catch a glimpse of it. Once you have seen it just for one second you will be drunk the rest of your life.

And then the next poem: "Atom, you want to flee the Sun? Madman, give up!" I love it when Rumi gets angry, and Rumi gets brilliantly angry in his poetry. He is not a sweetheart. He is wild with love, he wants you to wake up.

Rumi is not playing. He gets very angry and he is very insulting when he is angry. He is not insulting your Divine Self, not our Divine Self, but the ego that is trapping us. So he has to be angry and he uses all the different powers that a Master uses to wake us up.

If you have had a relationship with a Master, you know that a Master can be very, very sweet to dissolve you. He or she can be totally reticent to make you crazy. He or she can hit you over the head a thousand times with the saucepan of Divine Knowledge to blunt your egotism. He or she can and will do anything if you let him or her, to wake you up to the madness of what you are doing. And if you love the Master deeply, one of the things that you give him or her is total permission because you know that his or her anger is kindness.

"Atom, you want to flee the sun? Madman, give up." You want to flee the Divine Presence? Where do you think you are? Who do you think you are? What do you think is going to happen when you die? You are going to have this vision of the Divine Splendor, and you are going to be terrified out of your wits because all of your life you were just looking at the world with the pitiful little searchlight of your own ego.

> You are a jar; fate is a stone
> Kick against it, you'll waste your wine.

That is a terrifying line. If you are a jar, you are very fragile. You are in a dying body and you are going to die. You are going to be shattered many times by the loss of friends, by the chaos of the culture, by everything, then you are going to die, lose everything, be broken. So if, idiotically, you bash yourself against fate, thinking that you are the master of fate before you are awake, before you truly are the master of fate by being one with the Beloved, then you are going to be shattered and all the wine in you, all this precious substance, is going to drain away.

Then Rumi says:

> Reason, leave now.

Just get out, don't bring your tiring quibbles, don't bring all that. *Leave now.*

Wisdom is not what you are going to find here. You are going to find madness here, total insight. That won't be "wisdom." It will send you out of your mind, so go away. Don't play around here. You are not going to be able to fiddle with these concepts, arrange them in a nice, decent, tidy formula. If you want tidy formulas, go somewhere else.

> Were you thin as a hair, there would still be no room.
> The sun is risen! In its vast dazzle
> Every lamp is drowned.

How can you presume to bring the mind, that tiny, pathetic little firefly, into the blaze of the *Kibriya,* and expect this tiny firefly of the mind to give you some special light by which to study the *Kibriya?* With which to make comments about the *Kibriya* such as a friend of mine made last year, saying, quite seriously, that if he had organized the world, he would have done it a great deal better? That is the madness of what happens to reason. Rumi is saying that reason itself is absolutely mad, because reason attempts to examine the Divine Light from beyond and outside it, while it itself is only a very dim and minor reflection of that Divine Light.

The sun is risen.

The *Kibriya* is risen and "in its vast dazzle," in its universal and infinite radiance, "every" individual "lamp is drowned." Drowned forever.

The only way by which we unite ourselves to the Divine in us is by longing with every cell of our body and our mind to be one with the Beloved. It is the only way. And that longing has to be perpetual, permanent, it has to go on as a river in the heart, a cry in the heart, saying endlessly: Take me to you, take me to you.

That is why in Sufism and in Islam there is the practice of *dhikr,* which is the saying of the sacred name over and over again, so that the sacred name can infuse you with the sacred Presence, so that you can become drunk, so that you can drown, so that you can become one. Adoration and longing are the same thing; without longing there is no adoration.

What the Master tries to do is to take you to a place where it is simply unbearable to go on existing as yourself, and that is not a fancy theatrical word, it is simply unbearable. The pain of going on being in the ego, the pain of going on thinking your own dreary thoughts, the pain of going on imagining that you imagine something real, of being a slave to repetition and repetition, fear and fear, hysteria and hysteria, becomes literally unbearable. At that moment, you are ready.

A Zen Master says that when you want truth as much as a drowning man wants oxygen, then the truth can be given to you directly, and nobody can fake that moment. People can say, "Oh, I am just longing to be enlightened." They are faking it. If they were really longing for it, they would be burning, they would be prepared to die, to be drowned forever in the *Kibriya,* if necessary. If somebody says that they are cooking something and the stove is not on, wouldn't you suggest that they turn the flame up? That is what Rumi is saying to us: Turn the flame up.

And this is what he means in this next poem. Nobody has ever wept and sobbed and burnt so publicly and so extremely for his Beloved as Rumi has done, to enact this huge drama of adoration for the world so that we could finally see what it is to love in the Divine way, with the Divine passion.

> Over all the parchments of Egypt
> I've scrawled my cries and hungers.
> One hour of love's worth a hundred worlds.
> I have thousands of hearts; here, burn them all.

Until we mean that totally, we are not in the authentic state, we are still keeping something back, we are still not surrendering. The demand by the Divine is extreme because the gift is extreme.

Shams says to Rumi in one of the poems, "You ask me to give you Love but I can't hand Love like a stone." You have to vanish to be Love, you have to burn away to be Love. I will give you Love, but are you prepared to die? Until you are prepared to die you cannot be Love, because Love is not some sweet emotion, it is not some insight or series of realizations. Love is being the Divine Itself. How could the Divine give Itself to any created thing? You have to cease to exist for the Divine to exist through you as you. That is the price and it makes sense. Any teaching that is not telling you that is simply lying to you. And Rumi is enacting the passion that helps you get there, and that passion is to know that one hour of Divine knowledge and

Divine Love is worth 100,000 lifetimes, 100 worlds.

When you begin to feel these things, you are beginning the ascension to super-consciousness, the ascension to enlightenment. You have been preparing for that ascent for many lifetimes. When that ascent starts, know what it is worth, know that it is worth everything. And that if you have to die to start the ascent, that is nothing. That is the heroism required for the transformation. You have to be prepared to go through everything.

"One hour of Love is worth a hundred worlds. I have thousands of hearts." You want to break my hearts, break them. I have this heart, I have that heart, break them all—because I know that as you destroy me, you are making me live. I know that as you make me weep, you are building a joy beyond all tears in my soul.

Rumi was once asked, what is a Sufi? And he said, "A Sufi is a man or a woman with a broken heart." Someone who is always sensitive to the heartbreak of the world and who is always sensitive to the Divine Beauty of the world. Once you see it, your heart breaks open forever and goes on breaking at the beauty and majesty and agony of the experience.

Then he turns, and this poem is really one of his bravest, a poem of which we really need now to know the meaning.

> Desperation, let me always know
> How to welcome you
> And put in your hands the torch
> To burn down the house.

When you are desperate, it is often a clue that you need to leave an old way of being, an old way of life, an old understanding. After we smother that desperation, we cuddle it, we comatize it. But Rumi says, "Have the courage of your desperation" and put in the hands of your desperation the torch, the flame of Love and insight, and burn your house down. Allow desperation to be a Master instead of something that drives you deeper into coma.

We are at a desperate moment in human history. The world is in terrible denial of what is actually going on, because people are simply afraid of the level of desperation that they would feel if they faced what is going on. The point is that we have to face what is going on and allow that desperation to rise in us, and we have to follow that desperation right to its home which is in Divine initiation, Divine transformation. We have to let that desperation "take a torch and burn down" all our concepts, limits, fantasies, and banal solutions, because it is far too late and none of them are going to work.

> Light the incense!
> You have to burn to be fragrant
> To scent the whole house
> You have to burn to the ground.

Incense is made out of all sorts of dark things, just like the ego. If you want the incense to scent the house, you have to light it, light the ego. In disappearing, it releases the Divine perfume everywhere. If you want to scent the whole universe as Rumi did, you have to burn away. That is the Law.

"Like the incense, you have to burn to be fragrant." The seventeenth-century Japanese poet Bashō also uses the imagery of the burning house. He says in one of his last poems, "When the house is burnt down, you own a better view of the rising moon." That is the greatest enlightenment poem that I know. Burn the house down. You think it is a tragedy! On the contrary, you have a complete 360-degree view of the rising moon of enlightenment, the rising moon of Light, because you belong nowhere, you are a gypsy, no longer trapped by any convention or concept. You are free.

> You only need smell the wine
> For vision to flame from each void,
> Such flames from wine's aroma!
> Imagine if you were the wine.

Wine is the image of Sufi ecstasy. You have to smell the
wine. Even a sniff of bliss will give you so many astonishing
insights and perceptions, "such flames from wine's aroma."
But Rumi is saying, "Don't just be a hedonist of spiritual experience, don't just sip the wine, don't just smell occasionally the
wine, you have to become the wine. If you become the wine,
imagine what joy, what splendor, what energy will be yours."
Three last poems:

> The thread of your Love is thin,
> Far sharper than any knife,
> Wind it around my mind
> Pull it until I end.

> There's always another death to die
> Beyond the death you know
> Always another door of scars
> To open to another room.

Awakening is an endless process of opening, and there is
always a door of scars, of secret pain, secret terror, and secret
fear. So burn, always. A door of scars bars us from the next
room of revelation prepared for us. There is always another
death to die. Even on your deathbed, there will be another
death to die. On your deathbed there will be the death to die
into the Beloved as Rumi did, beyond the death that you already
know. And beyond that death there will be others we cannot
imagine, other deaths into other, wider rooms of light. This is
the Law, this is the Process, but you are always opening to
another room, another possibility, another vision, forever dying
and blossoming in the *Kibriya*.

> In the dryest, whitest stretch
> Of pain's infinite desert,
> I lost my sanity,
> And found this rose.

Chapter Three

Dying, Blossoming

RUMI'S LIFE, Rumi's work, Rumi's entire enterprise was inspired and utterly transfigured by his passionate and total dedication to Shams-i-Tabriz, the Sun of Tabriz, and it is his presence that I want to invoke now because it is his presence that burned Rumi's mind and heart away and recreated him in the image of the Divine. And it is Shams' presence, his glory, his splendor, his Divine power, and his Divine love that Rumi is transmitting to us in his poetry, a presence that Rumi discovered to be his own through the agony and ecstasy of Divine Love.

So let us begin by sweeping away the world as we now know it, by listening to a poem that Rumi wrote in an agony of love for Shams.

First, remember the story: Rumi met Shams when he was thirty-seven. Rumi's life was totally shattered by the power that Shams revealed to him. Shams was a wandering dervish, a poor, wild man that Rumi took in off the street, with whom he lived in the most intense intimacy and who transmitted to him Divine secrets.

The disciples grew jealous and Shams disappeared. In that first disappearance, Rumi tasted extreme desolation and madness. Out of that madness came his first poems and this is one of those poems. He loved Shams so much, he longed for Shams so intensely, he gave himself so totally to Shams, that this scholar, this famous man, wandered in the *caravanserai* begging people for news of his beloved, grabbing men who had

just stepped down from their camels, saying, "Have you seen
Shams-i-Tabriz? Have you seen Shams-i-Tabriz?" People
thought that he had lost his mind. He *had* lost his mind because
the beloved had shattered his mind with Love. And you hear
this mad thirty-eight-year-old man wandering in the *cara-*
vanserai out of his mind with pain and love for his beloved in
the poetry, in the pleading, weeping, and immense outpouring
of passion that this poem is.

> O whispering breeze, bring news of my beloved Shams.
> It would be worth more than all the amber and musk
>   from China to Constantinople,
> Tell me, tell me if you heard a word from his sweet
>   lips or a beat from his pounding heart.
> O just one word from Shams and I would gladly give
>   my life.
> His life is before me and behind me, and through his
>   love, my heart has become pure, my breast has
>   imbibed every virtue,
> One smell of his perfume and I walk light-headed on
>   this path,
> O cupbearer, enough of your wine, I am drunk on
>   the wine from his cup.
> My nose is so full of his fragrance that I have no need
>   for incense, musk, or the fine amber of Mongolia.
> Shams-ud-Din is alive forever in my heart,
> Shams-ud-Din is the generosity of every soul,
> Shams-ud-Din is poverty, Shams-ud-Din is the purest
>   of all wealth,
> I am not the only one singing, Shams-ud-Din, Shams-
>   ud-Din;
> The nightingales sing it from the garden and the
>   partridge from the mountain side.
> The beauty of a starry night is Shams-ud-Din.
> The garden of Paradise is Shams-ud-Din;
> Love, compassion, and gratitude, all, all, are Shams-
>   ud-Din.

Shams-ud-Din is the brightness of day,
Shams-ud-Din is the turning sky,
Shams-ud-Din is time everlasting,
Shams-ud-Din is the endless treasure,
Shams-ud-Din is the King of cups,
Shams-ud-Din is the Ocean of nectar,
Shams-ud-Din is the breath of Jesus,
Shams-ud-Din is the face of Joseph,
O God, show me that inner place where we can sit
   together,
Shams in the middle, my soul by his side.
Shams-ud-Din is sweeter than life,
Shams-ud-Din is a hearth full of sugar,
Shams-ud-Din is the towering cypress,
Shams-ud-Din is the flowering spring,
Shams-ud-Din is the world of clear water ...
Shams-ud-Din is the barrel of wine,
Shams-ud-Din is the bliss of my soul,
O Shams, you are the hope of every heart,
The one that every lover longs to hear,
O Shams, come back, come back, don't leave my soul
   in ruins.

Now you have heard what Rumi means and what the Sufis mean by longing—the music of extreme pain and extreme love. You have heard what it means when every cell, bone, and minute particle of the body, soul, heart, and mind cry out with longing for union with the beloved. Hold that feeling at the center of your heart, because it is the feeling that Rumi had for Shams, and it is the fundamental feeling of the human soul for its origin. What Shams revealed to Rumi, what Shams gave to Rumi, what Shams was for Rumi, was the flaming origin, the Divine Beloved, the total lover who could give him everything: the knowledge of his Divine identity, the Divine vision of the world as a ceaseless dance and fountain of theophanies. So when Rumi longs for Shams, he longs on behalf of all of us, because all of us are longing for origin, longing to go home, longing to return to the place where we spring from in eternal freshness, longing to dance back into ourselves in ecstasy in every flowering event and thing.

Attar says that there are only three roads in the universe of Love: Tears, Blood, and Fire. There are no other ways to burn down the madness of the false self, to throw it into ruin. And when you have allowed that Divine Love to pierce you, you then have to open with everything that you are to It, so that Its passion can become your passion and your passion for It can excavate in your heart a vast emptiness into which It can pour Its Divine Fire. This is an immense labor, an agony, a road of tears, blood, and fire.

Shams had made a bargain with God. He had wandered all his life, a totally realized being, unendurable to most people. He had made a bargain with God that if he were allowed one person to whom he could transmit everything that he was and everything that he knew, he would offer his life. And God said, "Go to Konya and there you will meet a young man called Rumi; to him you can give everything." So when Shams met Rumi, Shams knew that there was very little time for the transmission to be given, a transmission that was destined to transform the whole religious understanding of mankind and add a new instrument of love, passion, and glory to the orchestra of Divine awareness. And at that moment he seized and dragged Rumi into an overwhelmingly agonizing and glorious process which Rumi totally gave himself up to, a process that went at a speed that would have slaughtered anyone else, because Rumi had to be transformed before the knock came on the door, as it came in 1247 when Shams got up, said, "It is time. I am going," went out, and disappeared forever, probably murdered by Rumi's own son. The drama of this terrifyingly fast transmission is the subject of Rumi's poetry.

To transform Rumi, Shams had to checkmate every move that Rumi made to escape him. He had to slaughter Rumi's intellect, he had to show how each so-called spiritual position that Rumi took up vis-à-vis him was another evasion, another inauthenticity. He had again and again to bomb Rumi out from where he was standing and from where he imagined himself to be. Rumi's poetry is a long ecstatic account of those bombings, those incinerations in Shams' fire, of being continually emptied, continually stripped, continually burnt away, again and again, so that more could be given. Shams was dedicated absolutely to the total annihilation of Rumi. He had to murder Rumi to transform him. He had to murder Rumi to transmit his own absolute vision to Rumi. He had to murder Rumi for Shams to be reborn in Rumi and for the transmission to be given to the world. And Rumi had to love him enough to let that annihilation take place, because only insane, boundless, ecstatic love can give you the courage to endure that extreme a process. Shams' responsibility was to stoke that love, to keep it burning; every time that Rumi grew slack, flay him so that he would dance further, and every time that the fire damped, throw more fire into it, burn down everything that remained so that, in the end, only love and gnosis and the Divine Presence would remain.

The love between Shams and Rumi is the supreme human love affair. All other love affairs look small because the stakes in this love affair were not some private vision to be shared between two people only; the stakes in this love affair were a transmission of sacred identity, in ecstasy, to the entire human race. And they both knew it.

> Reason says, I will win him with my eloquence,
> Love says, I will win him with my silence.
> Soul says, How can I ever win him when all I have is
> already his?
> He does not want, he is not worried. He does not seek
> a sublime state of euphoria.
> How then can I win him with sweet wine or gold?
> He is not bound by the senses. How then can I win
> him with all the riches of China?
> He is an angel although he appears in the form of a man.

Even angels cannot fly in his presence. How then
can I win him by assuming some heavenly form?
He flies on the wings of God, his food is pure light.
How can I win him with a loaf of baked bread?
He is not a merchant. He is not a tradesman. How
then can I win him with a plan of great profit?
He is not blind. I can't fool him. How then can I win
him by lying in bed as if gravely ill?
I'll go mad, I'll pull out my hair, I'll grind my face in
the dirt, but how will this win him?
He sees everything. How can I fool him?
He is not a seeker of fame. He is not a prince addicted
to the praise of poets and how then can I win him
with flowing rhymes and poetic verses?
The glory of Shams' unseen form fills the whole
universe. How then can I win him with a mere
promise of Paradise?
I may cover the earth with roses, I may fill the ocean
with tears, I may shake the heaven with praises,
and none of this will win him.
There is only one way to win him, this beloved of
mine: become his.

Every possible diversion, every possible evasion from the
outrageous demands of unconditional love are placed in this
poem. Every way that Rumi possibly tried to wriggle away
from Shams, to deny the Sun, to wear dark glasses as he stared
into Shams' eternal sunlight—"I'll be eloquent, I'll dazzle
him"—Shams is not going to be dazzled by anything. Shams
has heard everything. "I'll win him with my silence." Shams
knows that you are playing a game, using silence as another
kind of seduction. "How can I ever win him who is already
mine," says the soul, but that is not enough, because the soul
has to enter into the Divine Presence, it has to go stripped naked
and utterly open into the Divine Presence. It can't just mimic:
"I am the Divine, the Divine is here, everything is the Divine."

Shams knows that Rumi does not know that yet and mocks him, because until you see the world streaming with Divine Light, until you know that no one is separate from you, until your every word is expanded in adoration and in service of the world, you simply do not know that you and the world are divine.

The Path that Shams has set down for humanity and that Rumi is talking about demands total sacrifice. Rumi and Shams are not talking about having mystic feelings; they are talking about burning away to become the Beloved, to live as the Beloved. So Rumi can't say as we so often hear in mystic conversation: "Well, you know, I do not have to do anything, because I am already enlightened, I am already divine, the whole world is divine." That is *not* the truth. It is the ultimate Truth, but that Truth has to be known in every cell of the body, with every breath of the body, and in every movement of the heart, before it is truly known. Shams knows how cheap words are and he knows what a wordsmith he has in front of him, and he will press, burn, deride, unsettle, expose, humiliate, and adore, love, and cherish just enough to make Rumi completely lose any sense of security, consolation, hope, help, or identification that he could possibly have. "He doesn't want, he doesn't worry." Shams is not in the state of wanting anything. "I can't give him anything. I can't make love to him, I can't give him a ticket to the ball game, I can't buy him a box at the opera, I can't give him money, my own wife, he doesn't want anything; that freaks me out completely." We are utterly at home in relationships where somebody wants something from us, then the good old market can go on. But the outrageousness of the relationship with a Divine being who loves us totally is that there is nothing we can give them except love. They compel us to be completely authentic; they force us by the ruthlessness of their divine beauty and their divine love, the ruthlessness of their presence, to go beyond all our evasions of authenticity to face naked and absolute love. And by facing naked and absolute love for them, letting it arise in flames in ourselves, feeling its burn, its rage, its glory, and its sweetness, a miracle can slowly be born, the miracle of becoming what we love, turning into the fire we are burning in. The alchemy works, the alchemy changes the entire being, but the burning is terrible and glorious. "He is not bound by the senses, how can I win him with all the riches of China, he is an angel." People smile, but Rumi was not making a joke; it was not just an image for him because he had seen this man burning in the Divine Light. He did not have sentimental feelings for Shams, he had absolute adoration, a totally different kind of emotion. His is not in any normal sense love poetry; compared to it, normal love poetry looks like nursery rhymes. His is a searing of the mind by direct visionary ecstasy, direct visionary knowledge.

When Rumi says about Shams, "he is an angel," Shams *is* an angel, he is not an ordinary human being, he is a being transfigured with grace. He has the *Kibriya* of the Divine Splendor, he is the King of the world. When you see and know this of the Master and it goes into your body like a permanent flame, there is no place to hide and nothing to give except your entire being, the total sacrifice.

"He flies on the wings of God. His food is pure light. He is not a merchant, he is not blind, I go mad, I pull out my hair." There is absolutely nothing you can do with a Divine Master! When the cobra has bitten you, you will die. "I will go mad, pull out my hair, grind my face in the dirt, he sees everything, how can I fool him?" The melodrama of the ego is not going to fool the Divine Beloved. You can fool human beloveds with the melodrama of the ego, because it is largely what they want. They want this massive soap opera to go on and on, to run for years like the TV show "Dallas." But the Divine Beloved is doing nothing except burning in total Love, waiting for you to become total Love.

There is a Sufi story about a Master and a disciple who are talking, and the disciple is going through an agony of love for this Master and has broken through into an understanding of the nature of the universe. He says angrily to the Master, "All you ever did was to sit there, year after year; you did not say anything, you just looked at me occasionally, you sat there as I vanished down trapdoors, as I went through hysteria after hysteria, as I saw my past lives in dreams, as my entire life boiled up again and again, as I lost my brain approximately 42,000 times, as I had fifteen nervous breakdowns, as I lost my wife, my family, everything, and I am grateful that it all happened because I got here—but damn you, you were doing absolutely nothing." And the Master said with infinite tenderness, "What a fool you are. I thought that you had understood something. Just think of a candle and the moth going round it. The moth is buzzing about, but the candle is burning away."

And when you realize that the Divine Master is in time with you, in a body, with you, burning away with you, then your heart breaks. There they are with you in the same dimension out of pure love, waiting for you to receive Pure Love, and your heart breaks. The Master said to the disciple, "What I have been doing is burning away, waiting for you to catch fire," and that act of immense burning, that act of incessant, endless love, streams out towards the entire universe. It is the sacred act of the Divine Master, the sacred agony of the Divine Master, and when you come to understand that, you will be destroyed. There are many minor destructions, but that is the real destruction.

Ramana Maharshi, or Shams-i-Tabriz, or Mother Meera, or the Dalai Lama are not out there floating about having an amazing time; they are here dying and suffering with us, out of absolute Love. That is what Rumi understood. Rumi knew that Shams was one with the entire universe, exploding and appearing in all things simultaneously because he had attained total Being. He understood that Shams was an Incarnation. Although Islam does not accredit incarnation, there is no doubt that Shams was experienced by Rumi as a living vessel of the Divine, and he knew that the passion and the sacrifice involved with that was of an extremity that completely broke his mind apart. He also knew that knowing this would mean giving Shams his entire being in Love.

Rumi knows that Shams' glory fills the universe. He has been initiated by his beloved into the Divine vision. He knows that Shams is one with the One, that he is one with Shams, and that grace flows from Shams. He knows that Shams is aflame like the Prophet in the very highest realm of illumination, and he knows that Shams contains the secret of the whole destiny of human life.

So he says this, and it is not a poem. "The glory of his unseen form fills the whole universe, how then can I win him with a mere promise of Paradise?" One of the most glorious Sufi sayings is, "If you went to Paradise, I will go, of course, but if you went to hell, hell would be Paradise, a Paradise of rose gardens, just because you were there." That is Divine Love. "Hell would be a Paradise of rose gardens, just because you were there." Everything transformed by passion. "There is only one way to win him, this Beloved of mine, become his."

The Sufis say that to become the Beloved, there are three stages. Of course, the Sufis, like the Hindus and the Buddhists, enjoy dividing those three stages into seventy-two stages, but essentially there are three: *Purification, Expansion,* and *Union.* And they correspond to the experience of all mystics, of all human beings who open to the Love of God.

The first stage is essential, and one of the main stupidities of modern so-called spirituality is that it does not consider this first stage essential. Purification has to happen. There has to be a commitment to some kind of discipline, some fundamental housecleaning, some commitment to prayer, to openness, to really looking at one's thoughts, to offering the heart incessantly through the repetition of the Divine name, to the Beloved. This is an immense work. Do not think that it is simple to purify the heart. It is not. Because what we are trying to do, the Sufis say, is to clear the mirror so that the Divine sun can be reflected in it. The mirror in most cases is filthy, and cleaning it takes an enormous effort of love and faith. In the first stage, it is often faith that will give you what is needed, because in the first stage, very rarely do you have actually any living mystical experience. So you have to slug it out in the dark, to open in the dark, to work in the dark. You have to learn how to be peaceful, how to empty your mind, how to offer your being. But until you understand that all worldly things are trash, that all worldly loves are transient, that you are in *samsara* and that *samsara* is destined and designed to break you, until you really understand those things without any illusion, you have not been purified enough to have the Divine experience. So purification is a very rigorous business because so much that you believe real has to be taken away. The Divine has to remove all the toys before She can place the diamond in your hands. You have to know exactly how precious the diamond is before God gives it to you. And when you are purified enough and when it is possible for the Divine to take you and use you and give to you, at that moment the second stage begins, which is expansion.

Sufis make a distinction, a subtle distinction, between what they call *hal* and *maqam*. *Hal* refers to the Divine states, moments of bliss, visions, dreams, sudden ecstasies. These are states that come and go. *Maqam* are stations. States are experienced by the grace of God; stations you acquire by work, by mystical work, inner work and transformation. The states give you a sense of what you are striving toward, of what you are longing to unify with; they are states of ecstasy, bliss, and peace, of suddenly seeing the world disappear and reappear, all the various extraordinary touches of the tenderness of the life of God. But you have to work with those glimpses by deepening them, meditating on them, expanding their significance into every area of your life, by using the mind to illustrate them and understand them in all their facets. God hands you a diamond, but you have to turn it in the heart and mind again and again until you really radically understand it and how the experience, for example, of bliss, goes down *into* the depth of being, radiates through being, and illuminates being. That is your work. When you have worked in the heart and in the illumined intellect to understand the *hal,* you acquire the *maqam,* you go into the station of bliss, or the station of awareness, and finally the ultimate station which is that of great peace, in which all is both empty and full and all appears always as theophany of the Divine. That is work. *Hal* is play, Divine play. In the second stage, the stage of expansion—a beautiful word—expansion of the heart, expansion of what we thought we understood, wild expansion of reason, in fact, a shattering of reason against the doors and the walls of bliss, endless expansion until you can hardly bear it any longer, the Master takes you to edges that you could not believe you could get to: edges of exhaustion, anger, ecstasy, bliss, suicidal despair, which completely expand your sense of who you are, what the world is, what your heart is, what your life is, and what death is. What the Master does, in fact, one Sufi Master once told me, is quite simple. In the stage of expansion, the Master takes the heart and opens it endlessly, tears it endlessly open. And when it is totally torn apart, torn open, totally ruined, shattered, totally expanded, then the whole universe can be placed in the heart. Then the Beloved, God, is in the heart, and the Divine Light is radiating in everything because you do not remain, and that is when the third stage begins: the stage of Union.

When expansion has destroyed you, then what the Sufis call *baqa* can take place, which is dwelling in the living Presence of the Divine, in the constant knowledge of the Divine Light, in the constant accompaniment of God. Then the journey in Union flowers endlessly. Union is an endless experience of bliss and joy, an endless theophany. In Union you partake of the emptiness, freedom, bliss, and playfulness of the Divine itself and therefore you can be expanded endlessly, because the heart has been shattered and has become the Divine Heart. And in the Divine Heart, supernovas explode, worlds are born and die, whole civilizations crumble, and Love goes on in peaceful ecstasy, singing the name of God.

As Rumi said in the poem that ended the last chapter, "In the driest, whitest stretch of pain's infinite desert, I lost my sanity and found this rose." Rumi has been right to the end of human experience and found where the rose blooms, the wild rose, the rose you cannot see until your eyes are loving enough to see it. The Divine secrets are all protected, the Divine Knowledge is protected, by ring after ring of sacred fire. And only the loving can get through that fire; only those who are totally in love with the Beloved can ever look at the Beloved's face. The Beloved will reveal many things to others, but the Beloved's face will only be unveiled to those who are lost in love. There is no other way to know these secrets than to become the heart where these secrets can dance. There is no other way to know the Divine Love except by opening to the great passage of love between you and all things. So when Rumi says, "In the driest, whitest stretch of pain's infinite desert," he is not writing a poem, he is telling you about a place of final disillusion, desperation,and hopelessness, which is also a garden of gnosis.

I have spent a lot of time recently at the deathbeds of friends who are dying of AIDS, and they are "in pain's infinite desert." But many of them use that infinite desert to get to a place where they are really receptive and utterly open in silence to the Divine, and the Divine can work with astonishing swiftness in the last five or six days of their lives.

Robert Lowell wrote, "Sometimes I am weak enough to enter heaven." When you are weak enough, you let go, and that is when you find the rose, that is when you know that it is not you living your life, it is the Divine. It is not you who are doing anything. You do not exist in the way you think you do. You are a wave on the great Ocean of Energy and that Ocean is carrying you at every moment. But you are also that Ocean because being a wave, what else could you be but the Sea? You *are* the rose you find, and that rose is blossoming in everything, always.

Rumi wrote of Shams,

> You see through each cloak I wear
> Know if I speak without mouth or language.
> The world is drunk on its desire for words
> But I am the slave of the Master of Silence.

Allowing oneself to become the slave of the Master of Silence is the ultimate discipline. Then Shams said to him, "Keep my mysteries in your soul's treasure chest...". If you think that Rumi is talking when he is writing his poems, you are wrong. This is not talk, this is Silence. Rumi is talking silently to our souls, out of the deepest, richest, wildest Silence that we can possibly imagine or know, and his words are soaked, inebriated with that Divine Silence. When you properly listen to them, they take you straight to the most silent, ecstatic part of yourself. They are initiatory because they are the instruments of Silence.

Rumi became Shams, became silent, and out of that Silence sprung this vast fountain of ecstasy that he played without end. But this ecstasy is silent.

> Keep my mysteries in your soul's treasure chest,
> Dissimulate my ecstasies even to yourself.
> If you find me, hide me in your heart
> Know my madness as absolute truth.

That is the most brilliant instruction from the Master to the disciple. Everything is in there. I will give you visions, I will give you mysteries, but keep them in your treasure chest, do not share them too soon. People will deride them, people will say you are crazy. Dissimulate my ecstasies, keep them hidden, even to yourself, because some may be so strong that if you take the full blast, you would be incinerated and would not survive. So learn how to survive. You are in the Sahara now—I am taking you into the desert of awakening and you had better be prepared for what you are going to find there. These are the rules: If you find me, hide me in your heart. This has a double meaning. Hide me in your heart from the others, from the vulgar so they cannot get at me; but it also means hide me right in the core of your being, because it is there that I will blaze and burn and irradiate you. And then, the last instruction, the most important instruction and the one that most disciples cannot keep, is "know my madness as absolute truth." The Master is operating from a dimension of Divine consciousness, and Masters, when they are real Masters, are always operating from a dimension that you, in your rational mind or even in the evolving mind, cannot possibly understand. The greatest act of trust, which can only come from Divine Love for them, is to say to them, "You know. I know that you know, I know that you can do this. I know that what looks to me like insanity is real."

It cannot be said too often: to find and be the rose you have to give up trying to understand. You have to give up trying to know anything. You have to give up all the ego's desires to control the experience.

The advice that Shams gives Rumi is always very extreme, but if you want extreme change, you have to take extreme advice. Rumi says in the *Discourses* that a great Master is like a very skillful fisherman. The fisherman throws out his hook, gets the fish, and then winds it in slowly until it is exhausted. So when he actually gets the fish out of the water, as it is dancing about, in fact it is bleeding to death. That is the joke. You think that you are evading and dancing away, that you are having a nervous breakdown, having hysterics. You are not. You are just bleeding to death, and when you get exhausted, the Divine is going to reel you in. This is perfect. The hook is in your mouth; you are hooked by Love and tenderness, you are hooked by Divine experience. The Master is just sitting quietly, reeling you in.

Listen to this poem: "You are the soul, you cannot leave the body." "How can you know the soul," Rumi asks, "as you know the body?" Shams replies, "What do you know, what do you think you know?" This is not an area where you make bargains. You do not bargain with the Master, you do not bargain with God, you do not bargain with the Beloved; you cannot suddenly appear with your list of requirements. "You are the Sea of goodness," Rumi says. "Silence," Shams replies, "Love is a jewel that you cannot hand over like a stone." That is one of the great lines in Rumi. Rumi goes overboard: "Shams, you are so fantastic; you are great." This is seduction. The Master cannot be seduced by anything except sincerity. That is what is so terrifying about him.

Shams says to Rumi, don't give me this bullshit about me being a Sea of goodness or an angel. That is your game; you are being Rumi, the poet, the wordsmith. Burn, and then we will talk. He says, "Silence, Love is a jewel that you cannot hand over like a stone." What he means is very profound. The Master is trying to give you a diamond. What you actually want is a new Chevrolet, or a new girlfriend or boyfriend, or both, or a new figure, or a new career. No, none of those things. None of the faked jewels. It is the diamond that the Master is going to give, so everything that you ask for that is not a diamond, you won't get, or you will get it only to show you that you do not want it. "Love is a jewel that cannot be handed over like a stone," because what is being given is nothing else than Divine consciousness. And what you so often want, right up into the last stage, is trivial approximation of an approximation of Divine consciousness. The Master will hold out until you long enough.

When you long enough, the Master can just breathe on your face and you will see the Divine vision. When you long enough, the Divine spirit can descend in dreams and teach you directly. But until you long enough, you are still relying on your own games, fantasies, and illusions, your own very limited intelligence, and all of these have to be taken away. The great acid to clean away illusions is longing, longing for union with the Beloved. This is why Rumi says,

Heart, be brave, if you cannot bear grief, go—
Love's glory is not a small thing.
Come in if you are fearless;
Shudder, and this is not your house.

There is a moment on the Path when you realize that you
are going to have to go through doors of fire, and going through
doors of fire means being burnt. There is a moment when you
realize that you are going to have to die in reality, not just pretend to die, not just read about dying, not just recite Rumi late
at night, but really, day by day, hour by hour, moment by moment, go into the darkness of the Love of God and really surrender, a moment when you realize that to do that, you will
need Divine courage:

> The report of a Lion spread to all parts of the world and
> a man, marveling at the rumor, made for that thicket
> from a far distance in order to see the Lion. For a year,
> he endured the rigors of the road and traveled from stage
> to stage, and when he arrived at the thicket and spied
> the Lion from afar, he stood still and could not advance
> closer. Why, they said to him, have you set out on such
> a long road out of love for this Lion? This Lion has a
> special quality; anyone who approaches him boldly and
> lovingly rubs his hand upon him is unharmed by the
> Lion, but if anyone is afraid and timorous, the Lion is
> enraged against him. The lion attacked some, saying,
> What is this bad opinion you have of me, for such a
> creature you have trudged on for years and now you
> have arrived near me. Why do you stand still? Advance
> one step more. But no one had the courage to advance
> a further step. All said, the steps that we took hitherto
> were easy, we cannot take one step nearer.

Faith is that step: to take that step in the presence of the
Lion towards the Lion.

There is a moment when you realize that everything that
the mystics have told you is true, so true that it is the only

truth. You cannot hide anymore from the reality of the Light, from the reality of the fire, from the reality of Divine Love. There is a moment when you have to face with every cell and breath in your body, and every thought in your mind, that everything that you have ever understood is unreal, and that the only reality is the Divine Knowledge, the Divine Love, and the Divine Light. And that moment you reel, because you are looking at the Lion in the face, the Lion of glory, the Lion of love, the Lion of passion, that is going to kill you with Love. It is going to kill you. Because if you really face what you are coming to know, you are facing the necessity of abandon, sacrifice, adoration, and transformation. You are committing yourself to the journey without end; you are taking all your clothes off like St. Francis and going completely naked into nowhere. But in that moment when you realize that you have to take one step towards the Lion, in the presence of the Lion, you say to yourself, "Heart, be brave. If you cannot be brave, just go. Love's glory is not a small thing."

I once saw in a cemetery in India an old woman just sobbing away at the grave of her son who had been tortured by Tamil terrorists. She spread herself over the whole grave and sobbed. She held the grave with two hands and sobbed and sobbed. And I thought to myself and said to my companion, "I don't want to love if that is what love is," and he said, "Are you crazy? What she feels is so immeasurably beautiful because she grieves that much, she loves that much, and love lives on in her." Love's glory was in her weeping, love's glory was in her sobbing, love's glory was in the abandonment of her grief. That is love's glory, and love's glory has blood all over it.

When somebody dies of AIDS in your arms, love's glory is the blood they spit onto your shirt as they are dying. Love's glory is holding the two-year-old child dying of AIDS against your breast so that he can have some warmth before he goes, but knowing that as he goes, he will break your heart in a way that you never had your heart broken. Love's glory is accepting the heartbreak and opening to it, not once, not a thousand times, but every second. Every second has a new heartbreak. Every piece of news has a new disaster. Every turn of this desolate world brings new agonies, and love's glory means accepting, opening, embracing them all, and giving love completely, unconditionally, at all moments to all, including the torturer and murderer.

In the leading image of our culture, the supreme avatar of the West, Jesus Christ, we have an image of what love's glory is. Love's glory is that battered body on the cross. He loved enough to give everything. So, "come in if you are fearless; shudder, and this is not your house," because this is the house of the Lion, and as Rumi says, "The step in the presence of the Lion, towards the Lion, is a great and rare matter, the concern of the Elect and intimate of God. This is the true step in a human life, the rest are mere footprints. That step comes to prophets who have washed their hands of their whole life." As Rumi says in these poems in *Love's Fire:*

> Have you no dignity, my heart,
> Scattering always like dust in wind?
> You are in the fire? Let's leave you there.
> Terror will make you subtle.

> Near truth's blaze what are "doubt" or "certainty?"
> Bitterness dies near the honey of truth.
> Doesn't the sun hide its face before his?
> What are these small lights that linger?

What is the mystery of Divine Love and loving the Divine? It is a very simple mystery. It is that the fire, the Light that is creating everything and in which everything is dying, is the fire of Love, ecstasy, bliss, and peace. But the fire that arises in the heart when the Divine Beloved is encountered, when Jesus or Mother Meera or the Buddha is really encountered, is nothing other than the light that creates the entire cosmos. That fire and the Divine fire are One. So as it rises, as it possesses the body, as it burns away everything that is not it, it joins with the fire around it and becomes one in union with that fire. It is the Divine Beloved burning in you, the lover, so that the lover can transform into the Beloved. You come to understand that the Love you are loving with is the Love of God itself, the Love that is creating and manifesting everything. And as you come to understand that more and more deeply, you become one with everyone and with everything eternally and the game is over. Rumi says:

> All the world's passions are simple
> Beside this passion; cool beside this
> Fire I am in that ignites the world
> And shall destroy it.

Anyone who has lived through an experience with a Divine Master will tell you that there is nothing more complex than the search for Divine simplicity, and anyone who has lived through the agony, tensions, and neuroses, the difficulty of all the different twists and turns of the ego as it burns to death, will tell you that you know nothing if you come to them and say they have been living some illusion, some fantasy. You do not go through all of that for a fantasy and in a fantasy. What you are going through is the most extremely difficult thing that you can possibly do. It is horrible to have the mirror of perfection staring at you and to see without any help or consolation exactly how futile everything is that you have been and done and thought. It is horrible to face just how little you want to love. It is horrible to face that behind all your protestations of love, there is a passion for control, that all of your ways of saying how loving you are can be ways of avoiding being destroyed to *become* Love. You want Love but you do not want to become Love. You want to be given the visions and the illuminations, but you do not want to become empty enough to receive them. You go through every conceivable game of your own darkness, of your own nature, of your own stupidity, and this is "a passion so complex that all the other world passions are simple before it." In fact, you train in the other passions to be able to bear this one. The secular, rational intelligence is totally banal, totally mediocre. It has no understanding of the massive effort of the heart and mind that goes into a transformation. None of the great poets of the twentieth century that we so revere have come close to understanding what Rumi and the great mystics understand, because we are living in a banal world that has lost this final sophistication, that has no understanding of crucifixion and transfiguration. This is why a poet like Rumi is so important because in him we find an entire spiritual culture: both the record of the bliss and joy of Union, and a record of the price, the cost, the stages, the evasions. When we read this poetry, we are educated in the highest sense to the entire nature of the Path, and we need desperately now to have this education.

> I groaned, he burnt me while I groaned.
> I fell silent, his fire fell on me.
> He drove me out beyond all limit,
> I ran inside, he burnt me there.

If you want to enter nowhere, if you want to build a tent in placelessness, if you want to be free, you must lose your chains.

> I groaned, he burnt me while I groaned.

You are groaning. Do you think that will do any good? You are just a depressive. Shams is so brutal to Rumi. Rumi groans and moans and Shams says, "Stop being a boring depressive, you are just dank wood. I am sick of your dankness, your endless growling, burn some more. You are not suffering enough; you are just groaning. It is revolting." Shams says these things. "I fell silent," because what can you do after this? I can't be depressive, so I'll go silent, I'll concentrate, I'll try to enter the mind, then fire falls on that. Why aren't you active? People are dying in the streets and you are sitting here in your stupid meditation, what do you think you are doing? Blissing out with your rosaries and your fantasies of God? Stop being silent, love, break your heart, grow up. "He drove me out, beyond all limit." The Master is there to put fire under every false step that you take.

> He drove me out beyond all limit,
> I ran inside, he burnt me there.

The last line is absolutely beautiful because, of course, it has at least two meanings. The first is: I ran inside, I cowered, I ran back into the house, and he burnt me there because he incinerated me with longing for him, for union, for bliss. So when I ran inside for protection, all I found was a longing so vast that the whole process began all over again. Or it can mean that when Rumi ran back knowing what he then knew, the true burning could begin.

Let us now talk more precisely about the burning. The best description of it I know comes from St. John of the Cross, and I suspect he was inspired to it by his reading of the Spanish Sufi masters. First, take a damp, dank log called Andrew, or Steven, or Sandra. Then put the damp, dank log into a roaring fire. There is a lot of spitting, and dark grimy smoke comes out of that dank log. The fire has to enter the log, but the log is damp and covered with grimy, old, dank moss—I am so depressed, my mother abused me, I lost my job, I lost seventeen girlfriends in a row, I want to kill myself, the world is ending, I am just sick of the whole experience, I want to die—that is the damp, dank log that we all identify with, that is the ego, the endless whining, self-piteous, dreary voice that goes on and on. What happens first is purification, to get back to the Sufi theme. Purification is frightening, because in the fire a lot of spitting and black smoke, a lot of difficulty happens. Then expansion: the fire enters the log and the Light enters. You burn in the fire and the blaze is without interference now because the impurities have been burnt away. The blaze is there, this great sunburst of the illumination of bliss which is the second stage. But this is not the final stage. The final stage can

never be talked about and no one, not even Rumi, has ever
described it. The Divine mystery is ringed about with silence
at the end and only the lover can go into the bedroom of Silence.
It is the last moment when the fire is dying and the love is ash,
an amazing soft, deeply tender, deeply radiant glow emanating from the log. This is union, this is oneness, because this is
a love so empty and so tender that the entire universe is always
dancing in it: *nirvana, baqa, moksha,* liberation, now.

Meanwhile, we are in the fire, spitting.

> I groaned; "Be quiet," he said,
> I was quiet: he said, "Groan!"
> I grew feverish, he said, "Be calm!"
> I grew calm, he said, "I want you to burn."

And when you have been through that, then you have to
make a commitment to suffering. You can't run away at this
point; you just have to say, "I am going to go through this."
You have to learn how to say what Rumi says:

> Pain is the wind his flags unfurl in
> The desert that the stallions cross and re-cross
> Without check or end,
> He is my anguish and I am his.

In that moment, the stupid, old, selfish ego begins to begin
to imagine something of the love of the Master. The Master
who says—remember the Sufi story—you think that I have
been doing nothing. I have been burning in love for you all
these years waiting for you to catch fire. You think that is nothing. That is infinitely vaster than you can even imagine. And
at that moment, when Rumi says, "He is my anguish and I am
his," you realize that there is a relationship going on, a love in
which there is tremendous concern from the Master in a very
strange and very deep way for your entire life.

I have seen that look on my Master's face sometimes, a look
of, "How long will it take you to understand? How long must
I go on loving you before you understand that you are love-

able? How long must I listen to the story that you call your life? How long? And it is not because I am impatient. It is because I absolutely love you, see you always as you really are, and I have been waiting all this time for you to turn up, so could you, please, turn up soon?" That is the Love of the Master. Masters are surrounded by ghosts trying to become human, and every so often, a ghost turns into a human being.

The process goes on in great intensity, great intricacy, and great subtlety. But as the process gets deeper and deeper, so the expansion, and the bliss and joy, get more and more profound. There are new griefs in expansion, new torments, but they are the torments of obvious love. The first stage is like falling in love which, God knows, can be very painful. The second stage is being in love and the third stage is being Love. From falling in love to being in love to being Love is the progression. And this is the stage of being in love, of being enraptured in the process, in the secret beauty and glory of the Master.

> Tonight is the night; sad, radiant,
> When our mysteries are fulfilled.
> All my mysteries are images of you—
> Night, be long! He and I are lost in Love.

The night comes up. The night for Rumi is always the time when the madness of the ego subsides, the Divine Beauty of the Beloved rises like the moon in the sky, and the perfumed night brings that beauty of the Beloved deep into the heart. And this night, he recognizes the onset of deep bliss. It is very beautiful; it is as if the poem is his going into bliss and as he goes into bliss, he is telling you what is happening, and it ends in the silence of bliss. Four lines that take you right into the heart and leave you there.

> Tonight is the night; sad, radiant,
> When our mysteries are fulfilled.
> All my mysteries are images of you—
> Night, be long! He and I are lost in Love.

"You could have had anything," you once said.
I laughed. What could anything be
Without you? All the world is driftwood
Thrown up from your sea.

You have in these poems fragments of real conversations
between these two supreme lovers. You can imagine a scene
when Shams is looking at Rumi with absolute love and wonder because Shams knew who was loving him, he knew that
the heart that Rumi was giving him was a heart big enough to
contain the universe that he was putting into it. And Shams
also knew that Rumi loved him with every part of himself, and
Shams basked in the glory of Rumi's love just as Rumi basked
in the glory of Shams' love. There are some amazing scenes in
Aflaki's texts when suddenly Shams and Rumi are dancing.
There is a Sufi feast, everybody is out of his mind with bliss
and joy, and Shams suddenly starts to sing and says, "You do
not know who Rumi is, you do not know who this man is.
You think that he is Rumi. This man has a thousand thousand
suns in his brain; this man has a thousand thousand oceans in
his heart; he is the glorious one." And Shams goes out of his
mind before his own disciple. There must have been a moment
when Shams held Rumi to him and holding him, said, "You
could have had anything, but you chose me, you chose me,
you could have had anyone, you could have had anything that
you wanted, but you chose me." And you can imagine that
moment, and Rumi laughing. "The world is nothing but you.
It is just driftwood flung up from your sea." Can you see what
a magnificent love play this is? This is like Tristan and Isolde
in the love duet from Wagner's opera: Tristan takes a phrase
and stretches his voice right until the end. Isolde catches the
phrase right at the end and flies and soars with it; she takes
off like a great eagle into the light, and then Tristan is there
right in the highest point of the sound and takes the last phrase
and dies further into music. What you are listening to when
you are listening to Tristan and Isolde's love duet is two beings

dying into love in sound. And when you are really reading this poetry, that is also what you are listening to. You are listening to two beings dying into love together. Shams and Rumi were both dying into love, they were both bleeding into love, they were both bleeding tears of fire into love.

Listen now to the next poem:

> Grieve for him all your life
> Make life your grief for him;
> Grief with its hidden smile
> Transparent as a twig in April.

Rumi missed Shams all his life. He may have become Shams; Shams may have entered into him, but there was a part of Rumi that always missed his beloved. We see it in some of the last odes when he says, "Today somebody said his name, Shams, and all the beauty of my youth came back and I was lost in tears." In that grief is a very profound tenderness. To accept that amount of grief is to allow yourself to be opened up to your own utter fragility. To accept that you can love someone that much and miss them with every cell in your being, to accept that you adore them, that their separation from you is actually killing you, is to be open to your utmost fragility, desolation, and loneliness, and therefore to be opened up to the loneliness, desolation, and fragility of the whole human enterprise and come into the space of love since love's glory, as we have said, has blood all over it. And now this poem:

> At the end of pain
> A quiet white exhaustion.
> Your ghost sits down
> To take my head in its hands.

Just listen to that. It is a final poem.

"At the end of pain," right at the end of the night, at the end of longing and immense mourning, "a quiet white exhaustion."

Emily Dickinson says this magnificent thing, "After great

pain, a formal feeling comes, nerves sit ceremonious as tombs." That is when you know:

> A quiet white exhaustion
> Your ghost sits down at the end of pain,
> To take my head in its hands.

The mystery of union begins when longing has softened you up enough to receive the tenderness of the Beloved. The mystery of union begins when you have been destroyed enough to be grateful for a blade of grass, for the wind and the freshness of the morning, for a beautiful face on the bus. Because at that moment, you are beginning to see that you are in a Divine world, surrounded by mercy. But how stripped you have to be to receive the mercy. To arrive at that point when you suddenly begin to see the miracle of everything around you, you have to lose all the false miracles of the ego. You have to die for the life which is trembling in everything around you to appear in its full miracle.

> When I am sad, I am radiant
> When I am broken, content
> And when I am tranquil and silent as the earth
> My cries like thunder tremble heaven.

He has come into the kingdom of paradox.

What is a mystic? A mystic is a king or queen of paradox. A mystic knows that death is not death, life is not life, the body is not the body, and the spirit is not the spirit. The mystic knows that the Master's abandonment is actually grace, and that a lesser kind of grace would actually be an abandonment. The mystic knows that he or she is an eternal being in a dying body, and that this is the supreme experience. To be an eternal being without dying in a body would only be to have one-half of the experience of God. But to be an eternal being in a body is to have both, to have the experience of transcendence and the experience of immanence, both the experience of the Divine emptiness that is creating and the experience of being the cre-

ation. Do you understand the gift? The gift is death, the gift
is time, the gift is pain, the gift is love, the gift is extremity.
When you receive the gift full in the blood of the heart you
dance as Shiva. You dance as the unborn one, you dance as
the Divine One, you dance as the child of the Mother, you
dance as Christ did, you dance as the liberated one in the complete divine experience, the complete divine madness, which
is to be in unity with everything that lives and dies, that has
ever lived or died. That is the supreme experience and that is
what is being offered to humankind.

God says to Mohammed, "For you, if you had not existed,
I would not have created the heavens and the earth." Think
what it means mystically. It means that this entire experience
is given to you as a feast of beauty, but to attend the feast you
must accept that you are dying and death is what makes the
feast so poignant, so exquisite, so extraordinary. "I cannot create unless I die," says Shiva, "so if you wish to be my beloved
and partake in everything that I am, create and die with me,
die as me and create as me, and be silent beyond all creation
and all death as me, and enter into my triple, simultaneous
being, enter into my smile."

Why is the Buddha smiling? Because the Buddha has become eternity in time at one nameless unnameable point when
neither eternity nor time exist, when both are dissolved in a
supreme deathless experience. That is why he smiles.

Tarif was a great early Sufi poet, and he said that "the cause
of creation is beauty and the first creation is love." The whole
of the glory of Islamic mysticism is contained in that phrase,
because if it is true—and it is true—that the cause of creation
is beauty, is to give the soul this experience of ultimate rapture, that is, to give the human being this experience of living
as the Divine in a Divine world, with Divine ecstasy, Divine
sweetness, and Divine peace, then the first creation, the pri-
mal, the source, is Love. What else could create beauty but
Love? And why was beauty created? To show Love. And how
can we come to see the beauty? By loving totally. If you love

totally, beauty is revealed and that total beauty has silenced everyone who has ever seen it. When you see what is really here, there are no more words. There is just an experience of endless rapture, wonder, and joy; and when the beauty that has been your destiny to see arises, it silences the heart, it silences the ego. The entire creation reveals itself as an endless net of jewels, as a series of diamonds all of which are sparkling and in which all are reflected. This is nothing other than God. And God is beautiful. This Divine Beauty is what arises in illumination and it is what arises in these poems. These poems are jewels of enlightenment. They come from the highest place and they are given to you, but you must know how beautiful you are to be able to receive beauty.

The tradition—the *Hadiths*—are sayings of the Prophet and they contain a whole universe. This one is very simple but very important: "My earth and my heavens do not contain me, but I am contained in the heart of my faithful servant." This is the supreme mystery of being human. The entire cosmos cannot contain God because God goes beyond the cosmos. But the heart—the open, illumined, and ecstatic heart—that can contain God because it can become God and God can appear in it as it, that is the mystery. "My earth and my heavens do not contain me, but I am contained in the heart of my faithful servant."

When you look at a sunset, you are looking at yourself flaming. When you look at rhododendrons in wild blossom, you are looking at your origin dancing, bounding in front of you. When you look at the grass awash in sunlight, you are looking at the Beloved which is you. You are looking at your own extreme beauty, and the love that awakens in you at that moment, the rapture that awakens in you at that moment, is your rapture at your Divine Self. When you listen to the music of sixteenth-century English composer Thomas Tallis, or Wagner or Beethoven, or Aretha Franklin, and the glory begins in your heart listening to that glory, you are listening to your own glory, the glory of the heart. So all of this is an immense experience of one's own

Divine Self, and in it, when you come to that understanding which is beyond any words, you may like Rumi say:

> "Come to the Spring garden," they said,
> "Its air is song; you can't hear the crow."
> In my soul there lives a marvelous painter
> Who paints on each crow feather a thousand gardens.

Rumi means that at that moment, the normal sense of good and evil is destroyed. When you see God dancing in everything, then the things you thought were evil or bad no longer seem evil or bad, because God is dancing even in them. There is no separation. Kali dances and you laugh even as she tramples you.

> I burn away; laugh, my ashes are alive!
> I die a thousand times:
> My ashes dance back—
> A thousand new faces.

Rumi has come to the stage where dying is easy, and when he dies a thousand times a second, his life is only this rapturous dying into a deeper and deeper life. So he says, "I burn away. I laugh." The ego mourns; the spirit laughs. If you are burning in the spirit, the spirit knows that some new dream, some new bliss, some extraordinary new theophany is being prepared for it, because that is the law of fire. "My ashes are alive." It is all alive. "I die a thousand times and my ashes dance back." Those who have been reborn in the fire of Divine Love are like the phoenix; they rise again and again, like the creation itself out of the fire of destruction. When you consent to dance and burn away, you become the creation—destruction and creation in one—and your ashes dance back with a thousand new faces. You go deeper and deeper into this staggering and outrageous realization that everything is nothing other than God, that you have to die and when you die and burn away, your "ashes dance a thousand new faces." It is as if Rumi has seen a thousand new Divine faces—every time I go through a death, a thousand new Divine friends appear. A thousand new origins, opportunities, a thousand new joys and dimensions, because you are, at this moment in this life, expanding at the speed of light to the edges of the universe.

> Cloud pregnant with a million bolts of lightning,
> Love gives birth to the philosopher's stone.
> My soul is flooded by your Sea of splendor,
> Being and cosmos drown there silently.

When the child is born in the heart, when the Beloved is born in the heart, the entire creation participates in this birth. In the Mahayana Buddhist texts, the moment of enlightenment is said to be accompanied by vast rolls of thunder, huge streaks of lightning, by the entire creation laughing with joy. At the moment when the Buddha obtained enlightenment, it is said that in that moment, nobody wept in the entire world, no one was unhappy, everything partook and drank of that extreme beauty and peace. The whole of nature worships the Beloved in you when the Beloved appears. So the "cloud pregnant with a million bolts of lightning" is Love, and Love gives birth to the philosopher's stone, the mysterious awareness of unity that is the philosopher's stone. At that moment, the Divine Light comes up, the world drowns in the Divine Light, and what the Sufis call the "Sea of splendor" is present.

> My soul is flooded by your Sea of splendor,
> Being and cosmos drown there silently.

This experience is absolutely beyond words or description. It is beyond Being and beyond anything that we know of nature. Nature reveals itself as transparent with light, and what you have imagined to be Being is revealed as a breath of God, nonexistence, an invention. The Sea of splendor that is manifesting both Being and the Cosmos drowns Being and Cosmos and you are initiated into the final and absolute reality.

When this moment comes, you will know that the Love of God is so immense that it prepares for every soul this final ecstatic experience at the end of the journey through *samsara*. When that homecoming happens, all the pain is forgotten, because all the pain was an illusion. The healing is final because the Love prepared is final. You realize the literal meaning of all the creation being created for you. You are it.

> On the Day of Resurrection, men will stagger
> Before you, pale and trembling with terror:
> I will hold up your love to you and say,
> "Ask it anything; it speaks for me."

Rumi has gone into the place of carelessness; he knows that he has loved Shams totally, that Shams has given him the Divine gnosis and that Shams will plead for him on the Day of Judgement. He has nothing more to fear, he says, "Your love will speak for me, because only you know who I am and only you love me as I need to be loved."

> Now I know that Love is with me always,
> Its soft and fiery curls always in my hand;
> However drunk the wine made me yesterday,
> Today his wine is drunk in me.

I know now that Love is with me always because I am Love. Love can only be with you always when you are Love itself. No separation. And the soft and fiery curls of Love, the revelation and the bliss—because the curls are the bliss of Love in Sufi erotic imagery—are always in my hand. There is no more grasping, yearning, and longing, because the state of Love has arrived, and this is a supreme state in which you say, "However drunk the wine made me yesterday, now the wine is drunk in me." When you become Love itself, you become intoxicated in the secret wine of the Beloved, and that wine itself ferments and deepens and grows more powerful. And now this:

> In the end, I shall be at an end,
> Nothing but grief and love,
> Mixed in a dark transparent wine
> You down in one gulp.

And now this:

> To die in life is to become life.
> The wind stops skirting you
> And enters; all the roses, suddenly,
> Are blooming in your skull.

The Beloved is all around you wearing the absolute beauty of his absolute springtime. Die into the spring, become spring, then the wind you think is blowing around you will suddenly be in you; you will be sprung free of your body. You will be in the space of emptiness and all things happening will be happening inside you, as you. All the roses, both external and internal, the roses of spring and the roses of the Beloved, the roses of vision, enlightenment, and awareness, all of them will suddenly be blooming in your hollow dull skull. Through the door of death you will have entered the state of eternity. You will be in the eternal present. And in that eternal present, everything will be simultaneously burning with and opening in the Divine Light. And now this:

> The soul's extravagance is endless.
> Spring after spring after spring ...
> We are your gardens dying, blossoming.

Rumi has seen right into the volcano of creation. Gaze into a volcano and you see incredible shapes being spewed out of the fire and going back into the fire. Imagine this vast dance of fire—worlds arising and falling back—then you begin to have some sense of the immense and fabulous extravagance of the soul. Out of the soul is being created the oceanic trenches, supernovas, wars, madness, ecstasy, everything. This vast Energy is dancing out of the soul, out of the emptiness that is the soul, and out of it is being created endlessly, spring after spring after spring. In the mind of God, there is only eternal springtime, eternal freshness, the eternal fiery sweetness of the eternal experience. "Spring after spring after spring, we are your gardens dying, blossoming." To die is to blossom and to blossom is to

die. When you have entered, embraced, delighted in, found
the mystical meaning of, and enacted that paradox, then you
are becoming everything. And now this:

> Don't call him "this" or "that."
> In the Love I know, what word could stay?
> Language is just a handful of dust
> A breath of his blows away.

And now this:

> Whatever they say or think
> I am in you and I am you,
> No one can understand this
> Until he has lost his mind.

And now this:

> After the certainties, the visions,
> This final loneliness
> You flower in.

After all the visions, after all the ecstasies and merging,
what is called by the Sufis the great Peace begins. At first it
seems like a state of neutrality, almost of death, but it is a state
of infinite delicacy and refinement in which you are no longer
experiencing as a human being but as a Divine being. So you
experience everything with the restraint of the Divine, the infinite delicacy of the Divine, the infinite peace of the Divine.
When you are watching this film from the Divine seat, you are
watching it with enormous tenderness but also enormous de-
tachment and generosity, enormous calm and sweetness, but
also silence and peace. At that moment, you enter the final
loneliness. After giving you all the visions and the ecstasies,
the guru usually takes them away because the final state is not
ecstatic. It is beyond ecstacy. It is knowledge itself, it is awareness itself, it is consciousness itself. This state is sober, but with
Divine sobriety. It is normal. It is what the Hindus call *sahaja*.
It is as it is, just as the Divine world is as it is. And that moment

is as it is. And that loneliness in which the Beloved flowers becomes aloneness in which the Beloved is.

You have to go into that loneliness where you lose everything including your ecstasies, your visions, and your insights. Everything is taken away and you wait. And right in the center of that loneliness the ultimate mystery begins, the ultimate tenderness arrives. It is really like the end of the night in India. Right at the end of the night when you can't believe that the night can get any darker, any more intense, suddenly the most miraculously tender light appears, this very soft, very alone grey, subtly suffused with pink, and this extraordinary silence and peace open. And now this:

> This isn't spring, it's another season.
> A hidden union makes our eyes swim.
> All our trees' branches dance in this rain.
> Each, for a secret reason.

All barriers dissolve; all fears dissolve and reality itself manifests as Light.

> For days I am no longer in the world.
> Nor am I out of it.
> Not "here," not "there."
> Silence, light, air.

Ask an enlightened being, are you alive? They might say no. Ask them if they are going to die. They might say no. Are they in life? No, not as you know it. Are they dying? No, not as you know it. Are they in a body? No, not as you know it. Are they here? Not as you know it. Are they there? Not as you know it. In that state all that you can say of them is what they say of themselves. Silence, Light, Air.

I put the next poem at the end of *Love's Fire* because I really believe this is Rumi's springtime and that he has been waiting a long time to be listened to. And that this is the time when listening to him could change everything.

Those tender words we said to one another
Are stored in the secret heart of heaven:
One day like rain, they will fall and spread,
And our mystery will grow green over the world.

That day is here, is now. The secret words Shams and Rumi
said to each other are spreading now through every language,
and everyone who listens to those secret words receives news
of their own secret selves. And as the news spreads, the smiles
spread, and the mystery grows green over the earth. Human
beings return to what they always are, to the knowledge that
they are Divine children in a Divine universe, playing a Divine
game of Love for the Divine Beloved, as Love, in Love, for
Love.

Chapter Four

The Voice of Silence

ALL THINGS BEGIN and end in silence. All things are born from silence. Silence is the nature of the mind and of the heart of God.

> Lovers share a sacred decree to seek the Beloved
> They roll head over heels, rushing towards the
> Beautiful One
> Like a torrent of water
> In truth everything and everyone is a shadow of the
> Beloved
> and our seeking is His seeking and our words are His
> words.
> At times we fly towards the Beloved like a dancing
> stream
> At times we are still water held in His pitcher
> At times we boil in the pot
> Turning to vapor
> That is the job of the Beloved
> He breathes into my ear until my soul takes on his
> fragrance
> He is the soul of my soul
> How can I escape?
> But why would any soul in this world want to escape
> from the Beloved?
> He will melt your pride, making you thin as a strand
> of hair

Yet do not trade, even for both worlds
One strand of his hair
We search for Him here and there, while looking right
    at Him
Sitting by his side, we ask: Oh Beloved, where is the
    Beloved?
Enough with such questions
Let silence take you to the core of life
All your talk is worthless when compared with one
    whisper of the Beloved.

Let silence take you to the core of life.

Here are three stories about the power of silence.

When I went to Tiruvannamalai I met an old woman who
had been Ramana Maharshi's disciple who told me her story.
She had lived a worldly life which had been very happy. But
when she was sixty, in the course of one year, she lost her husband, four children, her fortune, and her house. The whole
world that she had built, through will, passion, and care,
through all the human virtues, crumbled around her. She had
heard of course of the great saint who lived in Tiruvannamalai
but had never gone to see him. Why would she need to see
anybody? She had everything she wanted: a husband, children,
safety. But when all those things were taken away, and as she
wept night after night, a longing grew in her to see the Maharshi
and to present him with all her grief and all her pain. So, she
went to the ashram where he was sitting. She poured out her
story in great detail to him and awaited his reply. He said nothing. She grew impatient and asked him again, "Don't you have
anything to tell me? Don't you have any solutions, any explanations? Can't you give me any real teaching so that I can go
on? I am in desperate straits." And he said absolutely nothing.
She started to sob and sob because she thought that even the
Maharshi, even this great saint had abandoned her. Then she
grew tired from sobbing and noticed that the Maharshi was
looking at her. And, very quietly and simply, she raised her
eyes and she looked back at the Maharshi. What happened

then, she said, cannot be put into words. Because what happened then was transmission.

There are no solutions to life, but there is an experience of wholeness, of bliss, of being, of the deathlessness of the Divine Self, of Silence in all its multifaceted, diamond splendor that heals all grief, all wounds, all questions. It is that Silence that Ramana Maharshi implanted forever in this woman's soul, gave forever to her mind, initiated forever in her heart. It is in that Silence that Job gazed upon the splendor of the creation after all his afflictions when he sat down before the Divine and said, "I am dust and ashes. Do with me what you will."

The second story about the power of silence comes from my favorite tale of Milarepa. Milarepa, the supreme yogi of Tibet, the great lover of the Void, the gentlest, tenderest, most far-seeing saint of the whole Tibetan pantheon, lived in a cave in the Himalaya wrapped only in a cotton robe. One day a robber came and took everything that he had: his one pot, his nettles, and perhaps an old battered Buddha statue or two. And the robber, feeling very happy with his morning's haul, started to walk down the mountain. After about a quarter of an hour, he heard something behind him and turned to see a most astonishing sight: the bony hermit running naked, smiling, down the mountain, holding out his robe. The robber looked at Milarepa's eyes, saw that there was nothing he could do that could in any way alter this unconditional love and forgiveness that Milarepa had for him, fell at his feet and became one of his greatest disciples. What had been communicated to the robber's heart was some taste of that great love that rises out of silence. That infinite and universal love that rises out of the silence of the Void, that great silent love in which Milarepa's mind was forever at peace.

The third story is just an anecdote about our beloved master, Rumi. He had a disciple who was stubborn, sceptical, cynical, loquacious, and vain. And Rumi loved this disciple because he was amused by him. But one day he had had enough of the endless questions, the theological disquisitions, the concepts, the deconstructions. And he said to the disciple after a particularly harrowing hour, "All right. I think we should go for a walk in the town gardens." It was twilight. Rumi said nothing. The disciple kept gazing at Rumi, expecting him to say something, to give some clue, some marvelous disquisition which would finally cure him of his longing. Rumi went on saying nothing. After a while, he raised his right hand and just pointed. It was at that moment that the disciple saw that all the trees and all the laden rosebushes in the park were bowing to Rumi. And what Rumi was able to communicate to his disciple at that moment was the wonder that rises out of the heart of silence, the sense of ecstatic marveling, that is yet another facet of the diamond of silence. What Rumi was able to transmit in that extraordinary moment was not awe at his power, but awe at that divine power that can at any moment make nonsense of all our laws, of all nature's laws, of everything that we think is real.

Three stories of what happens in silence. Ramana Maharshi's transmission of the entire experience to the grieving woman so that she saw beyond the ego and its agonies to the Divine Self that is forever stainless, pure, and serene, forever beyond as well as within the creation. Milarepa's transmission to the robber who was to become his disciple of the unconditional, wordless passion of true love that arises out of the heart of emptiness, of the love of the Buddhamind. Rumi's transmission, beyond all concepts, beyond all dogmas, beyond all disquisitions, of wonder and ecstasy before the divine magic of the Lord.

All true gifts are given and received in silence. Silence underlies, permeates all things, because the Divine is silent. The glory, the *Kibriya,* is a great, golden bed of silence from which all the rose gardens of all the world flower and into which they fade.

You may think Rumi is a great master of words. That is true, but he's a far greater master of silence. And in Rumi, we have an almost unique phenomenon in world literature. We have a totally realized being, a master of being, who is one with the One, using words, using the mask of Rumi to say words that themselves are soaked with the wine of divine silence, that issue out of silence, draw the silence out of us, and make us drunk on the silent Presence that is always within us, that wells up in us as we listen silently to the silence behind the words.

Now I want you to listen to what he himself says about his poetry. He is very harsh because what Rumi is attempting to do goes far, far beyond poetry. What he's doing in these poems, if we let him, is what those three stories were doing: using words as moons to shine with the sun of silence so that the Divine Light that creates all things can illumine our hearts and our being and take us to a state far beyond concepts, dogmas, or words.

First I'm going to take you through what Rumi says about language, his language, through different parts of the *Discourses*, the *Fihi-ma-Fihi* where he describes his attitude to language. Then we will plunge into the odes and I will show you how they are the architecture of silence, the music of silence, and how many of them end with a plea for silence — not, as many critics have said, because this was a convention in the ghazals and songs of Rumi's time and in Persian poetry generally, but because the poem itself is leading you, stage by stage, recognition by recognition, bliss by bliss, to a state in which, at the end of the poem, you are prepared to leap into what the poem has prepared for you: the ocean of silence, the ocean of *Kibriya*. So the poem becomes a magical, mystical object into which you enter — which then works upon you, vibrates upon your deepest self by images, by rhythm, by drawing on the different emotional colors of spiritual experience to take you to a moment of security and ecstasy where you are prepared to go directly into the Presence which has no words.

No other poet has ever managed this supreme trick — to make the words themselves soak you in a Divine Silence; to use the words to dissolve all words, to dissolve all need for images in the mind. This is an astonishing act, mirroring the creation itself. What is the creation? The creation is a manifestation of Silence and Light. The creation soars like a million-winged bird out of the womb of light, and returns at every second into that womb to be refreshed and re-created. And that is what Rumi's poetry does, because he is in the Divine Mind. He is speaking as the Divine. He is enacting in his poetry the divinizing process whereby we progress through different emotional states, different gnostic recognitions, different mystic illuminations, higher and higher until we are prepared to take the leap into ultimate being. That divinizing process is echoed, mirrored, reconstructed dazzlingly with infinite skill, wisdom, and unnerving love in the poems themselves. Silence dances its fullest dance in the poems, just as silence is dancing this full dance in reality. The poems and reality become one. One consciousness, one act, one silence.

Rumi never created a poem without knowing exactly the uselessness of words. He never used terms in his poetry without knowing that all those terms dissolved in an embrace of the Beloved and in the Divine Light and in the infinite peace of the Presence, so that everything he does, everything that he is, has this radiant doubleness of purpose. He was using what we need—words, images—to take us to a place where we did not know we could go.

Reading a poem by Rumi really means three things. It means entering as far as you can into that Divine Silence from which these poems and all things come. It means listening as far as possible from the awakening Divine Self in yourself, with total attention, devotion, and concentration. And it means submitting to Rumi as he himself had submitted to Shams, so that this supreme Master of Silence, through words, can take you into the very deepest place where the Presence is always. Submit to each turn and twist, each rhythm and image, because each turn and twist and rhythm and image has another design upon you, another way of leading you into the secret of silence.

Sacred art is sacred because it springs from the most devoted silence, the silence of adoration, and because it leads to that silence of adoration.

Imagine, now, what it must mean to be a sacred artist of the depth and scale of Rumi. It means going through a real, terrifying, glorious transformation. It means soaking your mind for years in the Divine Light and the Divine Silence. How else can you speak? What else can you speak about? It means developing every skill and talent, every possible virtue and power, because what you are celebrating is not a love affair or some philosophical insight you have in the mountains, but the Divine itself—the *Kibriya,* the glory of God. What you do has to be as perfect as possible. And as precise: you are trying humbly and passionately to mirror in whatever medium you choose the Divine Creation. And this costs everything: total stripping, total attention, total humility, and total talent dedicated entirely to the making perfect for God. And it is then that you begin to have some notion of the stature of people like Jalal-ud-Din Rumi, who lived and existed and worked here (and lives and exists and works) simultaneously on all levels, just as the Divine does. There is Rumi, the mask, and there is the Presence behind and beyond Rumi who is using the mask in the great Divine Dance of transformation of humankind. Rumi's poems are the words of God himself. They are sanctified by illumination. They are made holy by having been, each breath of them, baked in the fire of Divine Silence. So when you come into that vast, silent mosque of one of Rumi's poems, take off your reason and cut off your head. What you're listening to is the silent voice of the Beloved, speaking through the lover in time.

Still yourselves to hear these words. You will not hear anything of Rumi until you are still with Rumi. What I've been trying to do in the first chapters is to blast away rock. Now the rock is blasted away. And Rumi is going to guide you to carve your own Divine image in the golden rock of silence that we've blasted out of the rock.

This is Rumi in the *Discourses:*

A man is said to be absorbed when the water has absolute control of him and he has no control of the water.
The man absorbed, and the swimmer, are both in the
water, but the former is carried along and borne by the
water whereas the swimmer carries his own strength
and moves at his own free will. So every movement made
by the man absorbed and every act and word that issues
from him proceeds from the water and not from him.
He is present there as the pretext. In the same way, when
you hear words coming from a wall, you know that they
do not proceed from the wall. But there is someone who
has brought the wall into speech. The saints are like
that. They have died before physical death. Not so much
as a hair's tip of separate existence has remained in them.
In the hands of omnipotence they are as a shield. The
movement of the shield proceeds not from the shield.
Regard such a shield as God and do not use violence
against God.

Then Rumi says amazing things about his own poetry, in
a very riddle-like, paradoxical, intricate statement. The man
who is saying these words, remember, is the man who has created a body of poetry which is considered throughout the
Islamic world as being in certain ways equal to the *Koran;*
whose ghazals and odes are sung as no other poetry has been
sung across the entire world, not just as entertainment or as
beautiful, emotional experiences, but as sacred songs—songs
which inspire the soul to gnosis.

It is a habit with me that I do not desire that any heart
should be distressed through me. Sometimes during a
sitting a lot of people thrust themselves upon me and
some of my friends fend them off. That's not pleasing
to me and I've said a hundred times, "Say nothing to
that man or any man on my account." I am well content with that. I am so affectionate that when friends
come to me, for fear that they may be wearied, I speak

poetry, so that they may be occupied with that. Otherwise what do I have to do with poetry? By Allah I care nothing for poetry and there is nothing worse in my eyes than that. It is become incumbent upon me, as when a man plunges his hands into tripe and washes it out with the sick of a guest's appetite, because the guest's appetite is for tripe.

Then Rumi modifies that rather angry and contemptuous statement. There's a whole side of Rumi which is like a Zen Master, endlessly longing to shove us into the enlightened state, sick of our evasions and refusals, who wants that state to be present now, because it is present now for him. But Rumi is also the tenderest of beings, so he continues:

After all, a man considers what wares are needed in such and such a city and what wares its inhabitants want to buy. Those wares he buys and those he sells, even though the articles be somewhat inferior. I have studied many sciences and taken much pains so that I may be able to offer fine and rare and precious things to the scholars and researchers, the clever ones and the deep thinkers who come to me. God Most High Himself willed this. He gathered here all those sciences and assembled here all those pains so that I might be occupied with this work. What can I do? In my own country and amongst my own people there is no occupation more shameful than poetry. If I'd remained in my own country, I'd have lived in harmony with their temperament, and I would have practiced what they desired such as lecturing and composing books, preaching and admonishing, observing abstinence and doing all the outward acts.

Thank God he didn't stay in his own country.

And now Rumi moves even deeper, and this is the clue to both his anger at words and poetry, his potential anger at anybody who misreads or doesn't listen to the act of poetry, and his understanding of what must underlie both the creation and the listening.

> The Emir Parvana said to me: the root of the matter is acts, and I replied: where are the people of action and the seekers of action so that I may show them action? Where are they?

In one way, Rumi wasn't interested at all in poetry. He wasn't interested in giving the world a whole new feast of concepts and doctoral dissertations. He wasn't interested even in adding this great body of dazzling, wine-soaked imagery to the world. He was interested in giving a vision, in directly transmitting Shams, the Divine, the Presence.

Listen to the Silence behind Rumi's words and you can hear it and him saying: "Once the immense glory has made itself known in the heart, the heart who knows that becomes desperate to communicate it because just one drop of that divine ocean can heal an entire life. One minute in the divine consciousness can transform anyone. So anyone who is in that consciousness, even slightly, must yearn above all things to share it. Where are the people to share it with? Where are the seekers of action? Where are the readers of action? Where are the listeners of action? Come out all of you so that I may show you action. You want words. You want poems, I give you a poem, you want an ecstatic poem, you can have an ecstatic poem. If I do not speak you become upset. Become then a seeker of action so that I may show you action. I'm looking all over the world for one man to whom I may show action."

Silence longs for action. In every sublime mystic creator there is a fundamental iconoclasm, something that would be prepared to burn all the books, break all the statues, everything, if in their place could come the Divine consciousness.

People listening to Rumi came from miles around, thinking that they'd get something, their wishes would be fulfilled, they'd get a concept they could use, or they'd be elevated. After all, Rumi was a great holy man. But elevation is not what he was trying to communicate. He was trying to transmit directly the direct experience of the Divine.

> What do you know of action, seeing that you are not a man of action? Action can only be known through action. Science can only be understood through science, form through form, meaning through meaning. Since there is not one traveler upon this road and it is empty, how will they see if we are on the road and in action?

This action is not prayer and fasting. The action Rumi is asking for, that the poems are begging you to begin in your heart, in your soul, in the ground of your being, is not prayer nor fasting; it is something that goes far beyond rites and rituals, dogmas and concepts. These are the "forms" of action only. Action, he says, is an "inward meaning." And it is tuning your whole being to that inward meaning, transforming your whole being by that inward meaning, entering into the fire of that inward meaning, to become it, that is the only action worthy of a human being. Everything else is illusion, including reading the poems in an aesthetic way. It may be even more of an illusion to read these poems in an aesthetic way because they are sacred; it would be like going into a church to eat your picnic. Or like throwing a party in the center of the Ellora temple to Shiva.

What these poems are demanding by the majesty of the silence that inspires them is action. "After all, from the time of Adam to the time of Mohammed, God bless him and give him peace, prayer and fasting were not in the form we know, but action was. So this is the form of action; action is a meaning within a man." What a glorious phrase: action is an inward meaning and then "action is a meaning within a man." Action is the Divine Silence present and fully conscious and fully working within a human being. It is realization. "Similarly you say the medicine acted, but that's no form of action. It is its meaning. Again they say, that man is agent in such and such a city. They see nothing of mere form but call him an agent in respect of the works which appertain for him. Hence action is not what men have generally supposed. Men supposed that action is this outward show, but if a hypocrite performs that form of action, it does not profit him, since the meaning of sincerity and faith is not in him."

So sacred art demands action from within the ground of our being; it demands a return to that Divine Silence from which the art came; it demands as profound an act of receptivity as we can make and as profound an act of responsibility as we can make. Because receptivity has to lead to responsibility, if it isn't to be decadent.

There's a tremendous danger of releasing these poems at this moment in an atmosphere that isn't totally sacred. There's a tremendous danger of releasing these teachings at this moment in an atmosphere that isn't totally sacred, because these poems carry salvation. They carry the direct light of initiation, and if you are not receiving them then I am responsible for giving them in a way that enables you to use them corruptly, however unconsciously. And if receptivity doesn't lead to responsibility, and if reading these poems doesn't lead to plunging into the silence from which they spring, the whole process has been not only wasted but betrayed. But of course, there is a purpose to language and Rumi states this purpose very beautifully.

The purpose of language, he says, is "to show you something far off," to show you "something moving, trembling in the distance, like a heat mirage." And to inspire you with all your power to go to the place emanating that mysterious light. The Buddhists say the purpose of the *sutras* is to point to the moon, but when you have seen the moon, take away the finger that points and go on gazing at the moon. Rumi could add that when you have seen the moon, inspire yourself to go on looking at the moon. Go on reading those poems that come out of an ecstatic contemplation of the moon. Go on listening to the music of Beethoven or Josquin Després or the sublime masters of Renaissance polyphony. Go on enriching your mind with these works of art, with these fragments of the *sutras,* with those Zen poems, with all of those things that have a shaft of moonlight on them and in them, and through that your passionate dedication to gazing at the divine moon will be deepened, enriched, made more and more gorgeous.

Language's function is to point to what can never be said in words, and what can never be "had" conceptually, but can only be enjoyed by those who have been purified enough, those who love enough, and those who have sacrificed enough to enter into its gates. The other use of language is when that experience is beginning to be stable in the heart, to be able to encourage, infuse, nourish, and inspire it, so that the deepening of realization can go on and on.

Read Rumi to be so inspired by Rumi that you begin to be transformed by him into what he is—your Divine eternal heart. So that when you begin to listen to the poems, to yourself speaking to yourself, you grow drunk on the news of yourself that arrives, ecstatic at the news coming out of your great heart to your great heart, and you reel with the beauty of the information.

Rumi is trying to destroy the barriers between words and hearts, between silence and academia, concepts, dogma. He's trying to completely rubble the whole enterprise because he knows he doesn't exist in the way that you think he does. He knows the words are not saying what you think they are saying. He knows that you have to leap within to another dimension so that the great game can begin: listening to the One talking to itself through him and in him. And that dissolves category and boundary, dissolves words, academia, everything for that space of pure Presence in which the Divine can manifest and appear.

What he's asking for is "action." What is the action that we should do listening to Rumi? It is to receive him totally, to submit to his alchemical power and be divinized slowly by the effect of this poetry, by its goal. It is to fill all our relationships, our actions, our political and moral choices with the radiance of this poetry, with the power of love that is engendering this poetry. In every single corner and aspect of our lives, because every single corner and aspect of our lives, every single choice, will be different if we take the invitation of this poetry to act from the Divine Center of Silence and allow the glory of the Presence to soak our every movement.

> Keep silent, because the world of silence is a vast fullness.
> Do not beat the drum of words. The word is only an
>   empty drum.

Someone once said to Rumi, well, if you believe in all of this business about silence, why then have you done nothing but talk and talk all your life? Rumi gave the ultimate reply. He laughed and he said, "The Most Radiant One in me has never said a word."

Here are the first two lines of one of his odes:

> On the night of creation I was awake
> Busy at work while everyone slept.

Who was he? He is the Divine. He has entered the Divine. He has the right of Al-Hallaj to say that, because he is speaking from that place from which we all can speak if we give up everything. Al-Hallaj said, "Between me and you, there is only me. Between you and That there is only you. Remove the you, and That is here, always."

> On the night of creation I was awake
> Busy at work while everyone slept.
> I was there to see the first wink and hear the first tale told
> I was the first one caught in the hair of the great
>   impostor.

One of the glorious things about Rumi is that he really has attained the highest state. Ramakrishna would embarrass his disciples endlessly by getting out of carriages and worshipping prostitutes with no teeth, as if they were the Divine Mother—and of course they are the Divine Mother. He was seeing the Divine Mother in them and realizing that their work of endlessly taking on the lust of unsatisfied men was in fact a holy work, a healing work. Just as Ramakrishna knew the Divine in everything, so Rumi sees the Divine in evil. He admits joyfully that he was "the first one caught in the hair of the great impostor" of Iblis, of Satan. He exults in the madness of the game, just as Ramakrishna does, because he knows that the atheist is soaked in Divine light as much as the saint. They are radiating the Divine Light, what else can they do? Even the evil have the light they deny in them; their tragedy is that by following and doing evil they can never see it and so never be healed. Rumi's compassion is infinite. And that compassion— total identification with the whole creation—is what you hear in the first lines of this poem.

You are now in that state but you don't know it. Every cell of your body is interdependent with everything else in the entire universe. Every breath that you emit has a relationship more or less subtle with everything else that exists in all worlds. So where is your separate I? Where is your separate identity? It does not exist. It is empty. It is a fiction, an illusion. See that you don't exist, to reenter existence and exist with much greater humor. You are here and not here. You exist and you don't exist. And you neither don't exist nor exist. It is far more amazing than any of us dare to imagine, because we are, each of us, the full Divine. As Rumi says,

> The drop becomes the ocean
> But the ocean also becomes the drop.

This is final magic. This is the drop, as ocean, talking. This is you talking. This is I talking. If you heard what I said, we'd all be enlightened now. What I said is, "This is I talking." There is only I here. Nothing else is going on in the entire creation but I. "I am that I am," is what God says. This is the I in the poem, in the room, in the universe.

> On the night of creation I was awake
> Busy at work while everyone slept.
> I was there to see the first wink and hear the first tale told

> I was the first one caught in the hair of the great
>   impostor.
> Whirling around the still point of ecstasy, I spun like
>   the wheel of heaven.
> How can I describe this to you?
> You were born later.

Rumi doesn't mean that. He's saying we were all born at that moment. "But you think you were born later." And he describes it for us. He's saying, "to really understand this you will have to take a journey to the place from where I am speaking. Then you'll know." So the wit is there always to unsettle your identification with Rumi. Because what Rumi does, often brilliantly, is to say all right, you want total enlightenment? You want to know what bliss is like, what the Divine Light is like, I'll give it to you. I'll give it to you in absolutely amazing imagery. Then he says, "Ah, but you haven't really got it. To get it would mean diving into some place you've not yet been. Don't think that you've got it because you're hearing it, however beautiful it is." The beauty dissolves the beauty, to reveal the beauty that can never be named. It's the dance of the seven thousand veils. Taking off each of the different veils of beauty to reveal a nakedness that can never be talked about. And he does it every time he catches you nodding off into transcendence. He will immediately say, "Ah, you think you're getting it. You're not getting it." Or he will dissolve what he has just said, because what he's just said is a concept that your mind is springing to get at. "It's only the I speaking. I don't exist." And immediately as you say that, he will dissolve that concept, so that you're unnerved. So that you rest nowhere, and the mind's inveterate tendency to tabulate and conceptualize everything is dissolved in something like ecstatic wonder. And that is the movement of his poetry, just as it is the movement of trance.

This poetry and mystical states are very akin. What do mystical states do? As you sink into the silence, what happens? Thoughts start. Mad, cinematic projections are born. They go.

Images start being born, then they disappear. Sometimes they work with the silence to deepen the ecstatic understanding of the silence. Sometimes they just dissolve until nothing but the silence is there. So sinking into the silence is sinking through different layers of ignorance and illusion. Going through all the different stages of your own inner language until you reach the silence. And this is what Rumi's poetry does, through the images.

Having said you couldn't understand, because "you were born later," he goes on to describe again. Rumi is so drunk on the glory of the enlightened mind that he wishes to share that glory with every living, breathing thing. And he will do anything, even speak and write poetry.

> I was a companion of that ancient lover,
> And like a bowl with a broken rim I endured his tyranny.
> Why shouldn't I be as lustrous as the king's cup?
> I have lived in the room of treasures
> Why shouldn't this bubble become the sea?
> I am the secret that lies at its bottom.

At this moment, when he's coming close to saying the unspeakable, to saying what must never be said, what Al-Hallaj said (and what Al-Hallaj was torn apart for having said)— *An'al Haqq*, I am the Supreme Reality, at that moment when Rumi has led you deep towards that point, he says, "Shh. No more words. Hear only the voice within." Not my voice. "Remember the first thing he said was: We are beyond words."

Rumi's great poems corner the ego into a place where, blasted with love and bliss, roasted in perfection and beauty, it has no breath left and has to die into silence.

> On the night of creation, I was awake
> Busy at work while everyone slept.
> I was there to see the first wink and hear the first tale told
> I was the first one caught in the hair of the great
>   impostor.

Whirling around the still point of ecstasy, I spun like the
     wheel of heaven
How can I describe this to you?
You were born later.
I was a companion of that ancient lover
And like a bowl with a broken rim I endured his tyranny.
Why shouldn't I be as lustrous as the king's cup?
I have lived in the room of treasures
Why shouldn't this bubble become the sea?
I am the secret that lies at its bottom.
Shh. No more words.
Hear only the voice within.
Remember the first thing he said was:
We are beyond words.

Even the most glorious language, the most glorious concepts that the mystical mind can create, even the most glorious secrets, all without exception dissolve in the silence of the
Presence. All of them fade away like small candles when the
great sun comes up. Rumi is finally only interested in you entering that great sun.

What Rumi does is to awaken all of your secret knowledge.
First he gives you a sense of what Oneness in being would be
like. You are at the first day of the creation. You are in all the
workings of evil. You are hearing and seeing the first tale and
the first wink. Then he takes you deeper. He gives you another
image of what enlightened consciousness would be like.
"Whirling around the still point of ecstasy," being both that still
point and everything that whirls in all the worlds around it.

So Rumi takes you from an image of Oneness, all-embrac-
ing being, to an image of dancing and ecstasy, from Shiva to
Shakti. The two sides of the Absolute are given. From the
Absolute that is still, absolutely absorbed in everything and
one with everything, to the Absolute that is dancing and fling-
ing itself out in supernova after supernova. And just when you
think you've got it, he unsettles you and says, how can I describe

this to you? These words—they're glorious, these images, but they're nothing. They too are concepts. They too are yet more prisons. So Rumi stops you. "How can I describe this to you? You were born later." Wake UP! He gives you the gold and then he flings some cold water into your face. Because you're dozing on all these glorious images, in all these analyses and all this dogma. Shiva-Shakti, Oneness, etcetera. You're all asleep already. But Shiva-Shakti is the entire universe. It is beyond words, beyond concepts. So he starts again. But this time when he speaks, he takes you far more dangerously deep.

The first time he is one with the creation. Then there is the still point, and then he says:

> I was a companion of that ancient lover.
> A companion of the Divine Beloved.
> Like a bowl with a broken rim, I endured his tyranny.

At this moment, Rumi turns and says: I was there from the beginning. "I was a companion of the ancient lover." I paid the price for that love, the price that creation pays, which is death, again and again, burning again and again, fire again and again. Mountains are built in the agony of continents heaving together. They grow, they crumble. Everything dies and passes away except the face of God. And He is that Everything dying and suffering, loving and passing away from glory to glory, from everlasting to everlasting.

When the mystics speak of nonduality, they mean nonduality. Nothing that is not This and This Present totally, in its agony as well as its beauty. The entire sea, the storms, tempests, and tornadoes, all held and all happening within the Great Peace. That is the state. Nothing less.

And then Rumi says, "Why shouldn't I be as lustrous as the king's cup?"—the cup that the king himself holds? Because I have lived in the room of treasures. The treasures are the mystical states that Shams gave him again and again. The room of treasures is the rose garden, is reality when seen through the eyes of the Divine Beloved. Why shouldn't this tiny bubble,

Rumi, this miniscule, evanescent, transient creature, become the entire sea? What a wild statement. You could think of thousands of reasons why it shouldn't. But Rumi says, why shouldn't it? Because the universe is that crazy. Because fundamentally this whole game is that gloriously insane. The problem with the so-called "New Age" is that it doesn't carry the insanity of nonduality far enough. It doesn't show that nonduality is Auschwitz and Somalia, Dachau and Hiroshima, just as it is elation, joy, and peace. It is being both at the same time always. One with the One. That's what's terrifying about it, and that's why most people would do anything rather than have enlightenment. Because to have enlightenment is to be one with everything. In everything as everything.

So when Rumi is saying, "Why shouldn't the bubble become the sea?" he's saying that this is the insanity of the game: the bubble does become the entire sea. Everything that takes place within the sea takes place in the bubble and the bubble manifests all things, all worlds. And then he says, "I am the secret that lies at the bottom." The great peace in which all the sea's happenings are stored, upon which all the sea's storms rely. The wilder the storm, the deeper the peace that makes that storm possible. The madder Kali's dance, the more profound her silence from which that dance arises. Look at the creation of a supernova. Can you imagine the force of silence, of peace, which enables the huge amount of energy to be unleashed that creates it? Imagine what vast reservoirs of peace enable that energy to be. Then you have some sense of what the enlightened mind is. It is Shiva-Shakti, that peace and that energy in One.

I am the secret that lies at its bottom.

At this moment when you think you understand—because you've been taken very deep, you've been given the true delirium of truth, and all truth sounds mad to the rational mind—Rumi withdraws words altogether. He says, "No more words." No more words, because at that moment you're being tempted to conceptualize even this. You're being tempted to take "I am the secret that lies at its bottom" and make that into your own *mantra,* the ego's final *mantra.* And what Rumi wants you to do is go beyond your understanding of your understanding. You may have had a glimmering of what I'm saying through what you've experienced, what you know, but if you cling to that glimmering you are finished. Because then it cannot be fanned by wonder, it cannot be fanned by silence, it cannot be fanned by truth into another possibility.

At that moment when he gives you the ultimate secret as far as it can be put into words, Rumi says, "No more words. Hear only the voice within." That means scrub everything I've said up to this moment in the poem, everything. You've been taken by listening to a place where you don't have to listen anymore to the words that took you to that place. You've taken the bus to Moscow. When you're in Moscow, you don't hang around the bus stop. You're in Moscow now. You have arrived. You are at the bottom of the sea. Now stay at the bottom of the sea. It may of course not be the bottom at all: there may be another sea under it.

No more words. Hear only the voice within.

What has happened in the poem is that the "voice without" of Rumi has led you to a place where your voice within is starting to whisper. He knows exactly the moment when you could be tempted not to listen to that whisper and he brings that voice within immediately and leaves you absolutely at the center, not of his poem, but of your own being. Not of his construct, but of your own soul. This is what a Master always does. The Master creates an external space of words, of teachings which lead you slowly into the only space that exists— the interior space. And then suddenly he or she takes away everything to make you confront where you are, which is inside you, and where the world is, which is inside you.

Rumi's poems are mystical acts. They have the structure of a mystical state and the structure of a mystical transformation. So they are transformational. They move in time, move in the spirit, in the heart and mind with complete security and complete certainty, working on all of those aspects of ourselves, until they have brought us by their alchemical magic, by their total mastery of all of our different forms of understanding, to the place where we can leap beyond understanding, where we can leap into the silence.

Shh. No more words.
Hear only the voice within.

"Hear only the voice within." And then, just as you're sinking into hearing the voice within, Rumi whispers—the end of the poem is a whisper of love—he says, "remember, as you sink into the silence, remember, as you listen to the voice within, as you take all these initiations that this poem has given you, remember all the initiations of the deepest secrets and scrub them out, because they have taken you to the place where you can now plunge." As you do that, "remember, remember, the first thing he said was, we are beyond words."

That is a poem of about twenty-five lines, but in it is the entire mystical journey.

Are you "clear" about this extraordinary strategy of Rumi's? The poems are really the equivalent of what the Hindus call *Raja Yoga* or *Jnana Yoga*. They are a destruction of the mind and heart, leading to an opening at the end of the poem, upon total silence. They are living *Raja Yoga*. The Sword Dance in which the head is cut off at the end.

On the night of creation I was awake
Busy at work while everyone slept.
I was there to see the first wink and hear the first tale told
I was the first one caught in the hair of the great
    impostor.
Whirling around the still point of ecstasy I spun like the
    wheel of heaven
How can I describe this to you?
You were born later.

I was a companion of that ancient lover
And like a bowl with a broken rim I endured his tyranny.
Why shouldn't I be as lustrous as the king's cup?
I have lived in the room of treasures
Why shouldn't this bubble become the sea?
I am the secret that lies at its bottom.
Shh. No more words.
Hear only the voice within.
Remember, the first thing he said was:
We are beyond words.

And then this poem—another supreme dance of silence. Let your mind spiral with it into origin, in the silence of origin from which all worlds flower:

Don't hide. The sight of your face is a blessing.
Wherever you place your foot, there rests a blessing
Even your shadow
Passing over me like a swift bird
Is a blessing
The great spring has come
Your sweet air, blowing through the city,
The country, the gardens
And the deserts is a blessing
He has come with love to our door
His knock is a blessing.
We go from house to house asking of Him
Any answer is a blessing
Caught in this body, we look for a sight of the soul
Remember what the Prophet said:
One sight is a blessing
The leaf of every tree brings a message from the unseen
    world
Look, every falling leaf is a blessing.
All of nature swings in unison
Singing without tongues
Listening without ears

What a blessing
O soul, the four elements are your face.
Water, wind, fire and earth
Each one is a blessing.
And once the seed of faith takes root it cannot be
    blown away
Even by the strongest wind
That's a blessing.
I bow to you, for the dust of your feet
Is the crown on my head
And as I walk towards you
Every step I take is a blessing.
His form appeared before me, just now as I was
    singing this poem
I swear
What a blessing! What a blessing!
Every vision born of earth is fleeting
Every vision born of heaven is a blessing
For people, the sight of spring warms their hearts
For fish, the rhythm of the ocean is a blessing
The brilliant sun that shines in every heart
For the heaven's earth and all creatures
What a blessing!
The heart can't wait to speak of this ecstasy
The soul is kissing the earth, saying
Oh God, what a blessing!
Fill me with the wine of your silence,
Let it soak my every pore
For the inner splendor it reveals
Is a blessing
Is a blessing.

What we have heard together is the Divine enlightened mind adoring its manifestation in everything and receiving back from itself blessing after blessing from everything that is.

In this poem, we have the ultimate paradox that is the enlightened mind. The master and the slave, the omniscient one and the totally love-drunk, ignorant one, wandering from epiphany to epiphany. The timeless one and the one in love, madly, deeply, hopelessly, eternally in love with all the manifestations of time. Blake said: "Eternity is in love with the workings of time." And here is the voice of eternity, the I, being both servant and master.

The poem begins with the evocation of Shams, and until we have felt this for our Master, or for the Beloved, love is not complete. This is the love for Christ that transfigured Mary Magdalene, for the Buddha that transfigured Ananda, for Ramakrishna that transfigured Vivekananda, for Mother Meera that transfigures Adilakshmi.

Don't hide. The sight of your face is a blessing.

When Rumi is saying, *the sight of your face is a blessing,* he knows what he is talking about.

And wherever you place your foot, there rests a blessing.
Even your shadow
Passing over me like a swift bird is a blessing.

Think of the beauty of that. This reminds me of the woman in the Gospels who has been trying to heal her diseases for many years and has gone to every doctor. She knows that Christ is Christ. She doesn't want to disturb him. She doesn't want to interrupt him. She loves him so tenderly and so absolutely that all she wants to do as he passes is simply to touch the hem of his garment. And she does so. And he turns and he says, who touched me? And she's frightened and she says, I touched you. And he says, "Your faith has made you whole." She is cured.

That is how much we need to adore the Beloved. Her adoration at that moment, her total openness to him meant that she could receive everything.

Don't hide.

And immediately, this amazing shift takes place in the poem itself. It begins with Shams as a person, but immediately in the second verse it becomes the whole world, because Shams is the whole world for Rumi.

Your great Spring has come.

This Spring is Him, is Her. The sign of the freshness of the Divine Presence.

Your sweet air, blowing through the city, the country,
     the gardens
and the deserts is a blessing
He has come with love to our door
His knock is a blessing.

Do you know how Rumi's poems were made? They were often made in ecstasy. Rumi didn't write them down; sometimes he was dancing around a pillar. You can hear it in the poem itself. The poem engenders the poem. It begins with Shams, the Beloved, each moment, each aspect, even the shadow, and then suddenly, Spring, that being the Beloved also, and then all the different ways in which the Beloved appears. And suddenly, as he moves deeper and deeper into this trance, into this ecstasy, no more words, but the Beloved is there, in his glory. The Light is there. Shams is present. Shams is. Only Shams is. The poem dissolves into the Presence and then re-emerges out of the Presence. The poem stops being a poem. It becomes a sacred invocation which works. Rumi evokes the Beloved, every image of the Beloved, every adoring possibility of the Beloved. He throws himself out in love, he's dancing around the pillar, he's summoning, summoning, and then the Beloved is there. The Presence is there. There are no more words to say. He just cries out: Shams is here.

His form just appeared before me as I'm singing this
     poem. I swear.
What a blessing! What a blessing!

The blessings cannot be contained because they come from the Infinite. The blessings are continually bursting the seams of reality, the seams of possibility and language. The theophany is endlessly emerging. Breaking reality is its goal. Out of this extraordinary moment, when the poem has suddenly seemed to vanish altogether and only Shams is, Rumi says, "every vision born of earth is fleeting, even this vision that I'm giving you." It is as if he is saying to us, "The words that I am speaking are inevitably words of the earth, words, because they are of the earth and you are of the earth in one way listening to these, but don't think that even this vision of the vision I've just had of Shams is enough. Go deeper. Plunge. Don't just cherish my mystic ecstasy. Why I'm doing this for you is for you to see how extreme this experience is, how astounding this experience is, and how you can have it here on the earth because you, like me, are the child of the Divine."

He reminds us, just after that shattering moment:

> Every vision born of earth is fleeting
> Every vision born of heaven is a blessing

At this stage of the poem, we have to ask ourselves: what is the real blessing? The real blessing is to be in Rumi's mind. To be in Rumi's heart. To be in Rumi's consciousness, in the consciousness of the Eternal I that is creating this poem, that is invoking Shams, that is dazzled before Shams, before Shams-as-Itself.

> Every vision born of earth is fleeting
> Every vision born of heaven is a blessing
> For people, the sight of spring warms their hearts
> For fish, the rhythm of the ocean is a blessing
> The brilliant sun—

Whenever Rumi mentions the sun, you know that madness is about to follow. Now you are asked to go into the sun—

> The brilliant sun that shines in every heart
> For the heaven's earth and all creatures
> What a blessing
> The heart can't wait to speak of this ecstasy

And that, of course, is the clue to the whole enterprise of Rumi. He was so overwhelmed by what he was living, by what he was loving, by how he was living and loving, that he could not wait to speak of the ecstasy that filled his every breath.

But because you may get lost in the ecstacy of the heart, Rumi goes deeper. He is always going deeper.

> The soul is kissing the earth, saying
> Oh God, what a blessing.

The heart can't wait to "speak of" the ecstasy, but the soul is doing an even deeper act. The soul is kissing the earth and saying in silence, "Oh God, what a blessing." Kissing the earth. Rumi takes the two poles of our existence: the most transparent, infinite thing—the soul—and the most earthy, and he shows that when you have experienced nonduality, when you really realize where you are, the heart can't wait to speak of the ecstasy, but the soul doesn't float off into the ineffable. The soul gets down on its knees and kisses this earth, this place, here. Because here is the *Kibriya,* the glory of God. This universe is the place where the Beloved manifests at every moment. That is Rumi's ultimate knowledge and secret. And into this secret knowledge, at the end of the poem, he dissolves the whole poem and our minds:

> Fill me with the wine of your silence
> Let it soak my every pore
> For the inner splendor it reveals
> Is a blessing
> Is a blessing.

Don't move. Stop the mind. Enjoy the blessing.

Chapter Five

Springtime of Eternity

STUDYING, READING, AND celebrating Rumi is a discipline that aims at the renovation of our souls, at the reclaiming, for ourselves as human beings and for our culture, of sacred ideas, knowledge, and life-powers. The great mystical force field that is Rumi is being transmitted through the poetry, through the silences, through some of the things that I am saying, and through the quality of your attention. Many of you will be changed by your contact with him and by your contact with the shattering vast vision that he is. Your lives, your work in the world, will be different, because you will have come to understand something of the nature of sacred genius and sacred service, and of the nature of your obligation to both.

When you begin to grasp who Rumi is, you begin to grasp who *you* are. Rumi is at that level of transcendent omniscience, of transcendent love and awareness that is the secret part of each of us. He is the sublime friend who waits behind all the other masks in each of us, waiting to possess our lives, possess our bodies, to use this transient and fleeting life as an expression of eternal love, eternal power, eternal knowledge, eternal beauty.

This power of holy possession is the power of sacred genius. It is not merely the power to move, enthrall, or enthuse—it is an alchemical power. It is not merely the power to fascinate or give new sets of intellectual formulae or build new structures—it is the power to work directly on the ground of the soul and so transform the entire basis of our human lives.

The lamps are different,
But the Light is the same.
So many garish lamps in the dying brain's lamp shop,
Forget about them.
Concentrate on essence, concentrate on Light
In lucid bliss, calmly smoking off its own holy fire,
The Light streams towards you from all things,
All people, all possible permutation of good, evil,
    thought, passion.
The lamps are different,
But the Light is the same.
One matter, one energy, one Light, one Light-mind,
Endlessly emanating all things.
One turning and burning diamond.
One, one, one.
Ground yourself, strip yourself down,
To blind loving silence.
Stay there, until you see
You are gazing at the Light
With its own ageless eyes.

When you have undergone this annihilation, this grinding
down of yourself, this humbling of every instinct and every
desire in adoration before the Divine, when you have really
made yourself the Divine slave, child, and beloved all at once,
then the miracle happens—the power to cognize nonduality
directly, humorously, normally, arises in the divinized mind.
At that moment, an entirely new being is born within you, free
of pain, free of desire, free to contemplate the Divine world as
a conscious actor in it and as its secret cosmic source. For the
miracle is that we are, each of us, the source of the whole universe, the source of the entire experience. Because each of us
is one with the source of sources, a mirror in which each other
and all creation are reflected.

At that moment, in that state, you can legitimately say to
yourself what Rumi wrote in this mystical sister-poem of the
last one:

Define and narrow me, you starve yourself of yourself.
Nail me down in a box of cold words, that box is your
coffin.
I do not know who I am.
I am in astounding lucid confusion.
I am not a Christian, I am not a Jew, I am not a
Zoroastrian,
And I am not even a Muslim.
I do not belong to the land, or to any known or
unknown sea.
Nature cannot own or claim me, nor can heaven,
Nor can India, China, Bulgaria,
My birthplace is placelessness,
My sign to have and give no sign.
You say you see my mouth, ears, eyes, nose—they are
not mine.
I am the life of life.
I am that cat, this stone, no one.
I have thrown duality away like an old dishrag,
I see and know all times and worlds,
As one, one, always one.
So what do I have to do to get you to admit who is
speaking?
Admit it and change everything!
This is your own voice echoing off the walls of God.

We will return to this poem later after a journey in Rumi,
a musical journey. I invite you to follow as you would a piece
of music, threading all the themes together in your mind. For
this is the way Rumi writes his poetry. This is the way the
Mathnawi is constructed, the way sacred teaching and sacred
learning take place: in the vastness and abandon of the entirely
open musical mind.

You have heard two poems that come straight from super-
consciousness, poems about direct understanding of the nature
of reality. Now let's have three stories about Rumi himself.
When you read these stories, wipe your mind clean and imag-

ine the consciousness of the man who is the sacred actor in these stories. When you begin to imagine that consciousness, you will begin to imagine how you might act in the world.

In the first story, Rumi and his disciples are sitting around a pool at twilight. Rumi was talking about the nature of divine love and the nature of absolute reality, when suddenly the noise from the frogs of the pool became so loud that nobody could hear Rumi speak. Nobody could listen to anything else but the frogs. So Rumi turned to the frogs and said, "All right, shut up." And then the discourse took place in this amazing, fresh silence. When he had finished and everybody had absorbed what he had to say, he just clapped his hands and the frogs began again.

The second story is exquisite and in it you can receive a great deal of what Rumi was like. It has the flavor of that quality everyone remarked upon who knew him: his massive gentleness of heart. That heart that burned in Rumi was the reason why Rumi so slayed his world. Everyone could see that what was burning in him was the tender fire of the love of God. And that love didn't merely extend to all living human beings, but also to the whole of the animal world as well, the entire creation.

One day Rumi asked one of his young, snotty disciples to give him an enormous amount of rich and delicious food. This young disciple was rather alarmed because he thought Rumi was living an ascetic lifestyle. Rumi used to pray all night and eat hardly anything. The disciple thought, "Aha, now I've really got the master—what he really wants is to go off somewhere secretly and eat all this food!" So he decided to follow Rumi. He followed him through the streets of Konya, out into the fields, out into yet further fields. Then he saw Rumi go into a ruined tomb. "I'm finally going to unmask his pretensions," the young disciple thought. But what he found was a totally exhausted bitch with six puppies, and Rumi was feeding the dog with his own hands so that she could survive to feed her children. Rumi knew that the disciple was following him, of course, and turned to him smiling and said, "See?" The disci-

ple, extremely moved, said, "But how on earth did you know
that she was here? How did you know that she was hungry?
This is miles away from where you are!" Rumi laughed and
laughed, "When you have become awake your ears are so acute
that they can hear the cries of a sparrow ten thousand miles
away."

We don't hear these stories told about Robert Browning,
do we? We don't hear these stories told about Beethoven or
Mozart. This is a different order of genius which has its origin in super-consciousness, in the completely awake heart.

I feel about Rumi what Rumi felt about Shams:

> The light of the sun's face cannot do what your face does:
> The tumult of the resurrection cannot do what your love
>   does.
> Whoever sees your face will never go to a rose garden:
> Whoever tastes your lips will never prattle of wine
> When your locks arrive, musk withdraws its fragrance:
> Your radiance arrives and intellect pulls back its head.

In the first story Rumi is nature's Master: in the second, her
servant. He can be both because he is one with nature in Divine
Love. To the disciple in the second story, there is an abyss
between the dog and the divinized human being that he recognizes in Rumi, but to Rumi there is no such abyss, because
all he sees is himself. He sees himself in the dog, he sees himself in the woman, the child, the plant, sea, and the wind—it
is all himself, all his divine self. So everything calls out from
him that tenderness, that instinctual passion of the heart.

Rumi no longer exists to himself. He has become love and
"Love is the bottomless ocean of life—eternal life is the least
of its gifts."

The third story is wonderful from beginning to end because
every detail is essential Rumi.

One day, in the middle of the market at Konya, Rumi suddenly began to talk about the highest mystical realities. In the
middle of the evening prayer, when night fell, some dogs had

formed a circle around him. He looked at them tenderly and continued his explanations. They waved their heads and tails and uttered groans of pain and silence and deep joy. And he said, "I swear by God that these dogs understand our glimpses." Then he said, "This door and that wall proclaim the praise of God and understand the Divine secrets. That door and that wall are saying subtle things, and the fire and the water and the earth are all telling stories."

This is an especially marvelous and serious story for me, because it all unfolds in the heart of banality, the marketplace. And the most despised things, the dogs, come and form a circle around Rumi, who they recognize as the master, free of duality. For him all things are sacred, and the dogs and the animals recognize his *ahimsa,* his harmlessness. They all gather around and his power of love is so great that they "get it," far more than the people who are listening. All these disciples float about who have been with him for years and think that they understand what he is saying, but they are not listening to him! The dogs are listening to him, in the only way that listening matters, they are giving everything to him. They are adoring him, revering him, they are bowing down in their hearts before the ambassador of God. That is why they are having the experience. They have the reactions: they groan, they cry, they are being moved. That's why Rumi says, "I tell you, they understand my gnosis, they understand because they have the reactions of purity, and you don't because you are so closed in your minds."

Then, to take the whole story much deeper, he says, "Don't just think the dogs are getting it; the door and the wall are speaking, and subtle secrets are being divined by what you imagine to be inanimate! You think the world is solid! All of the information that we get through the ego is false. We are not dying as we think we are dying; we are not living as we think we're living. Nothing is as it seems, once the Light has come up in the mind, once the mystical senses are open." Rumi is saying the dogs are getting it, and the door, which seems to be silent, and the wall, which seems to be silent, are actually instructing everyone, if only people could be mad and sane enough to know it.

Rumi is also implying, I think, that the least thing we can be is like a wall, or a door. If we were really bone-stupid, still, silent, and absolutely given up, then we might begin to begin to enter the only dimension that is of any importance. If we were as intelligent as sea urchins clinging in complete dumb silence to a rock and opening to the sun, the miracles of comprehension that would be born in our minds would astound us! What are these stories about? Divine love and divine action. What all of us need to learn now in this time of external danger and ordeal is the path of divine love and divine action—the action that is divine love. That is why we are reading Rumi, because he was—he is—that divine love in action.

There is something that I have not said yet about Rumi that is very important: Rumi was also the founder of a great religious order. Rumi did not simply create this great body of work, he also created a living sacred order—the Mevlevis—and his work became a living part of that order. His work has been read by the Mevlevi order day after day, month after month, all over the world. The odes are sung and send people directly into ecstasy. The *Mathnawi* is recited, contemplated, mulled over, and endlessly enriched by commentary and by thought. If you go to a Mevlevi meeting in Paris, Istanbul, Lahore, or Cairo, Rumi is present. There are men wearing the same robes dancing the dance that he created. When they open the *Mathnawi,* they know who they are reading: they are reading their beloved, the sublime friend of mankind. They are reading someone who knew the direct truth directly and was able to express it with a fabulous array of imagery and wisdom. Through their dancing and reading and praying their beloved is making love to them. This divine lovemaking goes on and on, and it is going on in us now, in you and I. Rumi is not dead. Rumi is the transmitter of a sacred path, a fountain of continuous revelation.

In this plane, I am the All-Merciful's nightingale.
Do not look for my limit and border—I have no limits.
Shams-i-Tabriz has nurtured me through love—
I am greater than the Holy Spirit and the cherubim.

Now let us return to the second poem:

Define and narrow me, you starve yourself of yourself.
Nail me down in a box of cold words, that box is your
      coffin.

He's saying it aggressively, with wonderful rage, the amused
rage of the enlightened. Define and narrow Rumi, you starve
yourself of yourself, because if this news comes from a real
place, it is from our own real place. All the ways we could
define Rumi are the ways I am trying to stop you from defining Rumi. "Rumi: 1207–1273," "Rumi: Sufi," "Rumi: sacred
master who wrote poetry." Every time you make a definition
of Rumi you make a definition of yourself. Go through all the
definitions by all means, enjoy them, but then throw them
away, confront Rumi nakedly in the spirit and look directly
into his fire-mirror. "Nail me down in a box of cold words,
that box is your coffin!" This is what the ego is doing all the
time. It is making coffins of words and nailing you down in
them. These coffins of words are called ideas, concepts of yourself. They are what you think is your biography, what you
think is your identity.

Our world is where it is because we have defined ourselves
as dying, desperate creatures. What could dying, desperate
creatures do but destroy their environment, because they are
depressed? This is the modern calamity: we're depressed because we are given information about ourselves that is unbearable. It also happens to be untrue. Think what many people
in the world are believing: they believe that they are dying,
that their life is meaningless, that there is no God, no love, no
hope. People are desperate because this information is, literally, unbearable. But worse, it is untrue!

Life is not a meaningless experience, it is an experience in which every moment is brimming with sacred importance, in which everyone is living as God, in God, for God, whether they know it or not. We are destroying the planet because in our depression we believe we have nothing worth living for! The only reason for being alive is to have the experience that Rumi had, the experience of the Divine godhead in us, and the experience of that divinity in all beings, dogs and frogs included, and in the whole creation.

Then Rumi says, "I do not know who I am. You all know who you are." He's saying to us, you've got your whole biography pat, but I don't know who I am, my biography has been razed, I've had a million experiences which have told me that everything my senses were presenting me was rubbish, or a provisional arrangement. That's all the ego is—a provisional arrangement. So, "I do not know who I am." "I am," and the words are literal, "in astounding lucid confusion." That radiant bewilderment is the highest state that you can be in on earth. It is very important to know what the enlightened mind is like. The enlightened mind doesn't have the answers. It isn't omniscient in any sense that the ego understands by "omniscient." It isn't a hyper-sophisticated computer. It is an infinitely responsive and loving instrument capable of infinite lucid expansion. The enlightened mind is always responding to the Light, always dancing with the Light, always opening up to whatever situation is before it, always learning. As Rumi said: "The limit of the travelers is union. But what could be the limit of those in union?" Enlightenment isn't a fixed state. In fact, enlightenment is the knowledge that there is no such thing as a fixed state, that all places are placeless, that the possibilities of transformation in God are endless. That is why Rumi is saying, "I am in astounding lucid confusion." "I am lucid," he is saying, "because I know this is a divine experience; I know I'll be guided, I know the clues will come. I know the signs will be given me. If I am listening to reality I know I will be given very clear indications from my heart from the outside in about what I should do, if only I am still enough." Rumi says in the *Discourses* that because the universe is reinvented in every second, it is being refreshed at every second in its source of eternal light. And this means that every experience is "baked" in light; real divine life is a perpetual series of astonishments which goes on right until the "last moment," and beyond.

> From beyond the intellect beautiful Love comes
>   dragging its skirts, a cup of wine in its hand.
> And from beyond Love, that One who cannot be
>   described, who can only be called "That" keeps
>   coming.

"I am in astounding lucid confusion." Rumi says it in calm trust. The great secret of the mystic life is trust absolute. If you trust absolutely, you will always be receptive enough to the signals that life and God and yourself—your deep self—will be giving you. You will always be given the clue, the information, and the inspiration to carry you through. It feels like confusion because you are not the master. The master is "That." The master is God; the master is the Divine. You are not controlling this experience, you are becoming one with this experience, celebrating and adoring this experience and trying to serve the maker of the experience by becoming, as far as you can, that love and that fire that is the nature of "That." As Rumi writes in the *Mathnawi,*

> The heavens cannot contain me, or the void, or winged
>   exalted intelligences and souls:
> Yet I am contained, as a guest, in the heart of the true
>   believer
> Without any qualification, without any definition or
>   description.
> From this mirror, every second, appear fifty wedding
>   feasts for the spirit,
> Pay attention to the mirror, but never, ever
> Ask me to describe it.

Before we return to the rest of the second poem, let us stop a moment at these words from Richard of St. Victory, a great medieval Christian mystic, that take us further into "astounding lucid confusion":

> When the soul is plunged in the fire of divine love, like iron, it first loses its blackness, and then grows to white heat and becomes like the fire itself, and lastly, it grows liquid. And, losing its nature, is transmuted into an utterly different quality of being. And as the difference between iron that is cold and iron that is hot, so is the difference between soul and soul, between the tepid soul, and the soul made incandescent with divine love.

"When the soul is plunged in the fire of divine love ..."

This is marvelous, the soul is *plunged*. You can do a great deal of spiritual work yourself, but you can only take yourself to the moment and the place where the Power can seize you, "confuse" you gloriously. The awakening is always chosen by the Divine. We don't choose it. In the *Upanishads* it is said that the "*Atman* chooses the awakener." There's a massive amount you can do: you can meditate, you can clear up your life, you can examine your ethical motives, but only the Divine can plunge the soul into divine fire. You have to wait with total humility and patience for the moment when you are ripe. You cannot know that moment, only the Divine does. So "when the soul is plunged in the fire of divine love,"

It first loses its blackness ...

First the loss, the purification. The soul has to lose its blackness. It is a very difficult experience, losing the madness, desolation, cruelty, and limitation that have clung to the ego and soiled it. The soul then "grows to white heat." It is you who will have to grow to white heat. Everybody in this culture imagines that God is going to do it all. That there is going to be some massive descent of Light, and that we are not going to have to change anything: not have to meditate nor open our hearts, nothing. We'll just become enlightened. But the act of trying to enlighten yourself is a passionate act, the ultimately passionate act. You really have to strip yourself, to suffer and open, to love and love. You have to give immensely to the Beloved so that your heart can be big enough for the Beloved to put the universe into it. But how to make your heart big enough? By loving immensely the Divine from where you are. So that is the second stage: growing to white heat, allowing this fire of Love, the Divine Love, to take possession of you, to burn you so that you become "white heat," white, because the Divine Light is white. You burn with it to its total intensity. But you still, in that state, remain as the iron bar. The bar is white-hot, but it is still in a form. There is another stage that then has to happen, another stage before you attain the rapt fluidity of "astounding lucid confusion."

And growing to white heat, it becomes like the fire itself.

Identity with the fire is then realized. This means that within the conscious mind taken to a very high elevation, direct cognition of the godhead is given. Both externally in seeing the Divine Light and reality soaked in it—seeing reality as the theophany of God, as the manifestation of God—and in experiencing that reality in a divine way, through inner bliss and through the radiance of the heart. Lucidly and in "astounding lucid confusion."

... and lastly, it grows liquid. And, losing its nature ...

"It grows liquid," this blazing white heat that is still the ego, its final most perfect shape dissolves altogether. Rumi didn't stay Rumi. We use the word "Rumi" as a convenience, but Rumi became something other.

And, losing its nature is transmuted into an utterly different quality of being.

"An utterly different quality of being." It is the same being in one way, but it can be used for totally different things. Once iron has been liquefied, you can make the most amazing things out of it. You can make birds, iron bananas, airports, you can do anything with it, just as the enlightened person becomes able to radiate sacred joy at any level of the spectrum in any dimension, as Rumi can, from beyond time.

> And as the difference between iron that is cold and iron that is hot, so is the difference between soul and soul, between the tepid soul, and the soul made incandescent by divine love.

The soul made "incandescent by divine love" is the soul in "astounding lucid confusion." The clue to sacred genius is being made "incandescent by divine love." But divine love is also divine "knowledge." So it is not simply being made incandescent by divine love, but also being made incandescent by divine direct "knowledge" of reality. That can only come when all forms of ordinary knowing are burned away, abandoned in love. Up to this moment I've been talking about a supreme artist, master, and spiritual genius, Rumi. But don't think that the kind of knowledge that Rumi is radiating is only an artistic or mystical knowledge. It is a complete knowledge, and for the complete picture for the future, we need one more element, we need a supreme genius, a mystical *scientist*. We need scientists who have the courage to go on Rumi's journey. We need someone who can combine Einstein and Rumi, can become liquid, and can then use his or her divinized mind really to explore reality.

How are scientists going to discover the unified field theory without being mystics? How are they going to understand reality without understanding that reality is an emanation of divine consciousness that cannot be "understood"—and without really "receiving" this divine "knowledge" in "astounding lucid confusion," which you can only do by becoming it? How are they going to create a science that isn't potentially destructive unless their minds are divinized by divine love and divine "knowledge"? The knowledge for the sake of which Rumi says "You must pass beyond knowledge into madness:" the madness of the soul 'made incandescent by divine love.'"On these questions depend the future of our civilization, which is presently addicted to a very narrow vision of what science can be.

I have in my mind a vision of what a divinized science might be like. It will have all the precision of the science we now know, all the command of all the registers of precision, but it will be dedicated to the Divine and it will be open to "astounding lucid confusion." Imagine what great scientists, trained to illuminate their minds on a regular basis as servants and instruments of the Divine, could discover, both technologically and in terms of the laws of the universe. Imagine what a lucid scientific "madness" could give to the human race. We really need a notion of what sacred genius is, because we need to educate people in a completely different way, whether they are going to be physicists or doctors, lawyers or artists. We have to educate them in a profound mystical way, so that they know who they are, where they are, and what they are working for. Only then can the whole of human life, at all the different levels of human life and inquiry, be infused with sacred passion, with sacred purpose, with the divine light, and the world be saved.

How can we possibly save the world in twenty years—which is the most time we have—if we don't, all of us, infuse what we are doing and what we are learning with sacred fire, sacred passions, sacred purpose? If we don't put at the center of our minds this notion of what a sacred life and a sacred purpose are, and if we don't just scrap the whole Western notion of genius and start again? Real genius is not narcissistic self-torment; it isn't somebody burning himself or herself out in ignorance and misery, occasionally creating works of battered splendor. Real genius is what Rumi had. Real genius is what Christ, what St. Francis had. They are the real geniuses of humanity. They are the ones who have lived a complete life, who are completely wise. We have to celebrate that place where our inner qualities are given their most splendid and most complete representation. At the center of our education, at the center of our lives, at the center of our personal lives, at the center of our work lives. Then we can save this planet, because then we will really know what this planet is, which is a theater of enlightenment, of "astounding lucid confusion" in which every moment is agelessly fresh, alight with love.

Now back to the poem:

> Define and narrow me, you starve yourself of yourself.
> Nail me down in a box of cold words, that box is your
> coffin.
> I do not know who I am.
> I am in astounding lucid confusion.
> I am not a Christian ...

"I am not not a Christian." You'll notice immediately that, of course, Rumi knows that we're trying to define Rumi by saying, "Rumi lived in Konya, he was a Muslim, and he was a Sufi.... " "I am not a Christian." Neither are you. You're not just a Christian, a Jew, a Zoroastrian, or a Muslim—you are a divine being using a particular sacred way to get to the placeless, the nameless, and the wayless. You are not signing onto some religion in order to drearily prance about in its *nostra et vostra*. If you are very intelligent you are choosing the sacred technology which works for you, while knowing and respecting all the others. And this is the future! Rumi is the future. He says to the whole human race: stop identifying yourself with labels, you are beyond labels, you are the source of all labels. You are the Divine Sea in which all the rivers of illumination end, and from which they all begin.

> I am not a Christian, I am not a Jew, I am not a
> Zoroastrian,
> and I am not even a Muslim.

Mohammed wasn't a Muslim, Buddha wasn't a Buddhist, and Christ wasn't a Christian! So how could Rumi be a Muslim? Religions are a cosmic disaster because immediately when the sacred fire is lit, somebody steals it to illuminate some grim old sanctuary.

> I do not belong to the land, or to any known or
>   unknown sea.
> Nature cannot own or claim me . . .

Do you hear that? The full astonishment of what we are only dawns gradually. As Emily Dickinson says, "The truth dazzles gradually, or else the world would be blind."

> I do not belong to the land, or to any known or
>   unknown sea . . .

I'm not in the game of knowledge, I'm not in Columbus' exploration of a new continent, I'm not in the space shuttle. It is a direct result of our ignorance that we spend billions going to a place that is already inside us. Billions of dollars to create fantastically sophisticated machines to go somewhere that is already eternally within us. You laugh! Do you see what mystic knowledge could do in the world? It could redirect those billions of dollars to work on those people who are also inside us, who are starving, who are dying of diseases that need money and researchers to be treated, who are living in terrible, impoverished conditions. We cannot allow the human race to go on in this consciousness.

> I do not belong to the land, or to any known or
>   unknown sea.
> Nature cannot own or claim me . . .

I do not belong to the games of the scientists, the physicists, the psychologists, or the behaviorists. I don't belong to any of them. The mystery of the divine person in each of us cannot be exhausted by any explanation. It can be experienced as a mystery, but it can never be explained or completely understood. It can be lived. To live it is why we are here on the earth.

But Rumi says, "Nature cannot own or claim me, nor can Heaven." Rumi is not interested in "heaven," "liberation," or other-where. He's not interested because he's already "there," "*here.*" To be "there/here" is the whole point. To be "there" in divine consciousness, "here" in dying divine reality as a dying divine being who is not dying. This is the whole game, the whole *lila,* the whole revelation, the whole possibility. He's saying, wake up! You don't belong to what you think of as reality, nature, or that dying world out there; nor do you belong to that other concept that has tormented you for so long—Heaven. Heaven has been made a concept and then people have mortified themselves, tortured and killed those who did not have their own version of heaven, tortured life as the servant of some future life into which you'll get ... another dreadful prison, another nightmare of the ego. Forget it. Heaven is the mystic consciousness here. Heaven is living as the divine servant and child here. Heaven is living as Rumi's beloved here. This is heaven, and this has no word. This is an experience of nonduality, life, eternal life. This is what the Buddha meant by *nirvana,* what Christ meant by "coming into the Kingdom of God" and "entering the Kingdom of God as little children." All the major revelations and the Kabalistic ones also—the great fountain of Jewish mysticism—have been about living divine blessing as divinized beings, totally receptive to the Light, on this earth.

> Nature cannot own or claim me, nor can Heaven,
> Nor can India, China, Bulgaria,
> My birthplace is placelessness,
> My sign to have and give no sign.
> You say you see my mouth, ears, eyes, nose—
>   they are not mine.
> I am the life of life.

Rumi is trying to do something very profound and complex in his work. He realizes the innate divine nature of his identity and of all beings, but he is writing poems which we could easily treat as aesthetic objects. So, he's trying to make the poems as subversive as possible, to stop us from putting them into any concept at all, so that as we read them, we become one with him and one with them. Then by becoming one with them and one with him, we become one with ourselves. This is the alchemy of sacred genius, When the sacred genius participates in the life of the godhead, the Divine gives the sacred genius the divine power to transform, illuminate, and directly initiate.

> Shams-i-Tabriz has nurtured me through love.
> I am greater than the Holy Spirit and the cherubim.

> You say you see my mouth, ears, eyes, nose ...

We are all in a fantasy, the fantasy of separateness. "I am different from you, you are different from her, she is different from the blackboard, the blackboard is different from the tree!" They are, but only in the relative consciousness which is based on separation and difference; this is useful up to a point, because it enables us to maneuver this reality that we are also in. But the paradox is that you can only understand that reality when you know the source of that reality. You can only be truly at home in this reality when you know the reality that is continually emanating it. You have to know, beyond any kind of linear knowledge, that you and the blackboard and that person and this person and you and me and this and that are all one! You have to become one with the One before you understand anything. The consciousness of the ego, however elaborate, brilliant, and intelligent it may seem, understands nothing. I mean nothing as it really is. It cannot, because it cannot see the Light that is projecting the images. Rumi is saying, you think I'm Rumi, you think this is Rumi's mouth, you think these are Rumi's words, you've got it all sorted out, you've got it all tabulated into your tidy conceptual formats.

> You say you see my mouth, ears, eyes, nose—
> they are not mine.

Nothing is mine, nothing is yours. The reality is that we all are what he says, "I am the life of life." I am the source, I am the miraculous spring out of which all this is coming—so are you! Stop using these words, "mine," "yours." Try and go to that place beyond words where you see all this reality brimming with sacred energy, shimmering in the *shakti,* dancing, spiraling in the transparent fire of the Divine in which you know that everything that happens is another message from the beloved. That is when you find out that "this" is not "this," that you are not you, but that you are essentially and really behind all the names and forms, the "life of life itself."

> I am that cat, this stone, no one.
> I have thrown duality away like an old dishrag.

Who is talking in Rumi, who is talking now? Stop separating things and then you'll hear the news, which is not my news, nor your news. Just the news.

> I am the life of life.
> I am that cat, this stone, no one.
> I have thrown duality away like an old dishrag.

Do you see what he does? There is a cat running about, and that cat is reality. You don't think that stones are normally filled with consciousness, but of course they are. Stones dance away. Everything is in the whirlpool of tender transparent energy, everything is doing the dance—Shiva's dance.

So Rumi dances from the cat to the stone, and he dances into placelessness, into final identity, to no one. The person beyond the person, the absolute, the light. "I am that cat, this stone," getting nearer, and wilder, "no one." Rumi is always enticing you, charming you, outraging you into going deeper and crazier so that there can come a moment in your brain in which something can explode and be released, something can flower beyond words and concepts. He says again, as if driving it home so that you know who is speaking and who has been listening, "I have thrown duality away like an old dishrag." Duality is garbage. All the ego's fantasies and concepts are just like bits of used paper; throw them away. All of them are lies.

Imagine if you take that statement seriously what it means! It means you can have no superior thought about anybody, because they're all you. It means that no poor person is not also your brother or sister. It means that everybody dying on the earth is also dying in you. It means that you and the environment are one and therefore you will dedicate whatever your gifts are to saving the environment and the world. It also means that whatever you do, you try to do it in an atmosphere of sacred love, sacred worship of your divine self, which is everything.

These poems are nuclear, they are not about playing games with the mind, they are about entering into the fire. In the fire, you are burnt away and you are seared into servanthood, into the endless responsibilities of sacred love. The stories I tell about Rumi are all stories of service. Service to the disciples, service to the hungry dog, service to the whole world saying God's name, all endless service.

> I see and know all times and worlds,
> As one, one, always one.
> So what do I have to do to get you to admit who is
>   speaking?

At the end of the poem, after giving you all this information, after trying to shock you into losing, as far as you possibly can, your concepts and your sense of who you are, Rumi says, like every mystic and prophet, "What do I have to do to get you to admit who is speaking?" And immediately, if you're really listening, you think, "God, what am I going to answer to this question?" On your decision depends your life, your entire mental and spiritual life. "What do I have to do to get you to admit who is speaking?"

What does the saint do? The saint throws him or herself into the fire and becomes a living sign of fire for the world. What does the sacred genius do, who is a saint? That sacred genius leaps into the fire, becomes a living sign of fire, and speaks and sings of the fire with the fire's own voice. What do you have to do to get people to admit anything? You have to become the thing of which you are speaking, so that they will know that it is real, and that it is themselves. This is the madness of the life of love.

Mother Teresa isn't sitting around saying, "Jesus is love." She is *being* love, so that you can see Jesus in her. By seeing Jesus in her, you can see that Jesus is real and that Jesus does live. The Dalai Lama isn't simply talking about enlightenment, Buddha, and compassion—he is *being* Buddha, enlightenment, and compassion. He is enacting these in every gesture, with every look and laugh. Rumi, the man who is asking you this question, is asking you from the place of a person who has thrown himself into the fire to become the fire. He knows that all things burn in that fire, and he is asking you not to entertain his question as an intellectual proposition, but to take it in the deepest sense as an invitation to transfiguration. He is impatient, as all the sacred ones are impatient, because they see the world burning in illusory fires and want to save everyone, out of love and compassion, from burning in them.

> What do I have to do to get you to admit who is
>   speaking?
> Admit it and change everything!

This doesn't just mean change the furniture, change the bookshelves, it means changing the entire ground of our life and our actions, the entire ground of our political choices, the entire ground of our relationship with the environment, everything! Feed the poor, establish justice, save the forests, unpollute the seas, build cities in which beings can live fragrant and sacred lives. Set up educational institutions in which the sacred role of genius can be really known and understood and in which mystical discipline becomes the foundation of all the other disciplines. Start the new Renaissance. Rumi is speaking from the great mystical Renaissance of Sufism, directly to the new Renaissance that must happen now for the world to be safe. That means a complete and very rapid shift in the human consciousness, and a complete rededication of all the skills we have acquired in our disastrous Promethean search for self-glory to the Divine and the divine work on earth. If that rededication can be done, then the planet can be saved, and if that rededication is not done, then it cannot be saved.

> Admit who is speaking, admit it and change everything!
> This is your own voice echoing off the walls of God.

Rumi is a prophet, talking to us with poetry to inspire our transformation. All of this is God. Nothing else. I am the life of life, and so are you. I am that cat, the stone, and so are you. "I have thrown duality away like an old dishrag," and so can you! To know that is everything. "I see and know all times and worlds as one, always one." The madness that Rumi is inviting us to is the perpetual springtime of eternity. We are in the eternal. How can we be effective in time until we know who we are in eternity? How can we create in time unless we have the knowledge and love of the eternal to help us infuse time with its own secret sacred perfume?

For Rumi, 1993, 1271, 8 BCE, ancient Egypt—all are one fresh eternal moment. Rumi is in that one fresh eternal moment, so are you and I. All times and all worlds, not just this world, but all the worlds of Betelgeuse and the Andromeda Nebula, all the constellations, the entire universe, all the worlds of the different stages of consciousness, all of these are only always one, one, *one!* And one here, now, in the light-core of the age-less Rose of Love.

> What do I have to do to get you to admit who is
>   speaking?
> Admit it and change everything!

When we recognize who we really are, we will see that we are Rumi, we are the Dalai Lama, we are Mother Meera—we are all these messengers of ourselves to ourselves, and we are the Light sending them to us in us.

I've tried to take you from constellation to constellation of thought and feeling. We have moved in clusters because the enlightened mind does not move in a linear way. Rumi's poetry does not move linearly. It takes dazzling leaps, leaps which are always rooted in the real, but are always rooted too in a consciousness which dances far above normal consciousness, always rooted in a secret laughter of identity and unity. If you are allowing those constellations of thought and feeling to work upon you, you are allowing yourself to participate in the fringes of the enlightened experience because you are giving up control of what you expect or expect someone to say about Rumi. You are allowing the full madness of Rumi to begin to take place, and allowing what Rumi said of Shams to take place in you:

> When your image dances into my heart,
> How many drunken images seethe along with it!
> They whirl around your image, your moon-like glory
>   whirling at the center.
> When an image brushes against you, it displays the
>   sun's rays like a mirror,
> My words become drunk through one of your
>   attributes,
> Travel a thousand times between tongue and heart,
>   heart and tongue.
> My words are drunk, my heart is drunk, and your
>   images are drunk—
> They all pile up on top of each other, and just gaze.

So, from that "gazing" now listen again to the poem that began this chapter:

> The lamps are different,
> The Light is the same.
> So many garish lamps, in the dying brain's lampshop . . .
>   forget about them!

Rumi is saying, you are in a dying body, there is hardly any time. Don't think enlightenment is easy. You have to try hard, and you have got to choose the essential. He is saying, "The lamps are different, but the Light is the same." All the different concepts, ideals, and religions differ, but the Light that is manifested in them is the same. So, forget about the lamps, forget about all the fancy ideas and the metaphysical systems. That is all narcissism. That is all spiritual materialism.

If you really want illumination, go straight to the Light, don't go around the to lampshops looking at the various shades, the ones designed in Mecca, the ones designed in the Vatican. "Concentrate on the essence." The essence is the divine Presence. The essence is the essential reality. It says in the *Koran,* "Everything is passing away, except the face of God." The face of God is the essence.

Then Rumi says, "Concentrate on Light." Divine Light is what is animating this universe. Light is what is creating everything. "The Divine Love," he writes elsewhere, "is the sun of perfection, its Light is the command, and the creatures are its shadows." Everything that we are, everything that we see, everything that we know is the Light dancing and playing— the Light knowing itself in a thousand thousand different disguises. By concentrating on essence you come to learn about the Light that is manifesting everything, and you begin to concentrate on that Light. Not on the lamps, but on the Light itself. That is the great leap, in mystic life, when instead of concentrating on the Master, you concentrate on the Light that is manifesting the Master. That is what you're contemplating when you are in the presence of a great Master. Being in the Dalai Lama's presence is contemplating the Light. Being in Mother Meera's presence is contemplating the Light, manifested directly, in her every action.

And Rumi goes on to tell us exactly, lucidly, calmly, scientifically, what the Light is like, "in lucid bliss, calmly smoking off its own holy fire." This universe, this creation, is the holy fire and that holy fire is giving off the Divine Light at all moments. The Light registers in the heart as lucid ecstasy, lucid bliss. When the heart is pierced by the Divine Light, when the heart is seeing the Divine Light, a lucid sober bliss possesses all the body, mind, and heart. The whole being bathes in this sweetness—in what St. John calls "the tenderness of the life of God." And that Light that you are bathing in is creating everything and is calmly smoking off its own holy fire. The fire is peaceful. The key to the nature of fire can be glimpsed in the traditional South Indian way of representing Shiva Nataraja—Shiva the Dancer—in bronze or stone. The face of Shiva in these statues, as he creates with one hand and destroys with another, and as he dances the dance of cosmic creation, is utterly peaceful. He is in what the Indians call *shanti,* sacred peace. The Divine is always in that sacred peace. Out of that sacred peace the worlds are being created, and into that sacred peace they are being dissolved.

That is the foundation and ground of the enlightened mind: *shanti,* that essential nature of mind, that peace. This is where Light appears and reveres itself as the creation— "calmly smoking of its own holy fire, the Light streams towards you from all things." Everything that happens in life is this Light streaming towards you when you are awake and properly understand. Aurobindo was bitten by a scorpion on his balcony and he said, "Ah, my beloved has sent me a message." He wasn't being funny—he was telling the truth. He had gone to the place beyond pain or pleasure. He had realized that all things that were coming to him were the kiss of the beloved. What you think is good may not be good because there will be some consequence in it that you don't know. What you think is evil may have some fantastic birth, some creative possibility that you cannot in the ego-consciousness possibly understand now. You know nothing while you are in the unenlightened mind that divides things. There is no less Divine Light streaming from someone dying in agony than there is in somebody walking happily down a street. Dying of cancer, Ramana Maharshi was in pain but he was also not in pain. Pain is there in the creation, but it is also part of the overall peace and bliss with which it is essentially intertwined. Nothing is not God.

Ramakrishna was asked, "Explain to us the nature of the Divine Mother." He gave a terrifying explanation, which is of course the most joyful and exultant explanation of all. He said, "Imagine a woman who is pregnant, gorgeously pregnant, coming out of a river, naked, and giving birth in ecstasy to her child, her beautiful child." Up to this point everyone is smiling. But then Ramakrishna says, "What happens then is that the very same mother who gave birth to the child tears the child apart and just as blissfully and just as joyfully goes back into the river." What Ramakrishna is trying to do in that story is destroy our fear. This is an experience in which we are being torn apart, but the hand that is tearing us apart is also the hand that created us. The mother gives birth, the mother destroys, the mother lives beyond either of what we call death or what we know as destruction. We are living in that eternal process as that eternal process, partaking of the full life of the cosmos, its full divinity, both being born and dying. To participate in it, we have to do what Rumi and what Ramakrishna are asking us to do, which is extinguish reality as we know it. Extinguish our concepts of what good and evil are, and of what destruction and creation are, because the unenlightened mind does not know that the Light is working in death as it is in life, in pain as it is in joy, in destruction as it is in creation. When we know that, only God is here; we can, in the highest sense, relax.

This is not any normal form of relaxation. It is the relaxation of gnosis, the impregnation by the radiation of the Light. You soak the Light consciously, you become the Light, you radiate the Light. And then Rumi repeats, "The lamps are different, but the Light is the same," and it is only one matter, one energy, one light, all of this is one. All one dance. You are that dance. "One light-mind, endlessly emanating all things, one turning burning diamond." Rumi ends the second part of his poem with this second vision of unity. He can only babble, because you can never describe it. No words will ever be able to convey it, because words fall down before the throne of the King.

My words are drunk, my heart is drunk,
And your images are drunk—
They all pile up on top of each other
And just gaze.

One turning, burning diamond.
One, one, one.

This is the reality "gazed" at by enlightened mind, then Rumi can say no more. Because this is where "knowledge" ends. The end of "knowledge" is what Thomas Aquinas experienced at the Mass of Naples in 1293, after writing the *Summa Theologica*. He had an experience in that Mass—a direct experience of the Divine Presence—and he never said or wrote another word. There was nothing at all to say. Just wonder, just joy.

One turning, burning diamond
One, one, one.

Do we want to know, *really* want to know what Rumi knew in "astounding lucid confusion"? If we do, there is a way!

Ground yourself, strip yourself down
To blind loving silence.
Stay there, until you see
You are gazing at the Light
With its own ageless eyes.

As Sanai, another great Sufi Master, wrote in his *Hadiqa*: "If you ask me, Oh my brother, which are the signs of the path, I would answer you very clearly and without ambiguity. The Path is to look at the Truth and break with lies, to turn your face to the living universe, to despise worldly rewards, to spring your mind free from any ambition of glory and fame, to stoop to His service, to purify your soul from evil and fortify it with discrimination, to leave the house of those who talk too much and go to the one where people are silent, and to travel from God's manifestations to God's attributes and from there to His knowledge. Then, at that moment, you will have crossed the world of mysteries and arrived at the door of poverty. When you are poverty's friend, your deep soul will have become a penitent heart. Then, God will extract poverty from your heart, and when poverty is gone from there, God will stay in your heart." And when God stays in your heart, you will be gazing at the Light "with its own ageless eyes," for what is the heart? The heart, as Rumi tells us in the *Mathnawi*, as all the mystics who have come into reality tell us, "the heart is nothing but the Sea of Light ... the place of the vision of God."

> In the Ocean of the Heart love opens its mouth
> And gulps down the two worlds like a whale.

> Hear from the heart wordless mysteries!
> Understand what cannot be understood!
> In man's stone-dark heart there burns a fire
> That burns all veils to their root and foundation.
> When the veils are burned away, the heart will
>   understand completely ...
> Ancient Love will unfold ever-fresh forms
> In the heart of the Spirit, in the core of the heart.

Chapter Six

Perfect Being

THE CORE CONCEPT of Islamic mysticism, of that body of divine knowledge that inspired and illumined Rumi, is that of the perfect or universal human being, *al insan-al kamil.*

First let us listen to Rumi:

> Reason is powerless in the expression of love. Love alone is capable of revealing the truth of love and of being a lover. The way of our prophets and perfect men is the way of truth. If you want to live, die in love. Die in love, if you want to remain alive.

> God has created in all the earth and in all the sublime heavens, nothing more mysterious than the spirit of man, and when you enter into that perfection, which is your origin, you will find yourself outside this world, that was for you the breast of your mother. You will leave this earth to come into a vast open place. You will know that what the *Koran* says, "The earth of God is vast," points to that infinite region where the saints have come to.

> The individual hearts are like the bodies compared with the heart of the Perfect Being who is its Original Source.

Now let us hear what Ibn-Arabi tells us of the perfect universal human being. What he says arises out of a profound inner experience. Rumi's mind and voice are passionate and warm; Ibn-Arabi's voice is the voice of the diamond itself:

The perfect human is the perfect image of God and contains in him all things. He reunites in himself the form
of God and the form of the universe. He [or she] alone
reveals the divine essence with all its names and attributes. He [or she] is the mirror in which and by which
God is revealed to himself and by this becomes the final
cause of the creation.

The achieved one, the awakened one, the Christ, the Buddha, the universal human, is seen to have in Islamic mysticism
and in Sufism five main dignities, powers, and sublimities. Five,
like the fingers of a hand. The perfect human is the lover of
God; the knower of the divine secrets; the mirror of divinity;
the caliph and vice-regent of God and creation; and the mediator between this world and the world that manifests it, between humanity and God, between the human soul and the ego.

Five powers, all interdependent, all interlinked. All irradi-
ating each other, all buoyant with gnosis. Five powers: The
lover, the knower of the divine secrets, the mirror of divinity,
the caliph of God and of creation, the mediator between the
human and the Divine. What Rumi and the Islamic mystics
are attempting to communicate at this moment to the world
is this vision of the perfect human being. Returning mankind
to a vision of the perfect human being as the goal of life is
essential to the survival of the human race. What you worship
you become, what you admire you become, what you strive
for, you become. If what we worship, admire, and strive for
are the idols of the marketplace, the tawdry, flashy, and neu-
rotic lives of our leaders, film stars, and football players, then
we will be cut off from our sacred origin and from all the powers invested in that origin for us by the Divine Presence. We
will need these powers to save the planet.

Now let me tell you a Sufi story. When I was twenty-six,
I went on one of my periodic flights from Oxford and the West
and buried myself in India for three or four months. I spent
some time in Ladakh, and then distractedly went to Nepal. I

found myself living in a seedy old hotel by the lake in Pokhara. It was there that I made one of the most sublime friendships of my life, a friendship with a being whose fragrance has deeply and strangely influenced the rest of my life.

He was a young Persian man, about twenty-five. He was very beautiful, with a mysterious and intense face. He was living in the room next to me with a couple of Iranian friends. We quickly became very close friends. One day I went into his room as he was putting on his shirt, and I saw that the whole of his back was covered with scars. I asked him where the scars came from. He said, "Now I must tell you the whole story." He was a Sufi, he told me, he had been arrested by the police under the Shah, had been hideously and brutally tortured, and had fled Iran to wait in Nepal for a change of regime. I asked him if that terrible experience had shaken him in his faith. He smiled and said nothing. Instead he said, "It's six o'clock, let's go out on the lake and I will sing you a song." It was a breathtaking evening; the lake of Pokhara is flanked by snow-covered mountains, and all the mountains were glittering in the still lake. The lake was flooded by a red-gold light. My friend said nothing and took me out right into the center of the lake. There, with the tears pouring down his face, he sang me this song—an ode by Jalal-ud-Din Rumi:

> What I want is to see your face in a tree,
> In the sun coming out, in the air.
> What I want is to hear the falcon drum,
> And light again on your forearm.
> You say, tell him I'm not here.
> The sound of that brusque dismissal becomes what I
>   want.
> To see in every palm your elegant silver coin shavings,
> To turn with the wheel of the rain,
> To fall with the falling breath of every experience,
> To swim like a huge fish in ocean water,
> To be Jacob recognizing Joseph,

To be a desert mountain instead of a city.
I'm tired of cowards, I want to live with lions,
    with Moses, not whining teary people.
I want the ranting of drunkards,
I want to sing like birds sing,
    not worrying who hears or what they think.
Last night a great teacher went from door to door
    with a lamp,
He who is not to be found
Is the one I'm looking for.
Beyond wanting, beyond place, inside form, that one.
A flute says I have no hope for finding that, but Love
    plays.
Love plays and plays, and is the music played.
Let that musician finish this poem,
Shams, I am a waterbird, flying into your sun.

He sang with a high, fiercely clear, and tender voice which seemed to ring off the mountains and to be one with the stainless purity of the snow on the mountains. Then he translated the poem that he had sung. He then said, you know why your culture is sick? It is sick because it worships the rebel and not the lover and servant. It is sick because it worships the man of reason and not the naked and dancing slave of God. It is sick because it has lost the image of sacred perfection that every mystical culture has known, always. It is sick because it has chosen the path of futile domination over the Path of eternal Love. And, he added, that song I sang you, by my master, Rumi, is not a song. It is not a poem, it is a manifestation of the Divine grace and beauty and power of a perfect being. It is designed to lead the whole of humankind back to origin.

Rumi's poetry is a direct initiation into the inner states of that perfected being. Rumi's poetry is not only a manifestation of that great power invested in the perfect being, but a mirroring of the states of that perfection, a showing of it in all its lavishness, splendor, humor, delight, joy, rapture, and bliss, so that we can begin to participate in that perfection in our own selves.

Now I'm going to look at this poem in great detail and tease out from it the qualities of the perfect being.

What I want.

Those words, "what I want," indicate that the perfect human makes a decision. The perfect being, the person who wishes for that total status, clears away all other desires and all other possibilities except the ultimate possibility, which for Rumi is to see his beloved, Shams, as God in nature, and as God radiating through nature. This is what Rumi says, I want to see and know your sacred presence in the tree which is itself vibrant with sacred presence. To the awakened eye of the perfect being, all things in reality are pulsating in the Divine Light and flashing out the Divine Light as direct signs of their origin. That is what he is saying he wants. He does not want ordinary perception, he wants divinized perception—he is aiming his entire being at it.

What I want is to see your face in a tree,
In the sun coming out, in the air.

The perfect being is the mirror of divinity. When Rumi says this, he is making a pun on Shams' name, which means sun, but he is also aspiring to the ultimate state, which is to know that the sun rising over the sea is the Divine sun, and that they are not separate. The sun is the sun, but it is also Shams, it is also the life-giver, the radiant one, the soul of the universe; it is also our sign of the ultimate sun, which is the entire cosmos and in which the cosmos is always being manifested and into which the cosmos sinks at each second, to be reborn again. So what Rumi is asking for is that mirroring awareness of Divine Knowledge.

What I want is to hear the falcon drum,
And light again on your forearm.

God is the king, and he wears the soul like an emperor wears the falcon upon his wrist. It is a fabulous, proud, exultant image—the emperor, standing, having the drum beats call the hawk of the soul to fly through darkness after darkness back to its eternal home on his wrist of light. What Rumi is begging for is to hear at every instant, in every sound of the wind, every screech of a car, in every word and every breath, the drumbeat of the king. Always to make of this experience of life a constant yearning for origin.

The state of perfection is not static, it is a state of dancing, it is a state of infinite suppleness, alertness, and changeability, always changing as the universe is changing. If you as a perfect being come to mirror God, what you will mirror are the dancing moods of God, what you will become is all the different aspects of the divinity—the child, the old woman, the old man, the girl, the dancer, the priest, the poet, everything in a constant kaleidoscope of love. It has nothing to do with what the ego imagines to be omniscient or perfect strength. It has everything to do with yearning, constantly aspiring, and throwing yourself again and again into the fire of constant yearning and aspiration.

When you listen to the poem, you hear what it takes to live in that state of receptivity and rapture that is perfect being. You hear his prayer renewing itself with every second, with every heartbeat, "what I want," at every heartbeat, "what I want," at every pulse of the heart. Every time your heart beats imagine that it is saying, "What I want is to be in you, with you, deeper, deeper, deeper, further, further, further, to drown endlessly in the depths of the sublimity and the abyss of divine love."

I want to leave you with that thought and refer you to one of the miracles of the world, which illumines what I am trying to say and what Rumi is saying. *The Rose Garden of Mystery*, a book by Shabestari, is one of the diamonds of human gnosis. Lahiji's seventeenth-century commentary on it is a masterpiece of the kind of diamantine precision that Ibn-Arabi represented for us earlier. With Rumi's poem in our minds, listen now to Lahiji's commentary on two lines of Shabestari's text. First the two lines, then the commentary.

> By love has appeared everything that exists,
> and by love, that which does not exist appears as
> existing.

If you know the meaning of those lines, then you have seen the truth. "By love has appeared everything that exists," everything has been manifested out of the Divine Love. "By love, that which does not exist appears as existing."

This is Lahiji's ravishing commentary:

> Shabestari means here that man is the eye of the world, and that the world is the reflection of God, and that God himself is the light of this eye. Man is the eye which looks in the mirror, and like the mirror reflects the face of the person who is looking into it, the reflection possesses itself an eye, and in the same time that the eye looks in the mirror, the reflection of this eye looks at it also. God, which is the eye of man, looks at himself through man.
>
> This point is very subtle: from one side God is the eye of man; from another, man is the eye of the world, because the world and man are only one, man being its eye. This man is called the perfect man. Since man is a résumé of everything that exists, he is a world in himself, and the relation that exists between God and man exists between man and the world.

If you are following in your light-mind the way in which the light travels between all mirrors in this passage, you will be close to having an insight of the enlightened state. Lahiji has perfected the entire experience in a series of very simple images that become ever more resonant as you meditate upon them.

The perfect man, the perfect being, is the one who has understood consciously, through mystical relationship, dedication,

and the purity of a disciplined life lived in devotion and passion, that God is looking at himself through him or her; he or
she has understood that the Divine is tasting the wine of the
Divine Presence through his or her mouth. The perfected being
has understood that the sole purpose of being here is to live,
looking into the eye of the eye that is looking back at you, to
see that the entire swirl of life is the magic of Divine Love, that
Love by which everything that exists appears, that Love by
which everything that "does not exist"—this passing theater—
also appears.

Let us reenter Rumi's wonderful poem, because I want you
to take these crystalline insights of Shabestari and Lahiji, shatter them, and reexperience them moltenly from within the
poem.

"What I want is to hear the falcon drum and light again
on your forearm." When you are in a relationship of adoration with a Divine Being, everything that that Divine Being
does reflects itself magically in all dimensions to show you not
only their perfection and their power, but also your own secret
perfection as their lover, disciple, slave, servant, and child. So
you see what level this poetry is dealing with, what mysteries
are here.

> You say, tell him I'm not here.
> The sound of that brusque dismissal becomes what I
>   want.

When Aurobindo was bitten by a scorpion he said, "Ah, a
message from my beloved." That is embracing everything, all
the difficulties, agonies, and harshnesses of life, because in
them there also is the presence of the Beloved. In them also is
Shams, who could be so harsh with Rumi, who could hurt him
so much to awaken him. Rumi came, through mystical knowledge, to know Shams as one with life itself, which can be harsh
with us, which can hurt us to wake us up. Rumi understood
that the key to perfection lies in the complete embrace of what
we take as "brusque dismissals"—"when someone beats a rug

with a stick he is not beating the rug—his aim is to get rid of the dust."

Now I want to take another journey out from this text to a letter by Rainer Maria Rilke, the only poet in the Western tradition who can hold a candle to Rumi. In these letters, Rilke is dealing from a completely intuitive level of understanding with exactly this acceptance at the deepest level of everything that life brings, which enables you to participate in the oneness of creation. Listen to this glorious letter that he wrote to the Countess M.S. Museau on January 6, 1923 (Day of Epiphany).

> Woe to them that are consoled ... for even time does not console as one superficially says, at most it arranges, sets in order, and only because we later so little heed the order toward which it so quietly collaborates. ... What we have to do is to face the cruelty of life, and I reproach all modern religions for having handed to their believers consolation and glossings over of death, instead of administering to them the means of reconciling themselves to it and coming to an understanding with it, with its full, unmasked cruelty. This cruelty is so tremendous that it is just with it that the circle closes. It leads right back into the extreme of a mildness that is great, pure, and perfectly clear as we have never surmised mildness to be, not even on the sweetest spring day.

What he is describing is the rhythm of the transformation of acceptance. To shirk nothing, none of the brusque dismissals of Shams, none of the cruelty, none of the madness of life, to embrace it all, to accept it all. The religious way is consolation; the mystical way, the way of the perfect being, is an embrace that leads into mildness "great, pure, and perfectly clear."

Rilke goes on,

> But the experience of this most profound mildness, which were only a few of us to feel it with conviction, could

perhaps little by little penetrate and make transparent all the relations of life toward the experiencing of this richest and soundest mildness toward which mankind has never taken even the first steps unless in its oldest, most innocent times, a mildness whose secret has been all but lost to us. The content of initiations is nothing but the implanting and imparting of a key that permits the reading of the word "death" without negation. Like the moon, which must have a side permanently turned away from us, which is not its counterpart but its complement toward perfection, toward consummation, toward the really sound and full sphere and orb of being.

Prejudiced as we are against death, we do not manage to release it from its misrepresentations. Only believe, dear dear Countess, that it is a friend, our deepest friend, perhaps our only one that is never, never to be misled through our behavior and vacillation. And that, it is understood, not in the sentimental, romantic sense of denying life, of life's opposite, but as our friend just when we most passionately, most vehemently assent to being here, to functioning, to nature, to love. Life always simultaneously says yes and no. Indeed, death, I beg you to believe it, is the true yea sayer. It says only yes before eternity.

Now listen, with Rilke sounding within you, to Rumi:

You say, tell him I'm not here.
The sound of that brusque dismissal becomes what I
     want.
To see in every palm your elegant silver coin shavings,
To turn with the wheel of the rain,
To fall with the falling breath of every experience,
To swim like a huge fish in ocean water,
To be Jacob recognizing Joseph . . .

Many marvelous images, but I prefer the last one, because that is the state of the perfect being. Joseph is the child, the son of Jacob, who was betrayed by his brothers. He was sent into slavery and went to live in Egypt and became the vizier of Egypt. Then, after many years and vicissitudes, again the brothers came and met their brother, and Jacob was able to recognize his own beloved son. But to be Jacob recognizing Joseph is to be origin recognizing origin, the soul recognizing the soul, the lover recognizing the beloved, the awakened being seeing existence as one eternal flashing of the now, as one perpetual theophany. It is to be always seeing in everything that happens the face of that creature most beloved to you, your deepest self, your son, your child, your friend. When Rumi says that he wants to be Jacob recognizing Joseph, he means that he wants to be the soul of the soul recognizing that everything that happens springs out of that origin and is another dynamic, ecstatic manifestation of that origin, and that he and the origin and reality are one diamond turning, one diamond burning, one diamond flashing out with sacred power, sacred joy, at every moment.

And then Rumi cries:

I'm tired of cowards ...

I think it's very important to see this aspect of the man or woman of perfection, because it's very important not to sentimentalize our lions of the human race, our knowers of the secret, our caliphs and mediators. Rumi is a great roarer of freedom, and he has a majestic rage, disdain, urgency, wildness, and passion for courage.

I want to live with lions ...

Rumi wants to live with those like Shams, Moses, and the prophets, who roar with the roar of emptiness, love, and sublime freedom. In the *Mathnawi*, Rumi tells this story which illustrates the function of the perfect being in the human race and in our lives.

There was a young lion who happened to be left behind by a troop of lions and was reared by a flock of sheep. And this young baby lion, because it imitated everything that the flock of sheep taught it, was a helpless and ridiculous animal. Imagine a lion *baa*ing, a lion shambling along in a scruffy kind of way, like sheep do. Imagine a lion running away in panic and fear from the wolves just as sheep do, imagine a lion whimpering and being terrified, banal, and obsessed with stupid goals just as sheep are. One day, a great wild lion happened to be passing and saw this astounding sight: a lion shambling, whimpering, and *baa*ing. This lion, Christ or Mohammed or Mother Meera, swooped down and took the lion/sheep by the scruff of its neck and dragged it to a clear, still pool, and said, "Look, you—me—same." Me—free—wild—rapturous—King. You—free—wild—rapturous—King. Me—ROAR! You—*baa*." He said to the sheep/lion, "Now, you start roaring." Of course the sheep/lion made a pathetic little sound to begin with, but after seventeen years of discipline, prayer, fasting, and vigil, the first signs of a real roar started to appear.

This is what the perfect man or woman is doing. They are living like lions, roaring like lions, and dragging anybody they can get their hands on to that still pool, where they are saying, "Me—you—the same." The prophets and the great saints, like Rumi, are doing that in all of their work and in all of their being, just that. Again, and again, and again.

This message has extreme importance for us now. Look at us, in this culture: "whining teary people," as the poem says. Look at the apathy of our depression, the desolation of our apathy, our boredom with ourselves. Look at how easily and fatuously we are distracted from anything serious by the dancing trivia of a trash culture. Look how we have been enslaved by the stupidest, most banal, and worst in ourselves, how we refuse again and again to take the journey into ecstasy which costs everything, the journey into joy which is really demanding, the journey into the kind of transcendence about which Rumi and Rilke and all the mystics are talking and which will demand of us that we make one decision—to live in happiness and in origin, not in the depression, doubt, and desolation that we have mistakenly deified as wisdom in our culture. The perfect being is challenging other human beings, and saying, if I can do it with this body, this head, this brain, you can do it. You and I are here as one reflection of the One. We are all this great secret. Man is the mystery and God is the mystery of man's mystery. But to *know* that the journey has to be undertaken in all its pain, in all its suffering, and in all its splendor.

> I'm tired of cowards, I want to live with lions,
> With Moses, not whining teary people.
> I want the ranting of drunkards ...

What we are longing for, what we are praying for, is the return of the drunkards of God, the return of those—the scientists, artists, dancers, and musicians—who are drunk on the Divine and who can communicate that drunkenness. In order to go through the terrible fight for the future, we will need the drunkenness of God to be able to bear our wounds. We will be battered, knifed, speared, derided, humiliated, and endlessly insulted. But what will it matter if we are really drunk on the wine of gnosis, if we really know what we are and where we are? Rumi's injunction on us to bring back the drunkards is really what all visionary artists are trying to do at this late moment, because we need the power of drunkenness. We need the glory of drunkenness boiling in our veins. We need to go on like the drunk man goes on, into ultimate danger, fearing nothing, drunk on the glory of his or her Beloved.

> I want to sing like birds sing ...

Only very great stability, great sobriety, great peace could permit this extravagance of birdsong, just as only the great silences of the sea can permit the enormous storms that rage on its surface.

> I want the ranting of drunkards,
> I want to sing like birds sing ...

There is nothing fresher in the creation than that sound of birds singing at dawn in spring. What Rumi is really saying is that he wishes to be like a bird in the sunlight, singing in ecstasy. As Shelley wrote in "Ode to a Skylark," "ascending joy." To be that ascending joy, always singing of the freshness of the creation.

> I want to sing like birds sing,
> Not worrying who hears or what they think.

The perfect being has gone far beyond shame. His only reference is the Divine Itself. The truths of the Divine are madness to all human beings who aren't in his state, and he has to consent and consent willingly to appear mad, crazy, in the hope that others will catch the craziness also. Then these amazing lines:

> Last night a great teacher went from door to door
>   with a lamp,
> He who is not to be found,
> The perfect one, is the one I'm looking for.

The perfect being never ends the journey looking for himself or herself. The journey towards ultimate being is endless and involves a constant appraisal, examination of everything, and overturning of everything, a constant burning away of everything in the Divine Fire.

Right at the end of the poem, Rumi describes exactly the qualities of the perfect being who he is looking for, who he has found in Shams, who he is striving to become, that the poetry is manifesting.

> Beyond wanting, beyond place, inside form, that one...

"Beyond wanting," that is beyond the whole psychosomatic burden of desire, having seen that desire only arises in the mind. "Beyond place," that is no longer identified with the body or with the body's surroundings, knowing that the body, its surroundings, and the whole creation are all passing manifestations of Divine Light. "Inside form," that's the joke: being beyond place, yet still inside form. Inside form, not in ignorance, but as the Divine is inside every form, with total consciousness, with rapture, with blissful consciousness. Then he says:

> A flute says I have no hope of finding that, but Love
> plays ...

A poignant part of Rumi (that is part of us all) that doesn't believe in this journey says, "This is so great, so vast, this concept of perfection, I have no hope of reaching it. I have no hope of reaching it ever, even if I give my life in this way, even if I open my life in this way." The perfection that Rumi and the mystics are aiming for has humility as its very ground, its basis, root of light, and light-spring. It is the perfection of the lover, the servant, the dancer, and the child, not any other kind of perfection. A perfection, in other words, that is endlessly examining itself, that is endlessly offering itself to be transfigured more deeply into mirroring the ultimate perfection. A perfection that is totally daring in its constant exposure to criticism and transformation.

That is why Rumi is always acknowledging the voice within himself that does not want to go further. But that is also why he is always paying tribute, in all of the poems, in anything that he ever says, to that force which infinitely surpasses and transcends his own, of which he is the slave and servant.

> ... but Love plays.
> Love plays and plays, and is the music played ...

He is saying: "I cannot do it; I cannot transform myself. What I can do is to consent to be played by Love, the supreme musician. What I can do is to make my being totally receptive to the playing of Love. What I can do is to become more and more like that supreme musician, Love, to throw myself again and again into the fire of Love, to be transmuted into Love. In doing that again and again, deeper and deeper, further and further, a perfection in me is born by the grace of God."

Let that musician finish this poem . . .

Of course, Rumi doesn't mean just let the musician finish
the poem. He means: let that musician finish my life. I am no
longer playing my life, I am no longer playing this music. This
music is being played in me, through me; let the supreme musician play, play what he wants and what he wills. All I am is
God's flute, God's instrument, that's all. That is all the perfect
human being aspires to be, because it is everything.

Shams, I am a waterbird, flying into your sun.

Now some more quotations from the Sufi mystics about
this perfect man, this perfect being. Then the poem again so
that we bring to the final reading of the poem everything that
we may have learned until now. Everything that we might have
felt, everything that Rilke, Shabestari, Lahiji, and all the mirrors of our own life might have reflected, dance in this poem.
This is Rumi's son Sultan Walad talking, writing in his famous
Walad-Nama:

> The human being has to be born twice, once from his
> or her mother, and then out of his or her body and of
> his own existence. This body is like an egg, the essence
> of man must become in this egg a bird, thanks to the
> heat of love. And then he will escape this body, into the
> eternal world of the soul, beyond space.

I chose this quotation after the waterbird because this is
what Rumi is. He has become the bird, the ascending bird, the
Simurgh, the bird of paradise flying into the sun.

The next two quotations are from Rumi's *Discourses.* The
first, perhaps the most profound single paragraph in the *Discourses,* is the clue to the whole nature of perfection. It is paradoxical and strange, but totally accurate. It is accurate with
the same strangeness that Shabestari and Lahiji were accurate.

> Human quest consists of seeking a thing which one has
> not yet found. Night and day a man is engaged in search-

ing for that. But the quest where the thing has been found and the object attained, and yet there is one who is seeking for that thing. That is a strange quest indeed, surpassing the human imagination, inconceivable to man. For man's quest is for something new, which he has not yet found. And this quest is for something one has found already and then one seeks. This is God's quest, for God most high has found all things and all things are found in his omnipotent power. "For God has found all things, and so He is the finder." Yet for all that, God most high is the seeker, he is the seeker, the prevailer. The meaning of the saying quoted above is therefore, O man, so long as you are engaged in the quest that has been created in time, which is a human attribute, you remain far from the goal. When your quest passes away in God's quest, and God's quest overrides your quest, then you become a seeker by virtue of God's quest. That is what the perfect being has become. The search of the ego for transcendence has passed away into the transcendence itself. The quest of the individual has passed away into God's quest for God's own being, God's own experience of God in God, which is Reality. Then, you become a seeker by virtue of God's quest, because you are then living as a particle of God in God, for God, with God.

The second quotation, before we reenter the poem, is also from Rumi. And it applies to the Supreme Perfect Being, the greatest of those who have "passed into transcendence itself," into God's quest for God's own being—the Prophet Mohammed.

Mohammed is at the core of the Sufi search because in him the complete relationship of the perfect being is realized. Mohammed is the mediator between man and God, the bringer down of a revelation, the knower of the Divine secrets through love, the lover of God, the servant of God.

In these two *Hadiths* of the Prophet are contained the great secret of all Sufi mysticism, in fact of all mysticism. "The heart of the believer is the highest heaven" and "the heart of the believer is the throne of God." Mohammed's life and being proved the truth of these two sayings, the truth that the perfect being is an "astrolabe of God," a theater of all the revelations, the heart of the universe, a microcosm in which the essence and the Divine Names of Allah could be reflected. It was to Mohammed that God in the *Koran* gave the ultimate praise, "If you did not exist, I would not have created the world." In the perfect mirror of Mohammed, adoration, God could see his own face at last, and the glorious purpose of the creation was thereby fulfilled.

So for the Sufis, Mohammed is completely and always sacred, as he must always be for every seeker of whatever persuasion. Now let us hear what Rumi says about Mohammed's perfection:

Mohammed is called unlettered, not because he was incapable of writing and learning. He was called unlettered because with him, writing, learning, and wisdom were innate, not acquired. He who inscribes characters on the face of the moon, is such a man unable to write? What is there in all the world that he does not know, seeing that all men learn from him? What thing, pray, should appertain to the partial intellect that the universal intellect does not possess? The partial intellect is not capable of inventing anything of its own accord which it has not seen. The fact that men compose books, and set up new skills, is no new composition. They have seen the likeness of that and merely make additions to it. Those who invent something new on their own account are the universal intellect. The partial intellect is capable of learning and is in need of teaching. The universal intellect is the teacher and is not in need. So, when you investigate all trades, the root and origin of them is revelation. Men have learned them from the prophets, and they, the prophets, are the universal intellect. There

> is the story of the raven: When Cain slew Abel and did
> not know what to do, the raven slew a raven and dug
> the earth and buried that raven and scattered dust on
> its head. Cain learned from the raven how to make a
> grave and how to bury. So it is with all the professions.
> Everyone who possesses a partial intellect is in need of
> teaching, and the universal intellect is the founder of
> everything. It is the prophets and saints and perfect
> beings who have affected union between partial intel-
> lect and universal intellect so that they have become one.

So in the perfect being there is union with God and sponta-
neous wisdom always flowing from that union for, as the *Hadith*
says, "The heart of the believer is the throne of God" and all
the Divine Light and powers stream from the throne. Because
the perfect being actualizes through this union with the throne
and this mirroring of the essence, the perfections, which exist
in ordinary men as only potential, the perfect being is the final
cause of the universe. As Rumi writes in the *Mathnawi*:

> That is why in appearance, you are the microcosm, but
> in reality you are the macrocosm. From the point of view
> of appearance, the branch is the origin of the fruit, but
> in reality the branch has come into existence because of
> the fruit. Had there been no desire or hope for the fruit,
> would the gardener have planted the root of the tree?

Before we return to Rumi's great poem, let's look at the
conclusion of one of the most wonderful books by Nasr, *Knowledge and the Sacred,* in which Nasr mourns what has happened to us as a culture through not placing at the center of
our culture, of our aspirations and adoration, the concept of
a perfect being mirroring the Divine. As you read this, keep
what Rumi has just said about Mohammed, the Perfect Being,
in your heart.

> How strange it is that agnostic humanism, which remains
> content with the vessel, without realizing the origin of

the divine elixir that the human vessel contains, should be only a halfway house to that which is totally inhuman. Pontifical man, original man, man as the bridge between God and the world [the perfect being we're talking of], has lived on the earth for millennia and continues to survive here and there despite the onslaught of modernism. But the life of Promethean man has indeed been short-lived. The kind of humanism associated with the Promethean revolt of the Renaissance has led in only a few centuries to the infra-human which threatens not only the human quality of life, but the very existence of man on earth.

The reason for such a phenomenon, which seems so unexpected from the perspective of Promethean man, is quite obvious from the sacred point of view. It lies in the fact that to speak of the human, is to speak at the same time of the Divine. While scholars occasionally discuss what they call Chinese or Islamic humanism, there in fact has never been a humanism in any traditional civilization similar to the one associated with the European Renaissance and what followed in its wake.

Traditional civilizations have spoken of man and of created cultures and disciplines called the humanities of the highest order, but the man they have spoken of has never ceased to be that sacred pontifical man who stands on the axis joining heaven and earth and who bears the imprint of the Divine upon his very being. It is this basic nature of man which makes a secular and agnostic humanism impossible. It is not metaphysically possible to kill the gods and seek to efface the imprint of the divinity upon man without destroying man himself.

Those are very stern words and they are absolutely accurate. It is not metaphysically, physically, emotionally, or spiritually possible "to kill the gods and seek to efface the imprint of the divinity upon man without destroying man himself."

The bitter experience of the modern world stands as overwhelming evidence to this truth. The face which God has turned toward the cosmos and man is none other than the face of man toward the divinity, and in fact the human face itself. Remember Lahiji's commentary on Shabestari—the eye that is looking into the eye that is looking into it. Nasr writes,

> One cannot efface the face of God without effacing man himself and reducing him to a faceless entity lost in an anthill. The cry of Nietzsche that God is dead could not but mean in the end that man is dead, as the history of the twentieth century has succeeded in demonstrating in so many ways. But in reality, the response to Nietzsche was not the death of man, as such, but that of the Promethean man who thought he could live on a circle without a center. The other man, the pontifical man, although forgotten in the modern world, continues to live even within those human beings who pride themselves on having outgrown the models and modes of thought of their ancestors; he continues to live and will never die.
>
> That man, who remains man, and continues to survive here, even during this period of despiritualization and of the desacralization of life, is the being who remains aware of his destiny which is transcendence, and the function of his intelligence which is knowledge of the absolute. He is fully aware of the preciousness of human life which alone permits a creature living in this world to journey beyond the cosmos and is always conscious of the great responsibility which such an opportunity entails. He knows that the grandeur of man does not lie in his cunning cleverness for titanic creations, but resides most of all in the incredible power to empty himself of himself, to cease to exist in the initiatic sense, to participate in that state of spiritual poverty and emptiness which permits him to experience ultimate reality.

As the Persian poet Saadi says, "Man reaches a stage where he sees nothing but God. See how exalted is the station of manhood."

Let us now return to Rumi's poem for the second time with, I hope, a far more luminous clarity as to what resides in the mind of the perfected being—what is that mind and what is its origin? This is the way to read a poem like this: You spend hours with it, meditating on it, letting it travel to the furthest reaches of your own inner experience, the furthest reaches of your mind, the furthest reaches of your continuing exploration of mystical reality, and you bring that back and enter the poem again. Afterwards you learn; the poem becomes different, it changes, and you've become different and changed. What you do is dance with the dancer, participate in the Divine creation that is this divine poem by dancing in your Divine Self with it. You use the poem to evoke that Divine Self, to bring that Divine Self to the forefront of your consciousness, and then you explore the poem as it goes deeper and deeper into all the different aspects of that Self, and you enchant yourself deeper and become drunk on the secret wine that is hidden behind the words.

Let us enter the dance of the poem again:

> What I want is to see your face in a tree,
> In the sun coming out, in the air.
> What I want is to hear the falcon drum,
> And light again on your forearm.
> You say, tell him I'm not here.
> The sound of that brusque dismissal becomes what I
>   want.
> To see in every palm your elegant silver coin shavings,
> To turn with the wheel of the rain,
> To fall with the falling breath of every experience,
> To swim like a huge fish in ocean water,
> To be Jacob recognizing Joseph,
> To be a desert mountain instead of a city.

I'm tired of cowards, I want to live with lions,
With Moses, not whining teary people.
I want the ranting of drunkards,
I want to sing like birds sing,
Not worrying who hears or what they think.
Last night a great teacher went from door to door
   with a lamp,
He who is not to be found,
Is the one I'm looking for.
Beyond wanting, beyond place, inside form, that one.
A flute says I have no hope for finding that, but Love
   is playing.
Love plays and plays, and is the music played.
Let that musician finish this poem,
Shams, I am a waterbird, flying into your sun.

For me, all of us are waterbirds flying into the sun of Shams
and Rumi. And what you discover if you go on flying into the
sun, giving yourself with greater and greater passion to the
light, is that you too start growing the lineaments of perfect
being, becoming a ruby in the rock, learning slowly, and with
infinite awe, the truth that Rumi tells us in the *Mathnawi!*
"You are not only yourself, O my friend, in truth you are the
sky and the deep sea. This powerful You is a thousand times
bigger than the ocean, in which a thousand 'yous' could be
drowned." And as that truth deepens and expands in you,
slowly, in humility and infinite awe, you may find yourself the
lover, the knower of secrets, the caliph, the mediator, the one
who opens a door of hope and love to others, as Mohammed
and Rumi so supremely exemplified:

You are the Door to the City of Knowledge
Because you are the rays of clemency.
Be open, O Door! For the one who is looking for the
   door ...
Be open until eternity, O Door of Compassion ...

This destiny is open to us all who love and die enough. Don't take refuge from the struggle for perfection demanded of us by imagining that only Rumi or St. Francis or the Buddha could achieve it. As Rumi reminds us, after extolling the perfection of Moses:

> This mention of Moses can become a shackle on men.
> They can think these stories happened ages ago.
> The mention of Moses serves as a mask:
> Moses' Light is your own coin, my friend.

Chapter Seven

Apocalypse and Glory

THIS POEM OF Rumi's is not a mystical poem, but a call to awareness for our times, facing what we are facing. Rumi is speaking now.

> Everything you see has its roots in the unseen world.
> The forms may change, yet the essence remains the same.
> Every wonderful sight will vanish, every sweet word
> will fade,
> But do not be disheartened,
> The source they come from is eternal, growing,
> Branching out, giving new life and new joy.
> Why do you weep?
> The source is within you,
> And this whole world is springing up from it.
> The source is full,
> And its waters are ever-flowing.
> Do not grieve, drink your fill.
> Don't think it will ever run dry, this is the endless ocean.
> From the moment you came into this world,
> A ladder was placed in front of you,
> That you might transcend it.
> From earth, you became plant,
> From plant you became animal,
> Afterwards you became a human being,
> Endowed with knowledge, intellect and faith.

Behold the body, born of dust, how perfect it has
   become.
Why should you fear its end?
When were you ever made less by dying?
When you pass beyond this human form,
No doubt you will become an angel and soar through
   the heavens,
But don't stop there, even heavenly bodies grow old.
Pass again from the heavenly realm and
Plunge, plunge into the vast ocean of consciousness,
Let the drop of water that is you become a hundred
   mighty seas.
But do not think that the drop alone becomes the ocean.
The ocean, too, becomes the drop.

Each time you read and experience this poem, you will
find new insights and revelations clinging to its words. It is a
poem that springs directly from the joy, glory, and peace that
arise from a knowledge of inner immortality and knowledge
of the Divine Self. It is this knowledge that Rumi is holding
out to us, and it is this knowledge that we need now, for it
gives the only power that can help us endure and transform
what is coming, and to be ready for what is coming in every
dimension.

As some of you know, I have had the great grace of being
with Bede Griffiths, the Benedictine monk whose life and vision
of the world were transfigured by a long stay in India, from the
age of forty-nine to his death at eighty-six in 1993. During that
time he went on an immense mystical journey. I first met him
when I interviewed him for an Australian film project. He and
I fell spiritually in love, and we talked for many hours. At the
end of our conversation, he leaned across the table and took my
hand, and said, "Andrew, you know that the hour of God is at
hand. The hour of God that we have been waiting for has finally
arrived." I replied that I did know this. As we sat in the quiet of
his library at the ashram, the light came through the windows

onto his hands and face and also streamed from them, because he was a man purified and made transparent by love. Then I said, "What do we do, Father, in these last days, if they are the last days?" He looked at me, and smiled an indescribably radiant smile, saying, "What can we do? We can become a sign. Whatever happens, become a sign of divine joy and a fountain of divine love."

My second visit to Bede took place when his body itself had become the site of an apocalypse. Two major heart attacks had paralyzed his already spare frame and attacked his mind, that crystalline organ of perception that had been a vehicle of clarity for so many thousands of people. From his bed, where he lay paralyzed, he enacted another series of even deeper miracles which showed me beyond all words that he himself had taken his words literally and had become a "sign of divine joy and a fountain of divine love." Sometimes when he was unable to speak or even to recognize to whom he was speaking his entire being would flood with rapture and joy; he would reach out with his hands and take the head or face of the person he was speaking to and look at him or her with the look of a child gazing at an astounding jewel. Again and again he demonstrated the ecstatic wonderment at human perfection that is the core of the enlightened vision. As he held the faces of those near him, his eyes would stream with tears of bliss, as if he were looking at me or the others with the eyes of God himself, the eyes of that deathless enlightened passion which all the mystics assure us lies at the heart of God's love for us.

From this extraordinary place Bede Griffiths was inhabiting came these four words, his teaching for the time of the apocalypse. From this placelessness of love and from this fresh vision, he repeated, "Serve the growing Christ." These are four words you will never tire of meditating upon, if you take them to heart. The words mean two different but complementary things. They mean very directly that each being is Christ, Christ in the process of realizing Christhood, of ascending through and enduring difficulty to reach illumination and enlightenment. Each being seen with the eye of the enlightened heart is nothing less than a Christ growing. Each being deserves, because of that, ultimate respect and total reverence for the final radiance that is in them. In fact, such a being, a "growing Christ," deserves the service of an entire life, and an entire being poured out in love.

These words have another meaning also. Bede believed, as I think all mystics now believe, that there is a chance that the chaos, disaster, and misery of this time will bring humankind to its collective senses and show dramatically that only a major transformation of consciousness done very fast and with terrific urgency and passion can be adequate to the problems that are confronting us. If we can transform the situation that is given to us, enact our divine identity and enact the "charge of responsibility" that all the mystical traditions agree that God has given us, then the growing Christ will manifest. In Christian terms, the pleroma, the fullness of God, will be made evident. Mankind as a whole will go into a completely different stage of evolution, a stage in which Christhood is possible in all its resplendence. This possibility demands of us now absolutely everything, because we are the generation on whose sacrifice, passion, and courage for transformation that possibility will be built, if it can be built at all. Our hearts have to be where the miracle happens for the future to exist. That places on us a unique intensity of responsibility.

So, what of the apocalypse and what now must be done? First, we must accept, in the privacy of our hearts, that it is a possibility. Some of the great ecologists who are fighting and have been fighting tirelessly for years against our patriarchal ignorance to save the planet from greed and exploitation have announced that they now feel the fight is over, that the planet cannot be saved and that what we are living in is an immense hospital that is filling up with the dead and dying. We really have to consider that possibility and take on board, in the most profound sense, its agony, and not protect ourselves, not hide from it in apathy, denial, or the histrionics of heartbreak. Nothing should prevent us from feeling that outrageous suffering in all its horror.

Already as human beings we face the apocalypse of death. We live in a body that is continually falling from us. Already as human beings we face the precariousness, poignancy, and fragmentation of *samsara,* a dimension which is designed to defeat our false hopes and reveal all our illusions as fragmented and fake. Nothing works in *samsara,* and nothing is meant to work, because all solutions short of illumination—as the Buddha said—are like whitewashing a burning wall. We are already facing the extremity of death, and the extremity of a dimension in which all the hopes of the ego *must* be defeated. Sex will not work, career will not work, fame will not work. None of these things will work. *Samsara* is God's strange and frightening machine for making us open to a dignity and radiance far beyond what we actually want.

One day, one of his disciples came to Buddha and said, "You know *nirvana,* you live in *nirvana.* Why don't you give us *nirvana?*" The Buddha said, "I will give everybody *nirvana,* but first go around and ask everyone in the village what they most want. Come back and tell me what it is that they most want. Then I will give everybody *nirvana.*" This pleased the disciple, so he went around asking everybody what they most wanted. Naturally one said a Porsche, another said a girlfriend, another wanted a boyfriend, another said a raise of $3,000 more a year. No one wanted *nirvana.*

But this dimension is designed to bring us to the point where we do want *nirvana* and liberation. That is its cruelty and its blessing in one. It is only when we accept the reality and possibility of the apocalypse that we deepen our resolve to know and become love, to know and be that "sign of divine joy" and that "fountain of divine love" of which Bede spoke. The highest, most effective, passionate, and tender form of love is to serve the growing Christ, or the growing Buddha, or the growing Rumi, and to go on bringing the whole feast to the table, even to the very end. The feast is love and gnosis, humor and peace, revelation and ecstasy. Bring them all in your being to the feast of this destruction, spread them on the table of Now and display them. Even if the sceptics don't eat, they will be there, a testimony to the glories of the Divine in us all.

The situation is so extreme that we have no choice but to reach for the highest in us, because it is only that highest that can possibly give us the endurance, passion, courage, truth, peace, sobriety, and certainty that we will need to survive or to bear what may now happen.

There is another secret hidden in this paradox, the secret contained in Bede's last words to the world, "Serve the growing Christ." If we can accept and embrace without consolation the possibility of total destruction; and if we can awaken from the embrace of that unspeakable possibility and resolve to act and be the living Divine on earth, as the caliph of God, the mediator, the rapturous one, the lover, the child, here and now, for God; and, if we can, as in the practice of judo, take the full force of this continuing and growing atrocity into ourselves and use it against history to forever enact the eternal presence; if we can do this, then there is a possibility that through such an act of enacting and enshrining the Divine presence and opening every cell, every breath, every movement, every passion, and every desire to the instruction and radiation of the Divine Presence, time itself, history itself, can be transformed, and this massive engine of destruction that we have set on course be turned around. If we rise to this ecstatic challenge, devote every second to it, and turn the forces of madness, nihilism, and negativity against themselves, not in hatred and anger but in pure and sublime service and love, then we can become channels for divine grace and the divine power be given us to transform apocalypse into hope.

Studying Rumi, being with Rumi, and accepting Rumi into your heart plays an essential part in this massive transformation. In Rumi's poetry you are receiving a transmission, one of the most beautiful transmissions of our core of identity. How will we find the passion and the courage to save this world unless we know that this world is nothing less than a theophany of God? How will we find the courage and the passion to save ourselves unless we *know* that we are the vice-regent of the divine, the place where the Divine manifests itself in creation? How will we save this world if we continue to act, even from the best motives, even out of righteous anger, even from political necessity, but always out of a limited consciousness that has not broken the frontiers of the ego and has not passed through the barriers of selfishness into the radiant and selfless? Let us not doubt for one moment that only the radiant, selfless soul and heart can be of any use anywhere— whether in the spiritual world, the political world, the classroom, the office, or on the psychotherapist's divan—only they will help a situation as extreme as this. You have to transform the entire ground of your being in order to be adequate to the challenge of this extremity. You have to accept the extremity and be one with it in unbearable compassion to be able to enact the truth of divine love. Divine love is what Bede was doing and being on that bed; he was suffering again the crucifixion of Christ in his body to transform the world.

Whether we are Buddhists, Muslims, Hindus, or Christians, we are called upon to take the apocalypse into our heart, to face it, weep endless inner tears for the destruction of this gorgeous theater of enlightenment, and go on fighting with love, without anger and hatred, for the reign of God on earth. If we can accept that challenge, then we can go further than in any other lifetime. Then, even if the world has to end and this theater of enlightenment has to be destroyed, even in that unbearable possibility, two things will have happened. First, there will be calm nurses at the hospital. There will be those walking through the dying holding them to their hearts, breathing with them, loving them, and showing by the light in their eyes that death is not the final possibility. There will be those who will take the apocalypse to their hearts and irradiate each action with the urgency, purity, and calm of divine love, to console, strengthen, and enlighten. We are all called upon to transform ourselves to be a source of enlightenment at the end of the world if we accept the challenge and take the apocalypse into our hearts. The second thing that could happen is that we will use the carnage, destruction, and horror as a way of going even more deeply into the hidden, unseen realm of *nirvana*. Finally, *samsara* is showing us what it has always been: a place of death, desolation, and hopelessness, a place of total and futile vanity. If we can take all of that on, we can use that appalling knowledge to go straight for super-consciousness and straight for the Buddha-mind, straight for the heart of Rumi so that we can live in this body before it is starved, deprived of oxygen, or has to die with the plants and the trees that are being killed; so that we can live and know that what lives in us is immortal.

So, returning to Rumi's poem, we realize that there is no way out of confrontation with extremity. Apathy conspires with apocalypse to keep us in a state of ignorance. Denial traps us in its dark prison. Futile activity conspires with ignorance, as does political activity that isn't founded in the greater glory of the heart. All action that does not spring from the fundamental action of transformation is doomed.

The study of Islamic mysticism goes straight to the heart of the problems we face as a civilization because Islamic mysticism is the most apocalyptic of all mystical paths. This is not to say that it is the best way, but that Islam has rooted in its own revelation a sense of timeless apocalypse, a sense of what must be brought to bear on every moment, and a sense of that divine glory that at any moment could melt the cosmos. As Mohammed says in the *Koran:*

> At any moment, if God wills, the entire creation could sink into non-being.... At any moment, if God wills, the mountains could disappear and become as clouds vanishing.... At any moment, if God wills, we could be as if we had never existed.

What Mohammed, Islamic mystics, and mystics of all kinds know is the outrageousness of God's power, the outrageousness of the magnificence of the *Kibriya,* of the glory behind everything.

Teaching Rumi now is not an act of elitist frivolity, but an act that arises from an apocalyptic vision of the nature of humanity, at a moment in which that apocalypse is not purely mystical, but actual. All the mystical traditions have a vision of divine glory, but some others speak of it in negatives. Theravada Buddhism, for example, never names it. One of the glories of Islamic mysticism is that it does not cease to name it. It pours out towards the *Kibriya* all the treasures of its heart and mind. Here are three excerpts from the *Koran:*

> Oh my servants, you will never be able to harm or to benefit me by your thoughts or your actions. No amount of devotion or worship can increase the sublimity of my kingdom. No amount of negation or rebellion can decrease the sublimity of my love. Were I to offer every conscious being everything it requested, this could not diminish the abundance of my kingdom, any more than dipping a needle into the ocean diminishes its depth.

> If I love one of my servants intensely, I summon up the angel Gabriel and say, "I love this servant, so you, too, must love and support him." And then the archangel speeds throughout the heavenly realms crying, "Allah most high loves this servant, so all of you must love and support him." Thereafter, profound love for this particular servant is gradually established and all the beings on the earth rejoice.

> On the day of Resurrection, I will call out, "Where are those who love one another through my divine glory alone and for the sake of my glory alone? Today I am offering them refuge and sweet refreshment under my shade, for this is a day on which there is no shade but my shade."

We are on that day. We are always on that day "on which there is no shade but my shade." Read those excerpts again, because if you listen to them with your inner ear, you will be given a great clue as to what kind of action is needed.

Action can no longer be done simply out of even the most profound attachment to humankind. Action must be done from an even deeper source, an even deeper passion—the passion for the Divine. Action for humankind will be inevitably soured by disappointment and tragedy, darkened by the endless defeats that anyone fighting for peace or justice or love in this world is bound to suffer as we confront the stupidity of the politicians and the greed of the bankers and the death-merchants. As we confront the infinite lust for blood that still rages in the heart of humanity, we will know disappointment, tragedy, disillusion, the "Bosnia-zation" of the world as neighbor attacks neighbor, and the collapse of all values. And if we dedicate action at this late time to humankind, all that we are going to see would so radically dishearten us that we would every day cry for death. Action truly, deeply, and most effectively springs from an absolute passion for the Divine, not just for humankind itself; an absolute passion to be a clear mirror for the Divine, and a calm and absolute passion to be the channel through which divine justice, divine purity, and divine love flow. And we must now allow the Divine to flow through us so that we can act not for humankind alone but for the Divine, the Divine in us and in all our fellow beings.

As Rumi said, "Love man not for the corn that is splattered with dung, but for the diamond cup that is hidden in the corn." To see always that diamond cup, in the face of the banker, in the face of the mad soldier, in the face of the torturer, even in the face of the man or woman who finally presses whatever button is finally pressed, or who cuts down, laughing, the last tree. To go on gazing into the Divine in humankind, for the Divine's sake. To go on working for the Divine in humankind, for the Divine's sake. To go on offering to the Divine every breath, every movement, every hope, and every moment so that this immense disaster can be, if not averted, then sweetened by the presence of love.

This is the mystical law, whether in Hinduism, Sufism, or Buddhism; there is no other law. It is immensely demanding and it has always been so. All the "technologies of the sacred" that fall short of this immense demand are fooling you and are at this moment doing more than fooling you—they are enabling the destruction of the planet. It is time we face just what truth costs and accept the price, as Rumi did, joyfully, as part of our dignity. I'm going to recount four very extreme examples of what it means to work with the apocalypse in this spirit. These four stories come out of the hell of modern history—a hell that is going to get hotter. These four people represent for me the way through. Everything that I say or do I dedicate to the examples of these people.

The first story is about a woman called Lily. This story could have been enacted in Cambodia, Burma, in the gulags of the Soviet Union, or in the Chinese concentration camps of Tibet. It happened, actually, in Auschwitz. It is the story of a woman who had a major revelation of the Light in the 1930s as part of a very small group of people who withdrew into a Hungarian village to find the truth. Lily was possessed by an angel who gave through her an astonishing message of transformation that is contained in Gitta Mallasz's book, *The Dialogue with an Angel,* one of the important books of the century. This book contains a prophecy of transformation which echoes in the clearest possible way the other great prophecies of a possible new age in Aurobindo, Teilhard de Chardin, and the Buddhist prophecies of Shambhala. This prophecy comes right from the source of life at this moment.

Lily had been possessed and used by the Light as a medium. We have priceless testimony of her actions from one person who survived Auschwitz. Lily gave half of her food every day to whoever needed it. She gave her time ceaselessly to those who were tormented or dying, and also to the young children who were frightened. She would carry the children who were too young to walk, and walk with them to the ovens singing nursery rhymes or prayers to calm them. It was Lily who in that place of hell would again and again go out of her way to show the Germans that they were not defined by this atrocious mask they were putting on. It was she who would try to console those few guards whose hearts were riven by what they had to do. The same inmate of Auschwitz describes her comforting a young guard who was weeping as he was sending people into the ovens. Lily went straight up to him and held him in her arms, because she knew, of course, that the unspeakable atrocity that he was doing was against himself and against the dignity of the Christ in him, and was as great as the atrocities that he was doing against the others.

Lily's is the kind of knowledge we are going to need. We are going to need this knowledge, because we, too, are going to be in a holocaust. A holocaust of nature is happening now all around us. To every dying plant, to every starving person, to every banker whose greed is killing the world, to every politician, we have to extend our unconditional love. The Mother and the other avatars are here to show us how to do it.

The second story is about Mahatma Gandhi. I have a friend who was standing about eight feet behind him when Gandhi was shot. He saw Gandhi stretch out his hand and take the head of the assassin who had shot him, smile, and say, "Ram, Ram," the name of God. The last action of that great saint on this earth was to transcend the horror of the violence that was destroying him and to reach out in a final act of blessing and forgiveness, and also of recognition to the man in front of him. Even at that moment he kept divine clarity and love alive. Gandhi was once asked, "What is your message to India?" He replied, "My life is my message." His last gesture concentrates the entire vision of his life.

The third story is of His Holiness the Dalai Lama. If there is one being on the earth, apart from Mother Meera, who represents what it is to live calmly, decently, with compassion, with infinite lack of false hope, yet with real positive tender passion, it is His Holiness the Dalai Lama. One day in Dharamsala, he was teaching on compassion, giving the initiation into the Buddha of Compassion. It had been a sublime sunny day, and he had been, as he always is, joyful, funny, majestic, and hilarious, all in turns, a marvelous expansive space of joy. In the middle of the initiation, a monk rushed up to His Holiness. As the monk spoke to him, his face fell, and a pall fell over us. His Holiness buried his face in his hands, and we saw his body shaking with sobs. To see His Holiness weep is frightening, because at the moment when His Holiness weeps you feel that the world could actually melt and fall apart. What do we have left if His Holiness weeps? He raised his face and said, "Last night the Chinese tortured and killed sixty nuns and 120 monks. Now, let us pray for the Chinese."

We all should be practicing this alchemy of forgiveness by reaching out to the torturers, the killers, the maniacs, the bankers, and to all of those inside ourselves, perpetual hands of unconditional love. That is the only force that can swerve them now. It is not guaranteed to work, but it is the only force that can convince them of two essential things: first, of their own battered dignity, as they see it reflected in the love that is directed towards them, and second, that there is a power through which the Divine could transform their cold and ruined hearts. So when His Holiness said, "Pray for the Chinese," he was not being holy, he was being totally practical.

The fourth story I have kept for the last because it leads into a meditation on Rumi's vision of perfect being. The last three stories are examples of the mirroring of divine action in the human. In Lily you have someone who knew revelation and who lived revelation out into her final actions. In Gandhi you have a politician who became a saint, who sanctified and gave a direction to politics, and who gave his life to that vision, and who at the final moment showed that the light-spring of his vision was a divine knowledge of the sanctity of humankind. In His Holiness the Dalai Lama, you have an enlightened being working directly at all levels in the world with total awareness, humor, passion, and compassion. We have our heroes and we must not fail them.

My personal hero is someone whose whereabouts I don't know. He has probably been tortured and killed. He is the Iranian young man I mentioned earlier who initiated me into Rumi by taking me out onto the lake and singing me one of Rumi's poems. I'm going to tell you just one story about him, because it contains a real clue.

His Holiness the Dalai Lama once asked if I knew what the two masterpieces of the twentieth century were. He answered his own question: "Torture and genocide. Torture and genocide have always gone on, but now we have perfected the methods to carry them out."

My friend was tortured by having horse hairs shoved up his penis. This was repeated, he was put on the rack, whipped, and many more pains were inflicted on him. He said there were two things that helped him get through. One was the knowledge that the prophets and the martyrs had also suffered, that Christ had suffered on the Cross, and that Al-Hallaj, giving the sacred truth that birthed Sufism, was torn apart in the square of Baghdad. He knew that all mystics who go through the transformation for the world go through great suffering to take upon themselves the ordeal of the transformation. And it is an ordeal. There has to be a crucifixion for the resurrection. The knowledge that these great spirits had gone into the fire, had abandoned everything and sacrificed everything, was what gave him the courage, at that moment, to endure what was happening to him. A second insight gave him courage as well. One day the hood covering his torturer's face slipped, and while he was being tortured, he saw tears running down the man's cheeks. At that moment, he began a Sufi prayer for the mercy of God to save that man—an ordinary, plump man who might have been a grocer. He used the pain that the man was inflicting on him to deepen in the most passionate way the blessing that he was sending with his whole being towards him.

These four examples have been chosen to exemplify the Divine way. Each of these people refused self-righteousness, the easy gratification of rage and hatred. Instead, they offered their own lives as what Bede called "signs of divine joy and fountains of divine love." They did so, where we will have to do so, in hell; but hell is also heaven to the eyes of love.

If you ask me what there is to do, the answer is that there is nothing to *do,* but there is everything to be! All action will flow from that new being: the doing is consecration to transformation.

Let us return now and focus on the last half of Rumi's poem:

> From the moment you came into this world,
> A ladder was placed in front of you,
> That you might transcend it.
> From earth, you became plant,
> From plant you became animal,
> Afterwards you became a human being,
> Endowed with knowledge, intellect and faith.
> Behold the body, born of dust, how perfect it has
>   become.
> Why should you fear its end?
> When were you ever made less by dying?
> When you pass beyond this human form,
> No doubt you will become an angel and soar through
>   the heavens,
> But don't stop there, even heavenly bodies grow old.
> Pass again from the heavenly realm and
> Plunge, plunge into the vast ocean of consciousness,
> Let the drop of water that is you become a hundred
>   mighty seas.
> But do not think that the drop alone becomes the ocean.
> The ocean, too, becomes the drop.

Even in hell and even in the apocalypse we can attain enlightenment, be calm, loving, humorous, warm, tender, ecstatic (ecstatic above all), and free.

Imagine what it would be to accompany a child to the oven door, calmly. Many of you may have held a young man in your

arms as he is coughing up blood and dying of AIDS. Reenter
that heartbreak. Imagine what it would be to go on working
at the work of forgiving the Chinese, when you know the horror they are inflicting, and when you know how costly that
horror is to the world because it means the death or the potential death of a great wisdom and tradition, as well as the deaths
of thousands of ordinary humble people. Imagine what it means
to live through torture and to have to find in your heart the
courage not to hate, and the courage to extend even in that
final station ultimate forgiveness.

Imagine what it would be like, as you were stabbed or killed,
or shoved by a guard into an oven, to reach out to your murderer as your last act on earth and to bless them with one of
the many names of God. Imagine now what it will be like to
participate in the end of the planet, to know without panic
and anger that defeat may be at the end, and to go on loving,
always, because God is love. Then imagine that out of this
meditation arises the most urgent resolve to throw yourself
into the fire of divine love. Imagine that you finally see that
the only possible way of being of any possible help at this
extreme time is to become a "sign of divine joy" and a "fountain of divine love," and that you really take that with all the
seriousness, sincerity, and wild passion that Rumi exemplifies.

As Rumi says:

> It is a pity to reach the sea and to be satisfied with just
> a little water or a pitcher full. There are great pearls in
> the sea, and from the sea myriads of precious things can
> be produced. This world is just false coin gilded, it is a
> fleck of foam on a great sea of love. Man is the astro-
> labe of God, the astronomical instrument in which the
> heaven's movements are charted and reflected.

Man is the astrolabe of God, but it requires an astronomer
to know the astrolabe. This time is asking all of us to become
astronomers so that we can know that we do reflect the entire
cosmos and that the cosmos works in the most intimate, sub-

tle, and delicate way in each of us. Rumi goes on: "If a vegetable seller or a greengrocer should possess the astrolabe, what benefit would he derive from it?" This culture has made all of us vegetable sellers and greengrocers of the heart by cutting us off in a dreadful, nihilistic way from all the sources of divine awakening. We have this instrument which is incredibly delicate and precious, and we don't know how to use it. But this is why we are learning and doing the spiritual transformations under great masters, because we must learn before it is too late. With the astrolabe in our untrained hands, what would we know of the movements of the circling heavens, of the stations of the planets, of their influences and their transits? But in the hands of the astronomer, the perfect being, the astrolabe is of great benefit. "For he who knows himself knows his Lord."

If you penetrate to the core of your identity, you know that the Divine is that core and that you are one with the Divine in that core. Rumi goes on:

> Just as this copper astrolabe is the mirror of the heavens, so the human being is the astrolabe of God. When God causes a man to have knowledge of him, and to know him and to be familiar with him through the astrolabe of his own being, he beholds moment by moment and flash by flash the manifestation of God and his infinite beauty, and that beauty is never absent from his mirror.

And when that beauty is never absent from his mirror he realizes the truth of what Rumi writes in the *Mathnawi*:

> Know, O my son, that each thing in the universe is a vessel full to the brim with wisdom and beauty. It is also a drop from the river of His Beauty.... It is a hidden treasure because of its fullness, it has exploded and made the earth more brilliant than the skies. It is a hidden treasure because of its fullness. It has sprung up and made the earth like a sultan wearing a robe of satin.

What is our task now? It is to become that mirror from which the beauty of God is never absent, just as His Holiness the Dalai Lama is the mirror in which we can see in every gesture at every moment the presence, love, and humor of the Buddha of compassion; just as Sheikh Ben Toumes is the mirror in which we can see the laughter, joy, gravity, and poignancy of the sacred Sufi tradition which he so beautifully represents; just as Mother Teresa is the mirror in which we can see the torn face of Christ, the tears of Christ, and the love of Christ; just as Bede's massacred body and his hands stretching out to caress and bless each face are the mirror of the love of the Mother of God for all existence; just as Gandhi, in his stamina, in his patience, and in his forgiveness of the very people that were killing him and his world, is the mirror of a potentially saving form of political action.

Now, let us consider and meditate upon three aspects of this divine being that we all inherently are, to whom this poetry is directed, and which we all must become at this moment. In Islamic mysticism the first is known as "the knower of divine secrets." It is a beautiful title that is given to the saint, the man or woman who is sanctified by adoration and who has become the "knower of the divine secrets."

What does it mean to know the divine secrets? It means to be a knower of that ultimate divine secret: everything is God, everything is always taking place in God and as God, and everything, even the destruction of the world, will always be taking place in the silence, peace, and majesty of God which, as Mohammed told us in that meditation, can never be altered in any way. So to be a "knower of the divine secrets" is to be always standing in sacred unity and in the peace, majesty, grandeur, silence, and love of sacred unity; of always reposing the heart, soul, and body in that effulgence. In the Sufi sense it means to live in pre-eternity, in that space of ultimate awareness where all worlds and all realities dissolve. As Rumi says in the *Mathnawi*,

Before there existed in this world a garden, a vine, a grape, our soul was drunk on eternal wine. In the Baghdad of eternity, we all proclaim proudly, I am the supreme reality, long before the scandal and mystery of Mansur Al-Hallaj.

That eternal wine is still flowing, even in this abyss. Rumi goes on, "In the Baghdad of eternity, we proclaim proudly, I am the supreme reality, long before the scandal and mystery of Mansur Al-Hallaj." Let those words in their sublimity, in their transcendent sublimity, pierce right to the core of your fear of the horror that may soon unfold everywhere. The "knower of the divine secrets," the Buddha, the Christed one, knows that this world is not finally real before that face of God which is the eternal reality, that *nirvana* into which all things are dissolved, transcended.

Mohammed, in one of the most glorious moments of his ministry, said, "I was a Prophet when Adam was water mixed with clay." What this means is that the Light that is manifesting through him is the light of all beings and all reality. So the "knowers of the divine secret,"—the Dalai Lama, my tortured friend, Gandhi, Lily—all stand in an unshakable certainty. In Islam all the mystical stages are known as stages of certainty. This certainty is not about belief: it is about direct, naked experience so shattering that all conditions are transfigured by that experience and no possibility of any shadow of a doubt about your divine origin remains.

You could say that the knowledge of our sacred identity is an apocalypse in itself, because it is a burning and stripping away of all illusions, fake promises, and hopes. This sense of apocalypse is, as I have said, at the core of the Islamic revelation.

Islam is difficult to understand partly because we can't properly read the *Koran,* which at first seems to be a jumble of different unrelated chapters. In fact, the *Koran* is shards of divine revelations juxtaposed together in a mysterious polyphony. To understand the *Koran,* the seeker is challenged to go directly into the kind of consciousness that created it. The *Koran* is in many ways like *Finnegan's Wake*. Both attempt to represent what reality looks like after staggering derangement. The revelation that came to Mohammed was so deranging that his horse could not bear the weight of the revelation and fell.

Islam has recognized this intensity of the mystical life, and celebrated and sanctified it in a violently beautiful way. That is why Rumi is so thrilling, because in Rumi we hear a voice as brave as a lion, as brave as the soul really is, as naked and wild and passionate as the absolutely awake heart really is.

The *Koran* is altogether apocalyptic. It eschews the linear organization of time, revelation, and history that became the backbone of orthodox Christianity and remains the backbone of Western culture after the death of God. Islam is wholly apocalyptic, or eschatological, and its eschatology is not teleology. The apocalypse of Islam is always now, so we are always living in the last days. At any moment God can withdraw his mandate from the creation, and the creation will dissolve into the *Kibriya*, into the divine glory. It is a magnificent vision, because it shows man exactly how pointless any other existence is but that in God. Mohammed was doing nothing else but taking the desert and turning it into a blazing mirror, and showing the whole of humanity that blazing mirror, the Divine Light, saying, "Nothing but this is real. Everything but this will perish. Gaze into it, be transformed into it, become one with it, and act as it!" That is Islam, the desert become the burning mirror. In fully developed Islamic theology, only the moment is real. There is no necessary connection between cause and effect. One of the great strengths of Islamic mysticism is that it is not dominated by linear logic; it is quite clear that God can do whatever He wants at any moment.

The Islamic mosque discards the orientation toward time essential to a Christian church. "The space of a mosque is as if reabsorbed," says Titus Burckhardt, "into the ubiquity of the present moment." When you go into the mosque of Edirne, you go into a space which is nothing less than the desert made a mirror made light and space. Upon entering, if you are sensitive, a great silence falls and a peace is present. It does not beckon the eye in a specific direction, it suggests no tension or antinomy between the here and the beyond, between earth and heaven. It possesses all its fullness in every place. I am trying here to show you the interrelation between the essential apocalyptic vision of Islam, the space it arose out of, the desert, the burning sense of the present moment, the architecture and glorious art that Islam created, the poetry of Rumi, the vision of the perfect human being, and what we have to do now in the apocalypse in which every present moment takes us closer to the end of time. We need the Sufi revelation especially, because this revelation really sees the apocalypse of the present moment, the blazing of the divine glory, and the urgency of the need to fling the whole being into the fire and to dance as the fire devours and transforms. This revelation compels us to throw away our pettiness and our neuroses, and to accept and embrace every possible suffering that comes in the transformation, because the world itself is groaning and suffering beyond all imagination.

The Sufis really know in the core of their being what it means to live at the end of time, because they are always living at the end of time. Their entire vision is of dancing on the diamond point of no-time. That is what Rumi is doing throughout his works, with overwhelming intensity.

Now we as a species are at this no-point, literally, metaphorically, and mystically: that is why the Sufi vision is so sacred and so important. The following passage by Norman O'Brien about the *Koran* will give you a wonderful clue as to why Rumi speaks and writes as he does, and why the *Koran* is constructed in the way it is. The passage is about the *Koran,* but of course, it is not limited to the *Koran.*

> Many people, especially non-Muslims, who read the
> *Koran* for the first time are struck by what appears as a
> kind of incoherence from the human point of view. It is

neither like a highly mystical text nor a manual of Aristotelian logic, though it contains both mysticism and logic. It is not just poetry, although it contains the most powerful poetry. The text of the *Koran* reveals human language crushed by the power of the divine word.

When you are really reading the *Koran,* just as when you are experiencing the greatest of Rumi's odes, it is as if there has been an immense volcanic explosion. The *suras,* the verses of the *Koran,* are twisted shards of cold lava. The poems of Rumi are the strange, fabulous, ornate, baroque, and tremendously mysterious forms that the molten lava has taken. The molten lava of revelation cooled by the human mind takes on these strange shapes that themselves are full of majesty and invitation. The revelation that comes from that passion is a revelation of absolute light and glory. "The text of the *Koran* reveals human language crushed by the power of the divine word." It is human language, shattered into a thousand fragments like a wave shattered against rocks. You feel through the shattering effect left upon the language of the *Koran* the power of the Divine from which it originated. When you read the *Koran,* as when you read Rumi, the language is constantly stammering at the edge of language—imploding and exploding with cries of joy and pain. The words register with overwhelming vulnerable clarity what it is like to be in the clutches of the divine tiger, the divine lion of light. As Norman O'Brien says, "The *Koran* displays human language with all the weakness inherent in it becoming suddenly the recipient of the divine word and displaying its frailty before a power which is infinitely greater than man can imagine." He adds this marvelous sentence: "The bewilderment is part of the message."

This journey into the *Koran* and the nature of Islamic apocalyptic understanding is part of what it means to be the "knower of the divine secret." The knower of the divine secret is also the knower of the divine glory, and therefore is always on his knees before it, always stammering before it, always weeping inwardly before it, always opening with infinite humility and awe in its Light. "The bewilderment is part of the message." What is most glorious about Islamic mysticism is that the note of absolute adoration is kept alive from Mansur Al-Hallaj to Ibn-Arabi, to Jalal-ud-Din Rumi to Iqbal—that note which is the note of the human being that we are all called to become. As the destroyers destroy the manifestation of the glory that is our world, let us keep in our hearts, minds, and souls a permanent vision of the *Kibriya* of God!

The second characteristic of the perfect human being as seen in Islamic mysticism is the mirror of divinity. Rumi says:

> The saint, the *qutb*, the *pir*, the beloved, the person who has really made their lives over into the sacrifice preserves in his or her breast the infinite form without form of the invisible, reflected in the mirror of his own heart. Although this form is not contained in heaven or in the empyrean or in the starry spheres, or in the earth, for all these things are limited and numbered, know that the mirror of the heart is without limits. The heart is with God, or, to say it more truthfully, the heart is God Himself.

This is what the Dalai Lama knows, this is what the Sufi boy knew, this is what Mother Teresa knows, this is what everyone who comes to that station knows—the heart that has awakened to the presence of Christ, or Mohammed, or Buddha in the world, and to its own infinite space, is reflecting at every moment divine beauty, joy, and love, is God himself.

Our task is to be such a blazing sign of love and joy, such a mirror of the divinity, such a knower of the divine secrets, that anyone who comes into our presence feels everything that he or she has done is a waste of time: cutting down the rainforest is a waste of time, if you can dance on the diamond point of no time. Torturing is a waste of time if love can flood your being. Destroying, murdering, and raping the earth is a waste of time if you can live on this earth in love. That is what we have to be: the mirror of the Divine so that those looking at us can see the Divine in them mirrored.

What Rumi is telling us again and again is that we are at once love, the lover, and the beloved; at once the mirror, the beauty, and the eye that sees it. There is only one love and only one glory, reflected in a thousand million forms and situations. When you come into the presence of the glory, you realize that you are looking at the glory with the glory's own eyes; feeling the glory with the glory's own heart; loving the glory with the glory's own love; and dancing in the glory with the glory's own resplendence. That is what it means to be a mirror of the divinity.

A third category of perfect being reaches right to the heart of the problem of what should be done now, of how living the mystical life of action is the only way through for humankind. This third category that the Sufis say represents the perfect being is that of the caliph of God, the vice-regent, the representative.

In the most elevated forms of Sufism—and clearly in Rumi's poetry—Unity of experience does not consist for the finite ego in the effacement of its identity, by a sort of absorption in the Infinite Self; it is rather that the infinite goes into the ecstatic, loving embrace of the finite. It is not that the self passes out into the *Kibriya,* it is rather that the *Kibriya* can enter because the self is stretching out its arms to it with such passionate love that divine glory itself rushes into those arms, there to be embraced and to live, and there to take new divine energy from the energy of that passion and love. This is what it means to live as the vice-regent of the Divine. Without the human soul, the spirit could not be conscious of itself. The spirit can only manifest itself and see itself in its image that is the human soul.

What we know of the divine reality is reflected in His Holiness the Dalai Lama, in the body and presence of Mother Meera, in Rumi. What would we know if the divine light had not been enacted for us with total sacrifice by those who made the choice to do so and who gave up every moment to it? It is through these beings, the Sufis believe, and Islam believes, that the grace of God is literally dispensed to the world: they are the electrical channel through which it passes. So to become a sacred being, to become one of the perfect beings or to try and become one, is to become a focus of blazing grace, another point through which the power and love of God can literally *enter* the human race. These sacred, perfect beings are walking bombs, whose radiation transfigures everything around them. This is sacred action at its highest.

If you care about the future of the world, if you wish to save the world, become a vice-regent of God. If you wish to save the world, give your life over to that transformation which can make you in some part of your being a mediator, an intercessor, a channel for that grace which can only enter the world through you. Melville said, in one of his last notebooks, "The godhead is broken and we are the pieces!" The godhead, of course, is never broken, but it is true that we are the pieces of the godhead; we are the arms, eyes, limbs, and the embrace of the Divine, and the Divine is not going to save our planet for us. We have to do it for and as the Divine; that is our destiny.

There is only one real task before any of us, which is to go towards this union with God so that divine power can be real in us and so we can help.

I once asked His Holiness the Dalai Lama, "If it is the end of the world, what does that mean for the vow of the Bodhisattva? We won't be coming back again and again, will we?" He looked at me, smiled, and replied, "If it is the end, it has never been more important to become a Bodhisattva, because only the Bodhisattva will bring water to those on fire." There is no choice, thank God. Whether you die now, or tomorrow, or in the great burning of nature, jump now into the fire and know that you are immortal and then blaze on. Dance the dance of Shiva. Dance the dance of Kali. Dance the dance of Rumi:

> One day in your wineshop I drank a little wine
> And threw off the robe of my body
> And knew, drunk on you, that the world is harmony.
> Creation, destruction, I am dancing for them both.

Do everything to save this planet, but don't let this planet's death make you waver for one instant from the glory of
your origin. You will only be able to save the planet when you
reflect the glory of your origin in every action, in every moment.
To repeat Rumi's opening lines:

> Everything you see has its roots in the unseen world.
> The forms may change, yet the essence remains the same.

You have to find that out. You can't just listen to those
words, you have to go to the place where that becomes real.

> Every wonderful sight will vanish, every sweet word
>   will fade,
> But do not be disheartened,
> The source they come from is eternal, growing,
> Branching out, giving new life and new joy.

This recalls an image from a documentary I saw of a Muslim fisherman in the Aral Sea, which has been totally destroyed;
ecologically, it doesn't exist anymore. This Muslim used to
have a fishing boat. Now, every day, he goes out and sings
Rumi to the dead sea. He testifies; he witnesses the majesty
and the glory even in desolation.

> Why do you weep?
> The source is within you,
> And this whole world is springing up from it.
> The source is full,
> And its waters are ever-flowing.
> Do not grieve, drink your fill.
> From the moment you came into this world,
> A ladder was placed in front of you,
> That you might transcend it.
> From earth, you became plant,
> From plant you became animal,
> Afterwards you became a human being,
> Endowed with knowledge, intellect and faith.

> Behold the body, born of dust, how perfect it has
>   become.
> Why should you fear its end?
> When were you ever made less by dying?
> When you pass beyond this human form,
> No doubt you will become an angel and soar through
>   the heavens,
> But don't stop there, even heavenly bodies grow old.
> Pass again from the heavenly realm and
> Plunge, plunge into the vast ocean of consciousness,
> Let the drop of water that is you become a hundred
>   mighty seas.
> But do not think that the drop alone becomes the ocean.
> The ocean, too, becomes the drop.

Knowing this, let us drop our bodies now into the fire of
the end of the world and let what we cling to die now in the
fire of the end of the world. Let our false illusions and hopes
die now, with the last trees. Let us live now, in the fire and love
of God, all the while being signs, fountains, mirrors, nurses,
dancers, activists, psychotherapists, and above all, what the
Sufis call the children of spring.

I am tired of two things: I am tired of people saying that
the end of our world isn't going to happen. It is 80 percent
likely; the 20 percent is miracle. I'm also tired of people who
use that likelihood as an excuse for depression and apathy because its horror is so far beyond depression. Its horror requires
a leap. We have to rush out and leap into the divine fire. That
is what we have to do; what other truthful response is there?

Get out there and give real help! Get out there and love!
Get out there and testify! Get out there and create whatever
you can to inspire people to claim their divine being and origin. This is what has to be done now.

There is no time, there has never been any time. There has
never been any time for dallying and being depressed.

A reporter once asked Mother Teresa, "Mother Teresa,

don't you just weep all the time? There's so much poverty and horror. I can hardly look at it." Mother Teresa replied, "If you think I have time to cry, you are out of your mind." All any of us could possibly have time for now is to act as far as possible out of the passion of the enlightened heart, as far as possible and on every possible front.

> Lovers and men of intellect cannot mix:
> How can you mix the broken with the unbroken?
> Cautious, men of intellect shrink back from a dead ant:
> Lovers, completely carefree, trample down dragons.

> The intellect says: "The six directions are limits: there
>   is no way out."
> Love says: "There is a way: I have traveled it
>   thousands of times."
> The intellect saw a market and started to haggle:
> Love saw thousands of markets beyond that market.
> Lovers who drink the dregs of the wine reel from bliss
>   to bliss:
> The dark-hearted men of reason
> Burn inwardly with denial.
> The intellect says "Do not go forward, annihilation
>   contains only thorns."
> Love laughs back: "The thorns are in you."
> Enough words! Silence!
> Pull the thorn of existence out of the heart! Fast!
> For when you do you will see thousands of rose
>   gardens in yourself.

Chapter Eight

Sacred Art, Sacred Dance

> One day in your wineshop, I drank a little wine,
> and threw off this robe of my body,
> and knew, drunk on you, the world is harmony.
> Creation, destruction, I am dancing for them both.

IN THIS QUATRAIN, Rumi expresses the entire sacred significance of both music and dance. "One day in your wineshop,"
the mystical wineshop where the wine of gnosis, bliss, and
peace is sold, I, your disciple, drank just two sips of the sacred
wine, went into ecstasy, and "threw off this robe of my body."
This robe is the source of much ignorance, separation, banality, and closure, so I threw it off. I threw off the robe of my
body in which I could only hear the sounds of the ego, the
sounds of my own desires, the sounds of the banality of the
world. These are the sounds of the ordinary, dispassionate
mind. But because I was completely inspired, and filled with
you, and because I was drunk on you, I came to understand
the sacred secret: that the entire universe is harmony. This harmony is so extraordinary, so complex, and so vast that it is
infinitely unknowable to the ordinary mind, but knowable to
the mind steeped in gnostic ecstasy. I "knew, drunk on you,
the world is harmony." To know that the world is harmony,
you have to become drunk with the sacred wine. To know, not
to think, suspect, believe, or imagine, but to *know* beyond any
doubt that the world, this experience, life—the entire mani-

festation—is nothing but music, you have to be drunk on gnostic ecstasy and bliss.

> Oh daylight rise! Atoms are dancing,
> Souls, lost in ecstasy, are dancing,
> I'll whisper in your ear where the dance will take you.
> All atoms in the air, in the desert,
> They are all like madmen, each atom, happy or miserable,
> Is Passionate for the Sun of which nothing can be said.

When you come to know that the world is this passionate harmony, then you can comprehend the opposites, the two poles. What seems like terror, suffering, agony, disintegration, separation, and tragedy can be taken and cast into the last part of the poem, "Creation, destruction, I am dancing for them both." To dance in the Sufi sense is to dance as God dances, in agony as much as joy, in suffering as well as peace, in destruction as well as creation of the worlds, in the annihilation of supernovas as well as in their staggering birth. It is to know, in fact, that the conjunction of opposites is God himself.

> Your bitter cruelty makes me a pearl
> For pearls and corals live in the sea's bitter depths
> Your fidelity is another sea, so sweet to drink—
> And from it keeps flowing the four streams of Paradise.

Al-Ghazzali tells us in "The Alchemy of Happiness":

> The heart of men has been so made by God that, like a flint, it contains a hidden fire which is evolved by music and harmony, and renders man beside himself with ecstasy. These harmonies are echoes of that higher world of reality which we call the world of spirits: they remind man of his relationship to that world, and produce in him an emotion so deep and strange that he himself is powerless to explain it. The effect of music and dancing is deeper in proportion as the natures on which they act are simple and prone to emotion: they fan into a

flame whatever love is already dormant in the heart, whether it is earthly and sensual, or divine and spiritual.

These are the words of Al-Ghazzali, the Sufi, words that Rumi undoubtedly knew and loved, as his father was a great admirer of Al-Ghazzali. The words are reflected in two poems by Rumi which also explore the theme of music.

Follow the transitions, follow the different ways in which his imagery works upon you, and you yourself will become music played by him. Just as Rumi aspires, like every mystic, to be an instrument played in abandon by the abandoned hand of God, by the breath of God, so we, in listening to the poetry that is Rumi's music, can become that music if we allow it in all its subtlety, richness, and passion to play us.

How could the soul not take flight
When from the glorious presence
A soft call flows sweet as honey, comes right up to her
And whispers, "Rise up now, come away."
How could the fish not jump
Immediately from dry land into water
When the sound of water from the ocean
Of fresh waves springs to his ear?
How could the hawk not fly away
Forgetful of all hunting to the wrist of the king
As soon as he hears the drum
The king's baton hits again and again,
Drumming out the signal of return?
How could the Sufi not start to dance,
Turning on himself, like the atom, in the sun of eternity,
So he can leap free of this dying world?
Fly away, fly away bird to your native home,
You have leapt free of the cage and
Your wings are flung back in the wind of God.
Leave behind the stagnant and marshy waters,
Hurry, hurry, hurry, o bird, to the source of life!

Many different kinds of music are in this poem. We'll take each of the images one by one.

> How could the soul not take flight
> When from the glorious presence
> A soft call flows sweet as honey, comes right up to her
> And whispers, "Rise up now, come away."

That soft call, "sweet as honey," is always flowing from the glorious Presence. In the Hindu and Buddhist traditions, there comes a moment in the experience of meditation when you actually begin to hear with your own ears the sound of the Divine. The *Upanishads* describe very clearly and with great detail the different sounds that happen as the divine self wakes up in the mind, or rather, *as you wake up to* the divine self in the mind. You hear bells, singing, the sound of the wind, the sound of the sea, and most of all, as the clear and absolute sign—the final yogic sign—you hear all things shimmering with the sound of "*Om.*" *Om* is the sacred sound out of which the entire cosmos was created, and at a certain stage of development, you hear it as clearly as you can hear that tire screeching outside, the wind rustling in the leaves, or your own breath. It is a fact. Rumi is *not* talking about an image. It is not a metaphor, this is not poetry: it is direct mystical knowledge. If you still yourself, if you become quiet, your heart opens in love; if you try then to clarify the mind, you will hear the soft call that flows "sweet as honey" from the Presence. This will happen not just occasionally, but always, because it is the sound that reality is really making. There is a wonderful phrase by Rilke, from the first "Duino Elegy"—"What is our task? Our task is to listen to the news that is always arriving out of silence." This is the news of our divine self, the news of our divine origin and the Presence that waits to shine out in all things, when our minds are clear enough to see, receive, and finally accept it. So when Rumi asks, "How could the soul not take flight?," he is begging us to become so attentive to silence and the heart of the heart, so in rhythm with the light of lights, that we at every moment hear the call out of silence saying to us, "Rise up now, come away."

Then he switches from this actual mystical image of the call always flowing from sacred reality to talk about the fish: the soul, the spirit, the self separated from its source:

> How could the fish not jump
> Immediately from dry land into water
> When the sound of water from the ocean
> Of fresh waves springs to his ear?

When the *sound* of water from the ocean of fresh waves! That sound is a real mystical sound heard in meditation by yogis, Sufis, and lovers of God. That sound is the sound of the "water" that is drenching the universe at every moment. That water is the Divine Light, at every moment drenching, soaking, and saturating all things. Nothing else is going on but this rain of blissful Light that is soaking creation at all moments. When you begin to awaken, you hear that rain of Light as water. The sound of water—because God is kind and gives us sounds that we can be familiar with—alerts us to the secret endless ocean of Light that is the universe, "the ocean of fresh waves." This is a marvelous touch, because when you hear that sound—the *shabd,* as it is called in Indian tradition—what you are listening to is the eternal freshness singing to itself, the sound of the Divine, drenching all things with mystic Light. When you begin to hear that sound, how could you not want to "leap from the dry land" of the ego, desire, and ignorance, the dry land of this terrestrial, banal, separative reality, into the sea of gnosis and rapture, the "ocean of fresh waves"? But Rumi doesn't leave us there, he takes us deeper and deeper into the mystery. In the third verse, he says:

> How could the hawk not fly away
> Forgetful of all hunting to the wrist of the king
> As soon as he hears the drum,
> The king's baton hits again and again,
> Drumming out the signal of return.

In Sufism, the soul is thought of as a royal hawk, lost in the
shadows of a dark world, lost in mist and darkness. But through
that darkness, by the grace of God, the sound of the drumbeat
of return is always echoing mysteriously: reality is ceaselessly
echoing with that drumbeat. Once you hear it, whether in a
lecture, a poem, in Beethoven's *Missa Solemnis,* in a sudden
pause between the waves at Big Sur, in the wind through the
trees—wherever it is, once you hear that drumbeat, you are
hooked forever. Having heard the divine music, you will long
with all your being and every cell of your body to return to the
source of that divine music, to the wrist of the king.

After these three images, the soul itself taking flight, the
fish jumping from dry land into the sea, and the hawk flying
through the darkness, mystery, and agony of this world to the
wrist of the emperor, Rumi writes:

> How could the Sufi not start to dance,
> Turning on himself, like the atom, in the sun of eternity,
> So he can leap free of this dying world?

The soul, the fish, the hawk, all these images go behind to
create the inner state of the Sufi, the inner rapture of the one
who has made of his or her life a constant attention to the
music of the Divine. The dancing of the Sufi, as will be explained later, is itself the cosmos. It mirrors Shiva, the *Kibriya*
that dances always, and Allah himself—the dancer dances this
experience at every moment, dances for creation as well as
destruction, and dances for agony as well as peace. How could
the Sufi who is the hawk, the fish, the soul, *not* start to dance
awesomely, "turning on himself," turning around himself "like
the atom." The atom, a thoroughly modern image, is a solar
system in itself. We know that now, but this is actually pre-
figured in Rumi's imagery and in the imagery of the Sufi dances.
The Sufis believed, like the scientists of their time, that all atoms
rotated around the sun. Of course, for the Mevlevis that is a
very powerful image, because the sun, who is Shams, the sun
of the Divine Light, joy, and peace, is that force of passion

around which the whole universe constantly dances forever.

For the Sufi, dancing is the "leaping free of the dying world." It is the mirroring of the eternal order that helps us to leap free of this world in which everything is perishing, except His Face. By writing, reading, listening, and dancing in our own thoughts, we are all trying together to use our experience as a form of sacred dancing to leap free of this world caught in the spasm of apocalypse.

> Fly away, fly away bird to your native home,
> You have leapt free of the cage and
> Your wings are flung back in the wind of God.
> Leave behind the stagnant and marshy waters,
> Hurry, hurry, hurry, o bird, to the source of life!

Listen to those last lines because they are the clue to the Sufi passion for music and dance. It has nothing to do with a modern faddishness about using music and dance in flashy emotional ways to arouse vaguely spiritual emotions. The Sufis are after an experience of extreme passion; the dancing of which they are speaking can only take place if the soul is dedicated to God, if the soul is completely purified and awash with divine love. Otherwise, to use these great powers of music and dance simply to indulge one's own sensuality or, in a weak-minded and weak-souled way, to use that sensuality as a way of getting to God (as we see so often in half-baked versions of *tantra*) is a disaster. These powers are too great not to be respected. That is why, at the end of this poem about dancing, Rumi says. "leave behind the marshy waters," leave behind the ego, the selfishness and stagnation of the world, "hurry, hurry, hurry to the source of life."

> How could the fish not jump
> Immediately from dry land into water
> When the sound of water from the ocean
> Of fresh waves springs to his ear?
> How could the hawk not fly away

> Forgetful of all hunting to the wrist of the king
> As soon as he hears the drum,
> The king's baton hits again and again,
> Drumming out the signal of return?
> How could the Sufi not start to dance,
> Turning on himself, like the atom, in the sun of eternity,
> So he can leap free of this dying world?
> Fly away, fly away bird to your native home,
> You have leapt free of the cage and
> Your wings are flung back in the wind of God.
> Leave behind the stagnant and marshy waters,
> Hurry, hurry, hurry, o bird, to the source of life!

Rumi asks in the poem, How could the fish not jump, the hawk not fly away?, expressing perfectly the helplessness of ecstasy. Once the heart is a little open, once the mind is just a little open, once the soul opens its dark doors just a little, how could it not want to rush out? The beauty that it sees, the majesty that it glimpses, the ecstasy that pours in, are so vast that there is no hope for it; it must then stream out in dancing and burst out singing. Hearing the music of eternity, it must try to echo it in its every breath and movement.

If you listen to music in the Sufi way, you are listening with these questions—they roar in your heart. You are following the music in its intensity and poignancy right to the source of music itself, which is in the heart of the silence of God. If you are dancing in the Sufi way, you are dancing not only with your feet and hands, you are dancing with every atom in your body, because as Rumi says:

> Dancing is not rising to your feet painlessly like a whirl of dust blown about by the wind. Dancing is when you rise above both worlds. Tearing your heart to pieces and giving up your soul.

This kind of "dancing" is what Callas is doing when she sings. Someone once asked her, "Why did you lose your voice?"

She replied, "I pushed it into the fire, so it would burn hotter."

What the Sufis call us to do, what all mystics call us to do, what Rumi begs us to do, is to learn how to dance in this way, above all dimensions. Dancing is when you "rise above both worlds," both heaven and earth, here and there, now and then. You throw away this world, because you no longer want to be part of the madness and stupidity that is creating all this destruction; you also throw away longing for a transcendent *nirvana* because that, too, is an illusion, another fantasy of the ego; and you throw away the notion of safety. The truth is that there is no safety. There is nowhere to go. There is nowhere to be safe, except on the diamond point of this moment, where lunacy, ecstasy, and sober purity coalesce. This is where you must learn how to dance. It is there on the diamond point that the Divine is always to be found, in eternity. It is on that absolute minuscule atomic speck of *now* that you must dance, rising above both worlds, find the eternal, and enter immortality. Truth is not here, it is not there, it is not on earth, and it is not in some fantastic idea of heaven. It is in purest, wildest, most naked, most unsparing total honesty and passion.

Rumi says, dancing is when you rise above both worlds. Throw away your fears of this world, your petty little plans, your passions that drag you back, your hungers to be pious, throw away all of that garbage. Throw away your passion for heaven, your belief that if you are a good boy or girl you will go to some heaven. Get rid of transcendence in that petty sense and dance *here*. When you dance, see that you tear your heart to pieces. The kind of dancing that the Sufi is talking about is absolutely naked to the glory and pain of the world, so the heart is torn by that glory. When you actually see or glimpse even a part of the glory of the Divine, the heart is shredded by it; it is rendered mute, helpless, stammering, and babbling. But equally, allow your heart to be torn to pieces, to open to the suffering of the world, of the poor, of the forests, to the suffering of this terrifying moment in human history. You will find, as Rumi did, that the experience of having your heart torn to pieces is itself ecstatic! What keeps us from ecstasy is our clinging to a false identity, to an ego that believes it understands its limits, to an ego that is terrified of pain. Once you finally realize that you're going to die like a dog, that the whole world is going to be absolutely washed in fire—either in twenty years' time or a million years time when it goes nearer to the sun—once you realize that nothing works, that *samsara* is a long, crazy dream in which nothing can possibly come right, once you finally accept that, just tear your heart to pieces and enjoy the experience of having your heart shattered a hundred thousand times a day. That is where true energy comes from, because at that moment you stop living in the limited self and become one with the Divine who is shattering and creating, spinning out worlds in one hand and throwing worlds against the wall with the other, all the time. The universe is an immense blood bath, so dance in the blood. We all need to get to that point where we don't care what's going to happen in five minutes, because we're living so passionately this moment, that we are dancing, throwing away "earth" and "heaven," "now" and "then," "here" and "there," everything! It is that dancing *now* that is the entry into Paradise. Sustaining that dancing now is what Eden is. "Eden is a fiery city," says Blake. In that fiery city, the first thing you have to do, if you want to learn how to live in Eden, is learn how to burn. This is what Rumi means when he says, "Tearing your heart to pieces and giving up your soul."

I remember going to master classes taught by Callas at Juilliard, and there was a wonderful moment when this poor, unfortunate girl came out and tried to sing an aria. Callas just stopped her and said, "Stop it! Just stop it. I don't know what you think you're doing, but you're not singing. I'm not trying to be rude. I'm just trying to get across to you that singing and life are totally related. What do you think this girl in this aria is expressing? She's not talking about the grocer, she's not reading the telephone directory of Manhattan; she's expressing insane love for somebody which is breaking her heart. So . . ."

Then Callas sang just three phrases, and the whole place stiffened, because the majesty of abandon was then present. That is what great art is, it is that edge where you rise above both worlds, tear your heart to pieces, and give up yourself. That's what Rumi is doing with every second of his day, with every verse of his poetry. He is the supreme dancer, the supreme musician, an instrument in the hands of the Supreme Musician.

So now let us have a second poem:

> It is the day of great, great joy.
> Let us all now, become friends.
> Let us join our hands. Let us go to the Friend.
> We are all one, we are not two of one color and hue.
> Let us dance, let us go to the market, dancing.
> The beautiful friends now are starting to dance,
> So let's close the shop and dance, idle and free.
> Today is the day that the souls put on the robe of his grace.
> To mystery's side, to the side of mystery,
> We go dancing as God's guests.
> All the gods have pitched their tents in the garden
> And to see them, now we go to the rose garden.

"It is the day of great joy." It is always the day of great joy. That is why Rumi begins in the present tense, the great feast is always spread out for us, the great music is always playing, and the great joy is always dancing. It is we who are absent from the feast. It is we who run from room to room, claiming there is nothing to eat, when every object is a table glittering with the food of the Divine.

"Let us become friends"—the great Sufi call. Let us unite our hearts, so that you, I, and everyone else can do what we were meant to do on this earth, which is to dance together. "Let us join our hands," as dancers do in the dance.

> We are all one, we are not two of one color and hue.
> Let us dance, let us go to the market, dancing.

Rumi and the disciples often used to leave wherever they were and go dancing, which scandalized everybody. That's what the Sufi does—he enters the marketplace, the arena, he enters Manhattan, Tokyo, La Paz, dancing. He enters, doing the real dance, the dance of love, the dance of passion, at the heart of the market.

As the Sufi saint Abu Sa'id [d. 1049] said: "The true saint lives in the midst of other people. He rises in the morning: he eats and sleeps when needed. He buys and sells in the marketplace just like everyone else. He marries, has children, and meets with his friends. Yet never for an instant does he forget God."

I want now to tell you a story about the Prophet's son-in-law Ali. This man has a very profound place in the history of Islamic mysticism. Ali was married to Fatima, Mohammed's most cherished and beloved daughter. It is said that Mohammed taught Ali essential secrets on one condition: these secrets would be kept in a storehouse of mystical knowledge which would somehow permeate the world and transform it, but beyond language. So Ali learned them and followed Mohammed's instructions. Ali's heart was so drunk with love, so overcome by the majesty and the glory of these secrets, that he longed to share them. He knew that he couldn't give them to anyone, because if he gave them indiscriminately something terrible would happen to them. Mohammed's word was the word of God. So Ali ran out into the desert and found a deep well in an oasis. He buried his head down into the soft darkness and told the well in rapture all the secrets of his heart. He murmured all the things that Mohammed had told him in ecstasy into this fecund, secret, dark well.

As Ali told the secrets to the well, some saliva from his mouth dropped into the moss at the bottom of the well, and out of the moss grew a long, tall, sweet reed, a pure straight reed. Weeks later, a shepherd came to the well. The shepherd gazed into the well. He sees the reed and thinks, "Ah, this will make the most amazing flute." He cuts the reed, puts three holes in it, and starts playing to his sheep, all of whom immediately start dancing about like maniacs, and as he plays in the oasis, all the camels start forming circles and dancing and singing. The fame of the shepherd's mystical playing grew, until it came to the ears of the Prophet himself. The Prophet knew by now the whole story, by clairvoyance. He summoned the shepherd to play for him, and when the shepherd had finished, he said these wonderful words, which are a clue to the entire experience of the Sufis. The Prophet said, "These melodies that this flute are playing are the commentaries on the mysteries I gave to my beloved Ali in secret. If one among the people of purity has no purity, he cannot hear the secrets in the melody and the flute. He cannot hear them, and he cannot enjoy them because 'the whole of faith is pleasure and passion.'" By which Mohammed means the whole of faith is to be moved by sacred love for the Divine. Only when you are in a state of purity can you hear the flute's secret mourning for home. Only when you are in a state of sacred joy can the dancing become what it is, leaping free of the mortal body. Only when you are truly attuned to the divine silence can the music that is coming out of it really instruct and reach you.

Now, I want to focus on one central image, which in fact tells the entire story. It is a very simple image, and once you really begin to glimpse its significance you get to the core of Sufism. The great Sufi mystic Al-Hallaj cried out in the streets of Baghdad, "I am the supreme reality." The orthodox Muslims saw to it that he was hanged, drawn, and quartered. But he did something very glorious, which inspired all Sufis. Al-Hallaj went to his execution in chains, but with his feet free, and he danced all the way to the gallows. He danced and sang, and the chains danced with him. I wanted to give you this ecstatic image before plunging into the highest Sufi metaphysics.

The word for the sacred oratorio that Rumi and the Mevlevis instituted is *sama*, which actually means "audition" or "hearing." Hearing is at the core of the whole Koranic revelation of God. Hearing the *Koran* is what instills its sacred truths. Hearing is what the holy one, the mystic, is meant to do at every moment: to hear the instructions and the news that is always arriving out of the silence. Hearing is at the root of all transformation. So listen to what Ibn-Arabi has to say, in William Chittick's commentary on what is called "The Breath of the All Merciful":

> In one passage, Ibn-Arabi explains the mutual love that exists between God and the creatures in terms of visions (*ru'yah*) and audition (*sama*). God's love for the creatures stems from his vision of them within Himself as identical with Himself. Seeing them as the Hidden Treasure, "He loved to be known." The creature's love for God derives from hearing the sacred word "Be" which brings them into existence. They are in effect identical with this world: each is the word "Be" in a specific form.

All you are ever perceiving in the world, in the entire cosmos, and in the entire universe is "be" in a million different forms.

It is not "be" this or that, it is just "be." What everything has is this eternal fresh, wild being. There is no past, no future, there is just "be," at every moment. This is the realization of what dancing is, of what *listening* is, knowing this and being attuned to this. This is what Ibn-Arabi says and even if you cannot grasp it all immediately, let your minds move to the mystery, because one of the great marvelous powers of mystical language is its capacity to evoke in us things we did not know we knew. Dance with the strangeness of this language and with the strangeness of these concepts as they arouse odd knowledge in you. Who knows what you might discover as you read this?

> One of the characteristics of the Lover, should He possess Form, is to breathe, since in that breathing is found the enjoyment of what is sought. The Breath emerges from a root, which is Love for the creatures, to whom He desired to make himself known so that they might know him. Hence, the Cloud comes to be. It is called

the Real through which Creation Takes Place. The Cloud is the substance of the cosmos, so it receives all the forms, spirits, and natures of the cosmos. It is a receptacle ad infinitum. This is the origin of the Love for us. But as for our Love for Him, its origin is audition, not vision. It is his words to us while we were in the substance of the Cloud, "Be." Hence the Cloud derives from His breathing, while the forms which are called the cosmos derive from the word "be." So we are "His words which are not spent." And when we heard his speech, while we were changeless in the substance of the Cloud, we were not able to keep back from existence.

This is an amazing conclusion. When we were all of us there in the time before time, in the Cloud emanated by the Breath, we were enveloped in the cloud, ecstatic, lost in the Divine silence. But when the word "be" came, we could not but leap into existence, because that leaping into "be" is the sacred first step in the sacred dance, which the dancing of the Sufis mirrors and echoes.

The existent things, or words, come into existence within the breath as the result of God's speech. The *Koran* describes this speech as the single word, "be," yet this word is addressed to each thing in the state of its nonexistence.

God says, "Our only speech to a thing when We desire it is to say to it, 'Be!'" And "Be" is exactly what he speaks, through it that to which he says "Be" becomes manifest.... Thereby the entities become manifest within the Breath of the All-merciful, just as letters become manifest within the human breath. The thing that comes to be is a specific form, like a form painted upon wood.

The existence of the sacred speech, our existence, and interweaving of the two is very intimate. This idea is central to all the mystical revelations: that speech, the word, creates the cosmos. In the Vedic revelations, the Word is *paravak*, the sacred

Word spoken by Brahman and out of whose never-to-be-known silence comes the entire cosmos. It is also central to the Buddhist revelation. One of the highest tantric teachings is that at a certain stage if you say your *mantra* with enough devotion, you will come to understand that the entire universe is nothing but a creation of that sound. It is central to certain esoteric Christian understandings of what is meant in the first part of St. John's *Gospel,* when he talks about the *Logos,* the word that "speaks" the whole of reality. So music, by extension, becomes the most powerful way of drawing you back to that sacred Word, of making you aware of your sacred pact with eternity, of instilling in you the power to listen to the silent Word of your origin—that is what music is for the Sufis.

I would like to share with you an experience I had that I didn't understand until I came to read the Sufi mystics. It is the clue to what they believe music to be, and it is the key to the story of Mohammed and Ali. As I tell you my experience, remember Ali's story and what has been said about the cloud, the breath, the word "be," and the creation, and be open to what I am trying to evoke.

I was twenty-six and had absolutely no belief in any kind of mystical experience because, like most people, I believed that anything I had not experienced could not be true. Fortunately, I was in Pondicherry, in the atmosphere of Aurobindo, and I had a great friend who laughed at me a lot. Then, I had a series of very powerful mystical experiences which forever changed my understanding of reality. One experience happened when I was lying on my bed, and I don't think I was asleep. I had a very powerful vision. First, I went into a room where Aurobindo was sitting, where he blessed me and put his hand on my head. It was an ancient room. The moment he put his hand on my head, I went into what I can only describe as a cloud, that space of seething void, that strange, circling, and unknowable emptiness from which all things come. In that cloud I heard the most extraordinary and beautiful music I have ever heard. The only time I've ever heard music like it is in Tallis's *Spem in Alium*—this is, for me, the greatest piece of music I know, because in this piece you have a shadow of the divine music. The divine music does exist; the music of the spheres is real and it can be heard by the purified senses. I heard it for the first time that night, and I can only describe it as if everything in the universe was singing at the same time with unbearable tenderness its longing to be united in silence with the Divine. It is the universe singing in the purest, deepest, wildest, and most poignant imaginable bliss and ecstasy. It is singing *of* its origin, *for* its origin, and *to* its origin. All music, I've come to understand, is an attempt to reach that sound. I feel that all composers have somewhere, more than the rest of us, the memory of that central sacred sound to which they're trying to return. I hear it most clearly in Tallis, in Despres, I hear it clearly in the *"Et Incarnatus Est"* section of Beethoven's *Missa Solemnis*. I have also heard it in certain Sufi and Indian music. Very gradually, in my vision, the sound started to make sense. The worlds and the entire cosmos were singing words. What was being sung was, "O, my Lord, I do not want to leave you, I cannot leave you, I cannot bear leaving you." Then I realized that what was being sung was the song of the souls that are leaving the central Light to enter into matter. Then I plunged down a chute, my body hit the bed, and I woke up. I realized that I had been shown my origin, my origin in sound. Where I came from was that sound, that cloud of ecstatic rapture, although I had taken this road, the plunge into matter. It was a very extraordinary initiatory dream.

So what the Sufis are saying is that all real music reminds one of one's origins. To listen to real music is to listen to a passion for origin. Not just to listen with one's mind or heart, but to listen with an aching soul. It is the kind of listening I experienced that night in Pondicherry when the beauty of the music itself was so extreme that I became one with its agony and its bliss. Rumi once said, "A secret is hidden in the rhythms of music. Should I reveal it, it would upset the world." Music is as Mohammed says, "The commentaries on the mysteries of the secrets."

Aflaki tells us about Rumi:

> One afternoon, a musician was playing the violin and the Master was listening with great pleasure. A friend entered and said, "Stop this. They are announcing the afternoon prayer." "No," said Rumi, "This also is the afternoon prayer. They both talk to God. He wants the one externally for his service and the other for His love and knowledge."

Listen now to those first extraordinary lines of the *Mathnawi* in which this knowledge of music as mystery is expressed very clearly. Rumi began his greatest poem talking about music. He began it talking of the *ney*, a type of reed instrument like a flute. I'm going to dwell on this word, *ney*, to give you a sense of the complexity of the imagery around it. First read the opening lines of the *Mathnawi*. If we realized that dance mirrored the order of the creation, and that our music is an echo of the music that is creating the creation, what a transfiguration of our composing powers that would be, and what a transfiguration of our powers of listening. One of the messages that I hope to bring to you through Rumi is a knowledge of the sacralization of all the arts, a return of all the arts to their home in the opening of the divine senses, in the transfiguration of the divine senses themselves. That is what art is for. Art is to take us home.

> Listen to the reed. Listen to how it tells a story.
> And listen to how it complains of separation, saying,
> "Ever since I was parted from the reed-bed,
> My lament has caused both men and women to mourn.
> I want a bosom and a breast that is torn by separation,
> So I may unfold fully the pain of the desire of the heart."
> Everyone who is left far from his source
> Longs to have return the time when he, or she, was
>   united with it.
> The noise of the reed I am talking about is fire, not wind.

And who hasn't got this fire, who isn't possessed by
   this fire, will be annihilated.
It is the fire of love that is in the reed.
It is the fervor of love that is in the wine.
The reed is the friend of everyone
Who has been parted from a friend.
Its strains pierce our heart.
Whoever saw a poison, or a cure, like the reed?
Whoever saw a consoler and a longing lover like the reed?
The reed tells of the path full of blood,
And tells stories of the passion of Majnun.
Only to the senseless is this sense confided.
The tongue has no customer except the ear.

To cut a reed, you have to separate it from the place it comes from. The sound that the reed then makes, which makes it beautiful, is the sound of that separation.

But the reed removed from the reed-bed says, "My lament has caused man and woman to mourn." The reed that is used in the Sufi stories, the *ney,* is mourning our separation from the Beloved.

I want a bosom and a breast that is torn by separation,
   So I may unfold fully the pain of the desire of the heart.

If you read this poetry without any longing for God, what you will hear are a few wonderful images which might be interesting. But, if you listen to this poetry torn by a longing to be propelled into the presence of the Divine, then your whole being will be moved.

Everyone who is left far from his source
Longs to have return the time when he, or she, was
   united with it.

This is a key sentence to the understanding of music in Sufism, and its place in understanding Sufism itself. What the reed and its music are evoking is the sacred union that was before time. In that sacred union, the music of the spheres was heard. The voice, "be," was heard, and this essential gorgeous music was known simply. All human music is an invitation back to that sacred union, just as sacred poetry, especially by someone like Rumi, is an invitation back to silence.

The noise of the reed I am talking about is fire, not wind.

If you listen to the reed played in the Sufi ceremonies as if it were simply a musical instrument, you've missed it. The reed is fire, the sacred fire of passion and separation. That is what is actually playing the music and being transmitted by the music. That is what is the music itself.

And who hasn't got this fire, who isn't possessed by this fire, will be annihilated.

Rumi says that anybody who does not have this fire does not really exist. To have this fire is what it *means* to exist.

It is the fire of love that is in the reed.
It is the fervor of love that is in the wine.
The reed is the friend of everyone
Who has been parted from a friend.

You see how he shifts? First, the reed is mourning and needs pain in order to be listened to. But then the music itself becomes the friend of the person looking for the friend. This music and Rumi's poetry evoke in you a longing which is itself the first ecstatic step toward return. This is why the Sufis place so much emphasis on longing for the Beloved, on yearning for union, on this passionate, continual outpouring of the heart, because the passionate, continual outpouring of the heart is itself the shadow of the Presence. It is the beginning of the immersion in the Presence.

The sentence that follows is the subtle key.

Whoever saw a poison, or a cure, like the reed?

What tantrism does, whether it is in Sufi, Buddhist, or Hindu form, is to take things that would otherwise lead us into *sam-*

sara and desire, the very forces that tempt us, and use them as powers to *return* us to origin. The reed could be something poisonous, it could evoke sensual pain and play upon that sensual pain, since it is born from the pain of separation. In fact, it is the *cure* for our pain, just as Rumi's poetry is the cure for our pain because it helps us go to the place where we can be cured forever of our pain and of our grief.

> Whoever saw a consoler and a longing lover like the reed?

So the reed, in Sufi ceremonies, consoles us by reminding us of the sacred origin of music and identity, and it becomes the image of what the lover in Sufism should be like. The reed is literally someone whose entire being has become hollow enough to play the music of God.

> The reed tells of the path full of blood,
> And tells stories of the passion of Majnun.

The sound of the reed, that melancholy, poignant, piercing sound, is the sound that the Sufi makes of his life. This is the Sufi path full of blood, tearing the heart to pieces, dancing above both worlds, and giving up the soul.

Majnun was the great lover of Persia, whose love for Leyla is legendary. Leyla and Majnun were separated by their families. Majnun was transformed into a saint by his love for Leyla. Just one image of Majnun's love will give you the extent of his passion. He had become thin from longing. He lived among animals and wandered in the hills. He could never speak to anybody, such was the pain of his passion. His songs of love for Leyla were sung all over Arabia. Leyla would sit in her tent and weep, because her own relatives would sing Majnun's songs to her. One day, she was allowed to go and look at him across a lake as he sat under a tree, very thin and mourning. There was moonlight, and the moon had such compassion for her in her longing that it focused all its sacred beams upon her. She stood transfigured, unable to move, watching her lover across the lake glittering with starlight. Majnun just gazed upon her, and tried to sing but nothing came from his mouth. He could only weep tears of blood. He gazed across the starlit lake at Leyla transfigured in the moonlight. This great love is, of course, symbolic of the love of the soul for the Beloved. Nizami's poem of Leyla and Majnun is a marvelous masterpiece of the world, full of the excess and extremity that characterize the Sufi notion of passion.

You recall the different aspects of the *ney*. Here is a letter that was written to my great friend, Eva De Vitray-Meyerovitch (which she quotes in her book *Rumi and Sufism*), about the *ney* from someone who practices this particular instrument. You will understand how music, poetry, and the sacred path are all deeply aligned.

> The *ney,* the reed flute, and the *Isân-ul-kamil* (the man of God) are one and the same thing. Both are complaining of separation. Both have wounds in the heart and both are bound. Both are dried out because they are not nourished by the earth, and both are empty, filled only with the air of the musician. When they are alone, they have no voice. Their role is to find themselves between the hands and the lips of the musician, and to be for him an instrument to express his will and his desire. The perfect man has been brought from the garden of pre-eternity of the divine world and falls, by the force of destiny, into the material world. His heart is wounded by the burn of this separation. He empties his heart of the desire for all carnal things, empties his spirit of its imaginary existence, and abandons himself to God. He then is an instrument to manifest the will of God, and it is that that is his only duty. When the Divine Voice wants to express itself, it borrows the different voices of each spiritual man.
>
> When this latter speaks of his celestial origin and of the sadness of separation, his listeners, if they have a pure heart, feel the same sadness. But there are many

spiritual degrees among men, and everyone understands according to his or her own degree. This is why our master used to say, "who has seen a poison and a cure like the flute?" For some it is a poison, because it expresses animal desire. For others, it is the divine memory that is manifesting itself.

The *ney*, the flute, is like a friend, like a lover. In this age, lovers are separated and have their heads veiled. So, the flute is hidden and suspended in its sack. But the *ney* is made to sing, and it is only when it sings like this that you understand its secrets.

So you see how deeply for the Sufi are interwoven origin, divine truth, music, reality, and the end of the Sufi path, which is nothing less than to become the flute, "hollow in the hand of God."

We've gone from poetry, as an invocation of the soul, to an understanding of the Sufi vision of music as metaphysics, to an understanding of the deep correlation between the flute cut from its seed bed as an expression and symbol of the separation we all feel, to the role of the holy man.

Now we're going to go the core, an attempt to convey what is *sama*. I'm not going to convey it to you directly; I want you to read and understand. Part of you knows what this dance is about, because every atom in you is doing this dance. I will give you three quotations followed by three stories of Rumi that illuminate and orchestrate the *sama*.

Your knowledge of what Rumi is teaching comes from your own sacred memory.

> Oh brilliant sun, rise up now!
> The atoms are dancing.
> Souls drunk with ecstasy are dancing.
> Come here, I'll whisper in your ear where his dance is
>   dragging him,
> Each atom, happy or miserable,
> Is in love with that Sun of which nothing can ever be said.

Oh heaven, dancing round our heads.
For love of the sun, you are doing the same work as I
    am doing,
Dancing for love of you, for love of the sun.

I see the waters springing from their sources,
I see the branches of the trees dancing like penitents,
Their leaves clapping their hands together like minstrels.

Keep these three images in your mind. Let your mind and
heart become saturated by that divine dancing.

Rumi only began to dance when Shams left. Shams loved
to dance, but there are very few accounts of Rumi dancing
before Shams' disappearance, when the full pain and atrocity
of his disappearance came to Rumi and he realized that perhaps Shams had been murdered, that the thing he had loved
most in the world was lost. When Shams went, his world of
passion was gone, too. His looks, his presence, his laughter,
his amazing intensity, the light that streamed from him—all
that Shams was seemed to disappear from the world. Rumi
was left utterly bereft, heartbroken, shattered. For a long time
Rumi went out of his mind. It probably took him four or five
years to begin to establish any kind of normality at all, to begin
to live again. It was in this period that he began the dance that
the Mevlevis now use, the dance that symbolizes the dance of
the suns and the cosmos around the Beloved, of the atoms
around the sun, of Rumi himself around Shams. It was at this
time, too, that he brought in the minstrels and the dancers.
When you read this description by Sultan Walad of Rumi's
state, you understand it immediately.

Day and night Rumi danced in ecstasy. On the earth he
turned and turned like the heavens. His ecstatic cries
reached out to the height of the skies, and everyone heard
them, all around. He showered gold and silver on the
musicians. He gave away whatever he had. Never for a
moment was he without music and ecstasy, never for a

moment was he at rest. In the city an uproar of protest grew and the whole world resounded and hummed and bubbled with their uproar. Everyone was so surprised that a great *qutb,* a great Pole and *mufti* of Islam who is the accepted leader of the two universes should be raving like a madman, in public and in private. But the people turned away from ordinary religion and faith, and went crazy after love. The reciters of the word of God now recited erotic verses and mingled freely with the musicians.

Shams returned to Rumi in the ecstasy of the music and the dancers. Rumi was dancing his way back to Shams. He recreated the ecstasy that Shams had created in him by the music that he summoned from all the musicians, from all the corners of Konya, and by his dance. In fact, after Shams' disappearance, what Rumi put in Shams' place was the whole of human love, art, and passion, and these all together became the Beloved, reinstated and reintegrated the Beloved into his being. Rumi had worked out the science of transfiguration. He worked it out not through theory nor reading Ibn-Arabi, not because he had constructed a thesis about "music harking back to the sacred origin of the Divine." Rumi worked at it because he had to.

Rumi had to dance, sing, and listen to music day and night, because only the bliss of music and dance could save him and bring his soul back into the sun of Shams' Presence. He'd arrived at that place that every mystic yearns for, where you long so much for the Beloved that you pour the whole of your life into that absence and that absence starts to radiate with the Presence. People thought Rumi had lost his mind. On the contrary, what he was doing was discovering through the lucid insanity of his pain and through the extremity of his grief a form of healing through art that he would give to the entire world. Everything that Rumi has given us, he worked out along his own veins. All the techniques that he gave, he used them not to make himself happy, but to survive. He had to survive this horror. This is what gives the particular Sufi revelation that comes through him its extraordinary intensity and universality. The *Koran* says you should never pray when you are drunk or in a state of drunkenness, and the Sufi orthodoxy took this to mean that there should be no awakening of the senses through any "legitimate means in prayer," so that the state of sobriety and purity could be complete. But Rumi's desperation led him to risk that. So what Rumi has given to the world is a technology of sacred transformation through art, which is now central to the future, a future where all the arts must return to their sacred power, their sacred presence and origin, their sacred purpose.

Let us now go through what actually happens in the dance, the *sama,* in order to taste how intricate and rapturous the different stages of the dance are, and to appreciate the subtlety of the metaphysics that underlie it.

The dervishes enter into the room of the *tariqa,* the assembly, dressed in white which is a symbol of the shroud, covered with a large black cloak which represents the tomb, and wearing turbans which represent the stone that is placed on the tomb. So they offer an image of death—death to the world and death to desire. The sheik (originally Rumi himself) enters last, representing Rumi, the axis, the *qutb,* the point of intersection between the timeless and time.

First the dancers enter, then the sheik enters. The sheik is the secret center of everything and represents the eternal Rumi, whose message and inspiration is at the center of the dance, and who was the source of the grace of the whole order. On his high turban is rolled the black scarf that indicates his stature and dignity. He salutes the other dervishes who salute him back. He is seated in front of the red carpet, whose color evokes the colors of the setting sun, which spread its last fires in the sky of Konya when Rumi lay dying, entering the final union with the Beloved. Everything in this ceremony has the most tender and sacred significance.

Then an unaccompanied singer celebrates the praises of the Prophet in a text written by Rumi with music by Itri (a Turkish composer who lived at the end of the seventeenth century). It is a slow, majestic composition. The flutist begins improvising after a while, while the master of the kettledrums plays and the sheik taps out a rhythm on the ground. At that moment the dervishes advance slowly and turn three times round the dance floor. These three rounds symbolize the three stages that take you nearer to God: the path of science, the path to vision, and the path leading to union with God.

Then, at the end of the third turning, the sheik places himself on his carpet as the dervishes go to a corner. After the musicians have sung, the dancers let their black cloaks fall in a triumphant gesture, as if liberated of their earthly envelope for a second birth. The sheik raises himself and the chief of the dervishes advances towards him, bows, and kisses his right hand. The sheik gives permission for the dance to begin. The dervishes, with arms crossed and hands on each other's shoulders, begin to dance slowly. They extend their arms like wings, the right hand turned up toward heaven to receive the divine grace, the left hand turned toward the earth to direct the divine grace that is coming into the right hand down onto the earth. Circling, they dance around the room. This dance around the room symbolizes union in plurality: the dancers unite themselves with everything in the cosmos that is also dancing (union in plurality), but it is also the whole dance of existence, the dance of evolution through all its stages of ascension, from stone to man.

This circle dance also echoes the law of the universe, the planets revolving around the sun, each turning on its own axis. The three salutations exchanged symbolize the successive degrees of faith. The beating drums evoke the trumpets of the last judgment. The circle of the dancers is divided through the middle into two semi-circles, one representing the arc of descent that is the involution of souls into matter, the falling of souls from divine spirit into matter; the other representing the circling of the souls to the Divine. An ideal line separates them. Toward the end, the flute improvises for a second time. This moment, when the flute reenters, is considered the supreme moment, the moment of deep union with God, the realized union. By this time, the true listening to the music and the true dancing with true understanding of the sacred character of each movement of the dance has led to a moment in which the flute can enter again, and this moment can evoke the whole sacred glory of union with the Divine. When the flutist goes back to his place, the *sama* stops and the singer sings words from the *Koran,* and the word of God arrives at the end like the response to all the passion of the dervishes. Right at the end of this ceremony, the singer, without any accompaniment, sings in usually the most ecstatic way. Nothing in the world is like a great Sufi singer at the end of this vast divine feast singing ecstatically from the *Koran.*

Then the last *sala'ams* are made, and the *dhikr,* the singing of the sacred name, begins. But before this, there is always a silence. At the end of this vast unfolding of the dance and music of the cosmos, everything has to be taken into the core of silence, because it is that from which the music and the dance are born.

> What is the *sama?* A message from those hidden
>   within the heart,
> A message which gives the heart—that stranger-peace
> The *"sama"* is a wind that warms the branches of the
>   intellect into blossom,
> A sound which dilates the pores of existence.
> The cry of the mystic rooster calls up the dawn,
> The rat-a-tat of man's drum engenders victory.
> The wine of the spirit keeps on shooting arrows into
>   the body's vat—
>   and when the body hears the tambourine,
> It starts to ferment, longing for transformation.
> A glorious sweet fire arises in the body, for the flute
>   and the singer's lips give it all the sugar it wants.

> See how a thousand scorpions of heartache lie dead,
> How a thousand sessions of ecstasy flow without a
>   single cup!

Given the intense sacredness of the dance, there is only one way, Rumi says, to really enter into its transforming truth.

> Dance only when you are in a state of purification. The saints dance only on the field of spiritual battle and it is in their own blood that they are dancing. When they are sprung free of the empire of the ego, they clap their hands. And when they soar free of their own imperfection, they dance.

You are not dancing until you are dancing in your own blood,

> Dance while you can shatter your own self
> And pluck out the cotton from the wound of sensuality.

> Ordinary people dance and frolic in the square
> Men of God dance in their own blood.

Through dancing, music, and spiritual ecstasy Rumi himself had come to such a place that the entire world was music and dance for him. What is the aim of the mystical life? To become the music of the spheres, to dance out the dance of God, to make everything that you do ring with the sound of the eternal, and everything that you say resound with the music of the eternal.

What is wonderful about Rumi is that he found a place for everything. I'm certain that even the way he ate his bread conveyed a musical gratitude for God. Everything was invited in; the revelation that he is giving to the world is a dance that sanctifies every aspect of our experience and roots and relates them all in one silent harmony of adoration.

Many of Rumi's poems were composed when he was dancing. There are times when Rumi would be so drunk on the dance that he would have to hold onto a pillar and go on dancing around the pillar. As he danced and turned, he would sing, "How could the soul not take flight?..." Rumi's poems spring from dance and you can hear the dance of the heart in the poetry itself. There is a dance with God, there is a literal dance, there is a dance in the poetry's rhythm, and there is a dance with us, reading and receiving the poetry in us, as us, for us.

"I have not sung the *Mathnawi* for you to hold it or repeat it, but to put it under your feet, so you could fly."

In perfect love and perfect abandon, dancing and flying are the same thing.

Chapter Nine

The Divine Child

IT HAS BEEN a continual theme of this book that to live a complete life, you do have to go first into super-consciousness, into the dimension of mystical reality, into the Light, and then to return with the Light, fully conscious, into the body and into the most ordinary details of life, to infuse them with the sweetness and joy, peace and ecstasy of the Light's working. It isn't sufficient just to shatter the false self, just to take the enormous journey into the Light, into the mystery of the Light.

What the great mystics show us, what has to be done, is to unify the Light with our daily work and practice. Why? By doing so we share something of the completeness of the being of God. God is both immanent and transcendent, both in the world and beyond it, acting and thinking through each of our bodies, and at the same time entirely beyond the creation, lost in the eternal light, in the eternal glory of the eternal light. And so are we! We are both in this body and in the transcendent. To live at ease in all dimensions, and to let the transcendent dimension flood through our actions, thoughts, and feelings, is the key. This is the full life. It is to this full, complete life that Rumi is pointing.

What I want to be is a friend of the heart of the human race. But, to be a friend of the heart of the human race, you have to have been through a complete mystical illumination and you have to want to give that illumination away at every second to anybody who wants even a scrap of it. Total generosity is required for the path of the full life. What I want for myself, what I pray for myself and for everyone, is integration of all the different parts of life. I think that Rumi is an example of that integration carried to its final intensity, which is not a balanced integration in conventional terms of what the world means by balanced, but an ecstatic balance. This balanced integration can deal with extremity. It can open completely to extreme grief and extreme joy and not be unsettled by either. It can seem crazy at moments, but remains rooted in the peace beyond all knowing and words. This is the balance that Rumi and Mother Meera exemplify. What the human race is approaching is the calm, humble, and humorous living out of the divine life on earth, as our true selves—the children of the Divine Mother and Father, truly empowered with our own immortality. That is what is being offered, if we have the courage to assume it.

In one of the most beautiful and pregnant of Rumi's remarks in the *Discourses,* you will hear the final paradox: "When you give up everything, everything is yours." As Rumi says in the *Mathnawi:* "It is in the realm of the soul that we find the heavens that govern the skies of the world." The Divine is trying to hand each of us an immense diamond in which we can see the whole of reality reflected and dancing forever, "the heavens that govern the skies of the world." However, our hands are full of plans for the new house, the next raise, all the obsessions which keep us from being in love enough to stretch out our hands with nothing in them, and say to the Divine, "Fill these hands with what you will." At that moment, everything can be given: all the power, beauty, majesty, and glory of the world. The responsibility of the Master, it is said in Hinduism and in Sufism, is to burn away the ego completely, so that the Divine Presence can be present. The Master takes the lamp and burns away all the oil so there is none left. At that moment, the Divine pours in its own oil and lights the lamp itself. The Divine oil is eternal, the wick is eternal, and the flame is eternal. This beautiful story, told all over Asia, exemplifies this.

A king was passing in a chariot, and by the side of the road he saw a poor man with a bag full of corn. The king said to the poor man, "Give me some corn." The poor man said to himself, "He must be crazy, this guy, but I will give him some corn." He took the five least good ears of corn out of the bag and gave them to the king. When he returned home, he found that the five least good ears of corn had become five golden ears of corn. And he heard the king's voice say softly, "If you had given me the whole bag of corn, all of it would have turned to gold."

When you hand over everything you have—all your gifts, sadness, grief, paranoia, lust, everything, not just the good, but what you think of as bad as well—when you hand it all over to God and say, "You do it, you transform it, you take it, it is yours anyway, it is you dancing in me," it is then that all of it can be transformed and integrated into a balance that mirrors the divine balance, into a harmony that mirrors, in marvelous ways, the divine harmony, and into a joy that flashes with the divine joy and the wildness and sweet anarchic ecstasy of the divine joy. The more you expend yourself, the more is given you to expend. Living the eternal life is living in the eternal dance, in the *shakti*. The *shakti* is boundless and gives away everything so that everything can pour in, and then be given away again. We are here on this earth to live in this ecstasy, and the ecstasy itself grows deeper and wider, richer and more stable, if you keep giving away everything you have, everything you know. As Rumi says in the *Mathnawi,*

> By God, don't stay in any spiritual station you have gained, but desire more. The one who suffers from dropsy can never have enough water. The divine court is the infinite plane: leave behind you the place of honor. It is the path itself which is the place of honor.

What the Divine is doing at every moment is giving itself away in the tulips, in the hills, seas, and supernovas. It is giving itself away, bursting and flowering. Rumi says, "We are your gardens, dying, blossoming." We are here to learn how to be those gardens that flower carelessly just for the sake of flowering. That is the integrated life, the full life, the life lived in the divine joy. Rumi, again:

> Anyone who gives anything to the Divine will find that it comes back to them turned to gold. The way of poverty is a way in which you attain all your desires. Whatever thing you have longed for will certainly come to you on this way, whether it be the shattering of armies, victory over the enemy, capturing kingdoms, reducing people to subjection, excelling your contemporaries, eloquence of speech.... When you have really chosen the way of poverty, all these things come to you. No man has ever travelled on this way and had cause to complain. Contrary to other ways, for whoever has traveled on such a way and toiled, out of a hundred thousand, only one objective in the world has been gained, and that, too, not in such a manner that his heart should be happy and find repose. For every such worldly way has its subsidiary means and powers to the attainment of that objective, and the objective cannot be attained save by way of these subsidiary means. That way is a distant way, and full of pitfalls and obstacles.

So if you choose to realize yourself through the world, you will always be disappointed. The truth of happiness does not lie in any of the goals of the world. The truth of happiness lies in giving the whole bag of corn to the king for him to transform and give back to you turned absolutely to gold. The truth of happiness lies in knowing your divine origin and dancing from that origin through entering the world of poverty. It is not enough to simply enter it, but really to practice it. Learn that these are not fantasies. This is not just a story told by mystics. This is the way to become happy, to become gloriously, shamelessly, joyfully happy. "God most high gives you kingdom and worlds that you never imagined." The ordinary consciousness cannot begin to imagine the glory of super-consciousness. It is as if somebody had been living in a small room with only one window in the darkest place in the Gobi Desert and was suddenly transported to the Champs-Élysées on a beautiful summer day, full of happy people drinking champagne. It could not be believed that such joy, such glory and happiness, could be on this earth. The way out of ordinary consciousness to super-consciousness is to choose poverty: the poverty of the spirit, humility, adoration, love of God, praying to give everything that you have in the service of the divine will in the world. That is the only way. The Prophet says, "I will be Master of mankind on the Day of Resurrection, without boasting." As Ibn-Arabi explains, this is not true because he is a lord but because He is the Perfect Servant, who has actualized his own nothingness, and has become pure adoration.

So, when you have entered the world of poverty and practiced it, "God most high bestows upon you kingdoms and worlds that you never imagined."

You know, Mohammed could not read or write, and yet to Mohammed was given the empire of the worlds. Mohammed felt his lack of eloquence, his lack of training very acutely. He was a deeply humble man. This is what Rumi says about Mohammed:

> So it happened with the Prophet, God bless him and give him peace. Before he attained his goal and became famous, observing the elegant speech and eloquence of the Arabs, he always wished that he, too, might be endowed with a like elegance and eloquence. When the unseen world became revealed to him, and he became drunk with God, his heart turned completely against that desire and longing.

He didn't want the Arabs' elegance and eloquence anymore. When God came to him, what could he want but God?

> God most high declared, I have given thee that elegance
> and eloquence which thou soughtest.

So the gifts that are given fulfill even your most secret desires.
Even the ones you thought you had to give up are fulfilled and
given to you.

> The Prophet answered, "Lord, of what use are they to
> me, I am indifferent to them and do not desire them."
> God most high replied, "Do not grieve. That too shall
> come to pass, and yet your indifference shall still obtain
> and it will harm thee nothing."

You will get everything you want, and you can stay in-
different. It is very important to be detached. God says to
Mohammed, you can be detached and have it all as well. You
can rule the world and not care, because I will give you everything.

> God most high bestowed upon him such speech that all
> the world from his time down to the present day have
> composed and still composed so many volumes expound-
> ing it. And still men fall short of comprehending it en-
> tirely.

What Mohammed was given was the wisdom of the Divine
itself, in its infinite unknowability, in its infinite depths, re-
cesses, and strangeness. So, as soon as he "died" and became
utterly detached, then divine joy could dance through him,
and the words that were not his own could flow through him.

> I will publish thy greatness abroad to such a point that
> men will shout it aloud in sweet intonations five times
> daily on the high minarets and all regions of the world
> so that it will be famous in the East and the West.
> So every man who has gambled himself upon this
> way, to him all objectives, whether religious or mun-
> dane, have become available and attainable and none
> has ever had cause to complain of this way.

So, if you wish to change the world, give yourself over to that divine will that also wishes the transformation of all being. Let us all give ourselves over in our entirety, fearlessly, to God, to lead us forward from miracle to miracle, from joy to joy, from attainment to attainment. Fearless, we will play whatever part we can play in this great transformation, and know as we do so, "None has ever had cause to complain of the way."

Now to embellish this theme of the full and integrated life, below are certain evocative paragraphs from the last chapter of Evelyn Underhill's great book, *Mysticism,* which I recommend to everyone. It still remains, after eighty years, the greatest book on mysticism I know. It primarily describes the Christian tradition, but any tradition will find in it the deepest kinds of clues given in perfect prose and written from a full secret ardor of experience. One of the essential gifts of this book is that Underhill understands that the real mystical life is a life of action in the world.

The last chapter is entitled "The Unity of Life," and in it Underhill sets forth her vision of how the fully integrated life leads to divine action and to giving birth to divine action in the world.

> The mystic way is a progress, a growth in love. A deliberate fostering of the inward tendency of the soul towards its source. But the only proper end of love is union. Moreover, just as earthly marriages are understood by the moral sense less as a satisfaction of personal desire than as a part of the great process of life, the fusion of two selves for new purposes, so spiritual marriage brings with it duties and obligations. With the attainment of a new order, a new infusion of vitality, comes a new responsibility, the call to effort and endurance on a new and mighty scale. It is not an act, but a state, fresh life is imparted, by which our lives are made complete. New created powers are conferred. The self, lifted to the divine order, is to be an agent of the divine fecundity.

This fecundity creates the supernovas, the constellations, seas, and mountains, as well as the insects; this fecundity is the source of all, and to be its agent is to be, Underhill says, "an energizing center," a "parent of transcendental life."

Rumi too is saying we are to become "agents of the divine fecundity" and "parents of transcendental life." Aquinas says the last perfection to come to a thing is to become the cause of other things:

> A creature tends in many ways to the likeness of God, the last way left open is to seek the divine likeness by being the cause of other things according to what the Apostle says, *Dei aenim summus ajutores*. We are also his lieutenants.

First, we live the narrow and limited unconscious life. Then come the pain and difficulties that show us the limitations of that life and the beginning of a desire to deepen our acquaintance with the Divine. Then comes the long, arduous, painful, extraordinary, and ecstatic journey toward the Divine. Then slowly, with great amazement, wonder, and gratitude, there comes the gathering union with the Divine. Out of this union grows the sacred marriage of self and God, the world and the other, masculine and feminine, creation and transcendence, out of which is born the Divine Child secretly hidden within each of us. The ecstatic, playful, and trusting child knows that the Presence is always at home, and therefore has the freedom, joy, knowledge, and power to create in the world with the fecundity of the Divine itself. The *child* is the one to whom all is given, not the master, yogi, nor teacher, only the adoring and pure child.

As Rumi says:

> I do not speak these words, Love speaks them:
> This subject is something I know nothing about.
> You can only tell this story if you are a thousand
>   years old.

What can I know? I am a child of the present.
Yet the child I am is a parasite on the Eternal One
And my union with Him ages me centuries.

All the powers of all the worlds and ages are given to the child because that child will use them only in adoration and never claim them. This is the ultimate mystical secret—to the child is given the fecundity.

It is an extraordinary and dazzling system. You can only be given the world when you no longer want it. You can only rule the world, mystically, when ruling the world becomes absolutely irrelevant to you, and when all you care about is love for the Divine One. At that moment, all is given because that love for the Divine Beloved makes you one with the Beloved. And out of that oneness, that union which is a sacred marriage, a totally new being is born in your being. That being is the child—an awake, wondering, dazzled, and sometimes mischievous child. This is the secret of it all. This is what Rumi became, what Theresa of Avila became, what the Buddha became, what Ramakrishna started as and was all his life—a child of the Divine, fecund with the divine fecundity. Underhill continues:

> We find as a matter of fact when we come to study the history of the mystics, that the permanent unity of state or spiritual marriage does mean for those who attain to it, above all else an access to creative vitality.

It is time to end this fiction that the mystical life is some drab, dreary, passive thing! The mystical life is dancing in every direction; that is the mystical life. Look at what Rumi did: he composed thousands of great odes, started a religious order, healed twenty or thirty people a day, on and on for the last thirty years of his life.

And think of Theresa of Avila's life after her illumination. She did not sit around waiting for the angel to come and spear her again. She walked all over Spain, fought the Inquisition, told the Pope his business, built enormous Carmelite monasteries, infused people with sacred passion. Her life was one long passionate action. Mother Teresa sleeps only four hours a night! She has slept four hours a night for sixty years! If you are infused with mystical knowledge, and mystical passion, you give everything away.

Let us end forever this vision of the mystical life as passive; it is supremely active and supremely fertile. It means giving up your whole life and devoting yourself to serving the Divine tirelessly, with childlike abandon, on every possible front, in every arena. Evelyn Underhill again:

> It means man's small, derivative life invaded and enhanced by the absolute life, the appearance in human history of personalities and careers which seem superhuman when judged by the surface mind. Such activity, such a bringing forth of the fruits of the spirit may take many forms, but where it is absent, where we meet with personal satisfactions, personal visions or raptures presented as marks of the unity of way, ends or objects of the quest of reality, we may be sure that we have wandered from the straight and narrow road which leads not to eternal rest.

"Invaded"—because it is an invasion! Nothing to do with this dreary idea of rest, fashionable among many spiritual people. If we get out there and act, we will have all the peace we need; if we love very much, then we act, we serve, we give away. Peace will come from that action of giving away.

This is what the great Christian mystic Richard of St. Victor said:

> The fourth degree, the last degree of love, is spiritually fruitful. Wherever we find a sterile love, a holy passivity, we are in the presence of quietism heresy and not of the unity of life.

St. Theresa says:

I hold it for a certain truth that in giving these graces our Lord intends, as I have often told you, to strengthen our weakness so that we may imitate Him by suffering much.

Whence did St. Paul draw strength to support his immense labors? We see clearly in him the effects of visions and contemplations, which come indeed from our Lord and not from our own imagination or the Devil's paw. Do you suppose St. Paul hid himself in order to enjoy, in peace, these spiritual consolations and did nothing else? You know that, on the contrary, he never took a day's rest, so far as we can learn, and worked at night in order to earn his bread. Oh my sisters, how forgetful of his own ease, how careless of honors should she be whose soul God thus chooses for His special dwelling place. For if her mind is fixed on Him, as it ought to be, she must need forget herself. All her thoughts are bent on how to please Him better, and when and how she many show Him her love. This is the end and aim of prayer, this is the object of that spiritual marriage whose children are always good works.

This is what happens when you become rich in the spiritual marriage with the Spirit that makes you fertile. What you yearn to do more than anything else is to give it all away. I really do believe that if anyone on this earth could taste for two minutes the presence of the Divine Mother in her form as Mother Meera or the presence of the divine Buddha of Compassion in his form as the Dalai Lama, he or she honestly would become forgetful of his or her own fate, careless of honor like children, and work and serve in as many ways and dimensions as possible.

This is the object of that spiritual marriage, whose children are always good works. Works are the best proof that the favors which we receive have come from God.

Theresa of Avila says later in the same chapter:

> To give our Lord a perfect hospitality, Mary and Martha
> must combine.

Of course! Because what the Divine wants for us, especially
the Divine Mother, is the complete realization, which means
working in the world with all of our talents, whatever they
may be, for justice, for the reign of the Divine on earth now,
in this terrible time, with Her power and grace and love.

> The mature mystic, having come to his or her full stature,
> passed through the purifications of sense and of spirit,
> and entered on his or her heritage, must and does take
> up as a part of that heritage not merely a fruition of the
> divine goodness, truth, and beauty, his or her place within
> the eternal rose, nor the creative activity of an agent of
> the eternal wisdom, still immersed in the river of life,
> but both together: the two-fold destiny of the spiritual
> man or woman called to incarnate the eternal in time.
> To use the old scholastic language, he or she is at once
> patient and agent. Patient as regards God, agent as re-
> gards the world.

What do I want for you from this book? I want you to be
thrilled by the glory of Rumi and by the glory of your secret
self. I want you to enter into that glory and burn away in that
glory as you become one with it. I want you to work with the
knowledge of that glory in the world, in the darkness, in the
nightmare and madness, for the transformation.

> In a deep sense, it may be said of him, this person who
> has come into this nature now participates according to
> his measure in the divine human life which mediates
> between man and the eternal and constitutes the salva-
> tion of the world. Therefore, though his outward heroic
> life of action, his divine fecundity, may seem to us the
> best evidence of his state, it is the inner knowledge of

his mystical sonship whereby we feel eternal life in us above all other things which is for him the guarantee of absolute life. He has many ways of describing this central fact, this peculiar consciousness of his own transcendence which coexists with and depends on a complete humility. Sometimes he says that whereas in the best moments of his natural life he was but the faithful servant of the eternal order, and in the illuminated way became its secret friend, he is now advanced to the final, most mysterious state of hidden child.

This is the complete progression. This is where Rumi came to, where the highest beings all come to in the end.

The faithful servant begins by serving with true adoration and true love, and then, through illumination, through the waking of the Divine Light in his or her mind, becomes the secret friend, the one who knows that the Divine is always there. But there is a state beyond this, the most mysterious and final state of hidden child, the secret child of the Divine. The one who is always at peace and free in the body of the Divine, and knows the Divine as a child, knows its mother and father. This is what Ruysbroeck—for me, the greatest of all the Christian mystics—says about the life of the hidden child:

> How great, how great is the difference between the secret friend and the hidden child! For the friend makes only loving living, but measured ascents towards God. But the child presses on to lose his own life upon the summits in that simplicity which knoweth not itself.

These are divine words.

"But the child presses on to lose his own life," not anybody else's life, but his or her own life. The child is so in love with the Divine that the child just goes on following it. So if the Presence takes the child into hell, he or she goes into hell. What the child wants to do more than anything is to be united completely with the sacred Light, "in that simplicity which knoweth not itself." This is a very important phrase. What a paradox it is, yet one more of the extraordinary paradoxes of the spiritual life: at the summit of spiritual knowledge what you know is that you know nothing. But at least you know it! Most people think they know something. This is a fatal mistake. We know nothing, but what we have with that knowing nothing is complete trust that we will be led from state to state, from miracle to miracle. What we do know is that we are being led by the mysterious hand of the Divine, and that hand will always guide and help us. This we know. What is going to happen, we cannot know. What the consequences of our actions are, we can never know. What is prepared for us, we do not know, we can never know. What is God's ultimate nature, we will never know. However many visions we see, however profound our immersion in the peace of God, there will always be a dimension of God that remains absolutely beyond our comprehension. We do not know, cannot know, know we cannot, and do not care, because we are a child dazzled by love, dazzled by happiness, grace, and joy, dazzled by serenity and delight.

> How great, how great is the difference between the secret friend and the hidden child?

The hidden child is drunk with love! "But the child presses on to lose his own life upon the summits," and Ruysbroeck goes on:

> When we transcend ourselves and become, in our ascent towards God, so simple that the bare supreme love can lay hold of us, then we cease, and we and all our selfhood die in God. In this death, we become the hidden children of God and find a new life within us.

There is an extraordinary photograph of Ramana Maharshi on his deathbed. He was in great pain, in one sense, but in another sense, he was in no pain at all. He was lying on his bed, and he asked his doctors to allow everyone to pass by so that he could gaze at them and bless them for one last time, everyone who was there. In that photograph of Ramana Maharshi, you can see the essence of the divine child. On the one hand you see a totally burnt, emaciated, completely wrecked body that cannot move, that is in obvious *extremis*. His face is almost not there, it is so hollowed out by anguish. But on his face is the transcendent smile of the totally free child. The last smile of Ramana Maharshi, the last smile of the divine being that he is in his body, is the smile of a four-year-old child.

That smile is waiting for all of us at the heart of our heart. It is the smile on the Cycladic sculptures; it is the smile on the sculptures of the Buddha. That smile is the child's smile, the secret reality of this whole life. That smile is the smile of the Divine Mother, the golden thread through all the carpet of life.

Once in a carpet shop in Turkey, I saw a black carpet. I thought, my God, what a black carpet! The owner rushed out from the shop and said, "Ha! You think it is black!" And he raised the carpet to the light, and I saw that there were invisible gold threads which fell, changing the carpet into a molten sea of gold light. It was constructed in such a way that if you looked at it from the position of the ego, it was entirely black. But if you looked at it from the position of the soul, it was entirely gold.

The smile of the Divine Mother, the smile of the Divine Father, the smile of the child, is that golden thread in the black carpet. Instead of gazing at the carpet, "Oh my God, there's my mother, there's my abused childhood," our task is to take all of that with our own hands and lift it up into the light. When you do so, you will see all the golden threads that have always been there, without which the black carpet could not exist at all, are the secret lining of that carpet. Then, what will you do? You will laugh, you will smile and dance about like a child. At that moment, when you have finished dancing like a child, your mother or your father will call you to the door and say, "Here is the diamond of divine love and knowledge for you." You will know what you are getting, and you will

stretch out both hands, because it will be so big. Let us contemplate once again what Ruysbroeck says, followed by Underhill's commentary:

> How great, how great, is the difference between the
> secret friend and the hidden child? For the friend makes
> only loving living, but measured ascent towards God.
> But the child presses on to lose his own life upon the
> summits, in that simplicity which knoweth not itself.
> And when we transcend ourselves, and become in our
> ascent towards God so simple that the bare supreme
> love can lay hold on us, then we cease and we and all
> our selfhood die in God. And in this death, we become
> the hidden children of God and find a new life within
> us. [Ruysbroeck]

> Though the outer career of the great may be one of super-
> human industry, a long fight with evil and adversity, his
> real and inner life dwells securely upon the heights, in
> the perfect fruition which he can only suggest to us by
> the paradoxical symbols of ignorance and emptiness.
> [Underhill]

If you keep your mind as empty of concept as possible, then
you have the child mind, and into this divine child mind can
flash whatever needs to flash, at whatever moment, without
interference. As Rumi says in the *Mathnawi:*

> Like the hunter, the Sufi chases game:
> He sees the tracks left by the musk deer and follows them.
> For a while, it is the tracks which are his clues, but later
> It is the musk itself which guides him.

Unless you are childlike and let the Divine guide you, you
cannot be taught anything by the Divine. Unless you are totally
without concepts, the divine knowledge which is beyond all
concepts, the absolute which is beyond all form of mind, cannot flash itself and dance in your mind.

"And though the outer career of the great mystic be one of superhuman industry, a long fight with evil and adversity"— think of all Rumi and Shams had to put up with. Think of what we're all going to have to put up with. We are going to suffer a lot, it is going to be more difficult than any of us can imagine, but so what!

> He dominates existence because he transcends it. He is a son of God, a member of the eternal order, shares its substantial life.

Here again, Ruysbroeck comes to the rescue with a perfect sentence which expresses exactly all the poise and the interfusion of this life.

> Tranquility, according to his essence, activity, according to his nature. Absolute repose, absolute fecundity.

The essence of God is peace beyond all knowing, silence beyond all imagining, a depth of love and security beyond all possible description. That essence is always present, and that essence and the knowing of that essence bring the most profound tranquility. The quality of this tranquility, as Ramana Maharshi said, is like a man lying on the bed after a hard day's work, smoking his pipe. This is what enlightenment is. It is an intimate image—no flashing lights; it has nothing to do with flashing lights. It has to do with living in the secure possession of that peace and silence at every moment.

The nature of God is extravagant generosity of the most outrageous kind. The creation of millions of worlds and dimensions out of pure play, out of divine play, out of divine joy— that is His nature, Her nature, that's it.

Says Ruysbroeck again:

> This is the two-fold property of godhead, and the secret child of the absolute participates in this dual character of reality, for this dignity has man been made.

The search and struggle for justice in this world, and the search and struggle for union with the Divine are both equally important facets of life in this world, life as divine children.

The following poems of Rumi come from *Speaking Flame,* the second book of re-creations that I did. These poems exalt suffering, discipline, and intensity as a way to the purification that leads to the union, which leads to the birth of the child.

> Run forward, run forward, the way will spring open
> through you,
> Be destroyed, you'll be flooded with life.
> Humble yourself, you'll grow greater than the world.
> Your self will be revealed to you, without you.

Run forward and the way will not merely open before you, it will "spring" open, as when Aladdin rubs the lamp. You'll be flooded with life! If you accept the way of divine annihilation, you will be given everything and you will be flooded with life.

> Humble yourself, you'll grow greater than the world.
> Your self will be revealed to you, without you.

Mother Meera was once asked, "Who am I?" She answered, "Drop the 'I' and you'll find out!" If you drop the ego, you will find the "I." To live as the divine eternal being is to live as the eternal "I," which is to live as the whole experience, as the entire cosmos: gracefully, humorously, ordinarily, while cleaning your shoes as much as while reading Rumi. That is enlightenment.

> Blood must flow, he said,
> For the garden to flower,
> And the heart that loves me
> Is a wound without shield.

What stops the garden of all of our lives from flowering is being unprepared to suffer enough. We are not prepared to cry enough, to feel the depths and resources of our pain. Rumi is saying, open your hearts and accept that if you open your hearts there will be a wound. It is a wound, to love the world.

Sometimes, when people come to Mother Meera, her whole being has to hold itself, so as not to dissolve in tears in the intensity of her compassion. She feels everything at a level of feeling that is beyond our power to imagine. Her heart is a wound without shield. It is frightening. But this is the goal. You know how marvelously some children open completely to the sorrows of others. If you tell a child a sad story, she sobs, but then she has a meal, or a sweet. She cries, but then goes on. This is the gift of enlightenment: to feel everything completely, but to feel it appropriately, in the moment and for the moment's sake. This is why the child is the key to being enlightened.

> Stop learning. Start knowing.
> The rose opens, and opens,
> And when it falls,
> Falls outward.

The child falls into being with great rapture. Once I actually saw this: a rose falling, the last gorgeous, infinitely exhausted, infinitely happy petals of the rose, just falling with a sigh of release and peace onto the ground from which it grew. As I watched, I thought, please grant me a death like that. The rose will appear again, somewhere else, and do it all over again.

> Become the prey of God, and be freed from grief.
> Enter your own being, hurt holds you captive.
> Know your life throws a veil over your path,
> Linger with yourself, you will only grow exhausted.

You have to become "the prey of God." If you are obsessed with all the details of your life, this will veil your path. The path is light itself, transcending all biography.

Now let's move to the middle section of *Speaking Flame*. These are very frightening, glorious, burning poems which describe exactly the entry into the fire.

> Beauty harsher than a thousand suns,
> Broke into my house, asked, "How is your heart?"
> His robe of glory trailed the floor; I said,
> "Pick up your robe; the house is floored with blood."

Those four lines contain the whole relationship between the real disciple and the real Master. What the real disciple says always to the real Master is: "Kill me." I went to Mother Meera when I was thirty-five years old. I was not asking for peace of mind or happiness. I was saying, "Kill the old self, I cannot go on living as I am. I just cannot go on. I've seen it is an illusion. Kill me with love. Kill me with your beauty, kill me with perfection, kill me with the Light, kill me with honor, kill me with glory, but kill me." That is what the true disciple is saying to the Master. According to your sincerity, your passion in repeating that prayer, destruction happens. When someone really craves that from the bottom of their heart, they are destroyed and flooded with life. There is a moment when the pain is very extreme, but the beauty of the process is so extremely clear that you can say with Rumi these words,

> Beauty, harsher than a thousand suns ...

It is barely imaginable, what it is like to be with somebody the way Rumi was with Shams: to know that this person is the Divine in person. I have been with somebody who I knew to be the Divine in person, so that I knew as my eyes grew to see the great Light that shines through her that her beauty was more frightening than a thousand suns. The beauty of the entire *shakti*, the entire Divine Mother, blazing in the whole universe, is hers.

> His robe of glory trailed the floor; I said,
> "Pick up your robe; the house is floored with blood."

That last line is beautiful because it not only warns you not to get any of the blood on your robe, but also tells you to look around and see how much blood is on the floor. It says, look what I've been through for you. Of course, one characteristic of the relationship between the Master and the disciple, as between Shams and Rumi, is the profound recognition by the Master of the disciple's suffering. The Master knows, and is not grateful but rather deeply moved at a depth which the disciple does not suspect until much later, when the complete rapture of the Master's love arrives. In that moment, the disciple knows how he or she has been guided and guarded with infinite love.

> This Fire I crackle in is You.
> I burn as You, burning away myself.
> Mad lucidities! Triumphs without sound!
> Don't look for me; I am not here.

This poem is the recognition that when the Divine Fire comes, you crackle in it, but you know it is the divine that burns in you, so you burn as the Divine. You burn away yourself, and the fire is burning you away. Mad lucidities, triumphs without sound—nobody else sees this, nobody else will ever see this. It happens in the privacy of the heart.

> The Fire is one, one only, one always.
> Bird beating, red wings in each thing that lives.
> I am not a voice, I am the Fire singing.
> What you hear is crackling in you.

Where you essentially are is where Rumi always is. Where you do not know you are—in the Fire, as the Fire—is where Rumi always consciously knows he is. Rumi speaks from where he knows you are! If you can hear that, then you and he are "crackling" together, one flame, one Fire.

> What I tell about "me," I tell about you
> The walls between us long ago burned down.
> This voice seizing me is your voice
> Burning to speak to us of us.

Like a child, Rumi knows that he is us, and he wants, *burns,* to give us that transcendent news. We are in the position of imagining that we are we and he is Rumi! The voice that is seizing me, as Rumi, to write these poems, to be this poem, is my own voice, our own voice, "burning to speak to us" about us. Fire is burning away the safety of separate pronouns, all safeties and barriers altogether.

The last poem in this series of the fire, of the growing of union, before we go to the child speaking and singing the songs of eternal love and eternal joy, is the poem in which union is declared and in which the rapture of union in the divine fire is most clearly expressed. The whole of our lives is contained in these four lines.

> All my splendor is to burn in you.
> To know this Fire that eats me
> Is eating itself, to be this Fire,
> Dancing on my own bones.

"All my splendor is to burn in you"—it is not to rule the world, nor to be a famous poet, or whatever. From that burning comes the splendor of bliss, knowledge, and ecstasy. "To know this Fire that eats me is eating itself" is the glory. The Divine Fire prepares the fuel out of itself that it itself devours. We are in a feast as our own cannibals. Imagine the Divine laughing: "I am the Fire that eats the worlds, and the worlds are eaten by me, and the worlds are me. I eat myself." Shiva dances and devours Shiva and spins out of Shiva.

> To know this Fire that eats me is eating itself.

"To know" first of all, and then "to be"! No more knowing, that is too easy. From that knowledge of being the Divine, you have to become it! You have to become the fire "dancing on my own bones." To be the fire dancing on its own bones is to live life with the total intensity of divine splendor. That is why we are given this life: to flower completely in sweet child-fire in it! Watch the flowers: they open totally in their flower-moment. They hold nothing back, and that is our purpose too: to open fully in our human-moment, and by opening totally, to be in the eternal. Anything that opens totally opens into the eternal.

Dancing on your own bones cannot be faked, just as you cannot dance on other people's bones, although that is the preferred solution. In many modern relationships, we want other people to burn for us, whereas what we have to do is jump in and dance on our own bones. And everyone has their own set of bones, so everyone's dance is totally unique: you can't use anybody else's bones to dance with, and you can't even learn anybody else's music. You can listen to someone else's music, but the music that you are going to dance to will be your own unique, extraordinary music. That is when you become the child.

Every child is unique, and only the child is unique, because only the child is free to be completely itself. Being completely oneself means living inwardly beyond all conventions, beyond all guilt, beyond all religion and dogma, beyond all hierarchy, beyond all fantasy about heaven or earth, beyond all spiritual longing for spiritual achievement, beyond everything. Only the child is pure, naked and joyful in the present moment. This is what it means to be enlightened, to be Rumi's "child of the present."

> Tears at your tender glory
> Surprise me in each alley.
> I begged to go mad, I have!
> You've made my eyes a Sea.

When you have become a child, the whole world radiates with the beauty of the Beloved. The glory is so great and so tender that in each "alley" tears of joy and gratitude surprise you. If you are really looking at this world, you will be moved to your depths a hundred times a day by the flowers at the side of the road, by the people you meet, by the news, by the face of an old woman seen suddenly through a car window, by all the things that constantly bring you messages of your own origin and the origin of all things. Rumi says, "I begged to go

mad" in divine love, and "I have! You've made my eyes a Sea."
A sea of tears, but also a mystic sea, because when the mystic
eye is opened, it sees reality trembling as a sea of white light.
The eyes and the sea have become one. The eyes, tears, sea,
and Light have become one.

> I have seen death with his face.
> Heard death singing with his voice
> Songs that bring suns into my mouth,
> Burn all words to vision.

> No one ever sees that last moment,
> The eroded rock becomes sand,
> But if they did, they would hear
> The sea singing.

No one could ever see that last moment, because there is
no one to witness it.

Mechthild of Magdeburg wrote the motto for the child.
"Bei nichts stan, zu niemand gan." "Standing by nothing, I go
to no one." This is what every child has written somewhere
on his or her breast of light.

> Your Dawn in me ... I'm drunk, stammering,
> A thousand thousand words go dark,
> Lightnings are dark—to us —to this;
> Identity's boundless worlds-wide blaze.

This is a poem of total immersion in the sea of *Kibriya,* the
sea of Divine Glory. "Your Dawn in me," when the Divine
Light comes up, completely in the mind, then speech dies, "a
thousand thousand words go dark." Everything else, all concepts and ideas, everything goes dark and "lightnings," the
most violent lights that we can imagine in this dimension, "are
dark to us, to this," to this thing being born. Here is being
birthed "Identity," the "I-I" relationship, the oneness with the
one, in a "boundless worlds-wide blaze" of bottomless eternal Light that is all of our origin and all of our nature.

This miracle, daily as dawn and sundown,
Normal as bread, as sleep after love;
If I look at him, I see my own image,
If I look at my own, I see his, aflame.

Years ago I had the extraordinary experience of looking at
a photograph of myself and seeing Mother Meera's Light come
out of it. Then, I heard her laugh and her voice saying, "Ha,
I have even got into you, you see." That is when the miracle
starts really to happen. At that moment, not only do you see
it coming out of your face, but you see it coming out of everybody's face. The greatest sadness is that we do not see the divine
world with the eyes of divine love, because if we did, we would
be excited by everything, like a child. How many times Aflaki
describes Rumi and his lovers dancing days and nights away
in joy!

Live to give everything away,
So nothing keeps us apart.
Love brings you here; light-atom pulsing
Always at the Sun's heart.

I am trampled grapes,
Run where Love pulls me,
Why whirl round me? you laugh
I'm whirling round myself.

Leaping up onto the roof,
My head split open
On the moon.
Crying for joy; not a sound.

Wild peaceful days, where the slightest wind
Soars perfumed with your traces . . .
I am in a heaven of One,
Unable to talk, not to talk.

When love is in me, I am One with Love,
The lightning when I say your name,

> I roam, a dazzled drunkard in our dimension,
> Where each event is secret laughter.

These last two lines describe exactly what a child is awake to—"secret laughter." "A dazzled drunkard in our dimension." When you enter into that child-dimension, all the synchronicities start to dance obviously around you. You are given message after message, often in the most hilarious way, so the divine mind is always speaking to you. You just have to learn to listen to reality, to be open to the guidance you need. You will roam, "a dazzled drunkard" in this dimension of alertness, receptivity, and clarity. "We show them the signs," says the *Koran*, "on the horizons and in themselves." Every event, even the darkest, will be a source of "secret laughter." Whatever it looks like, each event is always bringing you something extraordinary and fresh. If you have cancer, the spirit in you knows that despite whatever your panic-stricken ego is telling you, you are closer to your union with the beloved. If you use your cancer, by giving it up totally to the Divine, by humbling yourself and using it to go deeper into compassion, by giving up and offering your pain to everybody else so that your pain can diminish the world's pain, then you can use that cancer to be transformed at every moment to go deeper and deeper into God. You start to laugh in some secret place because with this perspective even the most terrible thing becomes the child's way of entering deeper into the love of The Mother. This is an astonishing alchemy.

> One moon, blossoming in a thousand bowls,
> One water, laughing in a thousand thousand fields,
> One Sun with a million electric shadows,
> One Silence with these love-cries for children.

These last three quatrains need no commentary. This chapter sums up where we have gone so far. I've been talking of perfect being, mystic poetry, sacred art and dance, and the mystical journey, but all these things lead to divine childhood

and boundless trust, the foundation for all true energetic trans-
formatory action in the world. Think how powerful all of us
could be, if we had that boundless trust at the very core of our
being. Nothing could terrify or humiliate us—we could be in
prison, but we would still be praying for the transformation
of our jailers. We could be shot, but as we died, we would
speak the names of God and extend them to those who shot
us for healing and forgiveness. Abandon in God is the power
that changes all things. This is the nuclear power we need if
we are going to turn the world around in twenty years. This
power is given only to the child, because only the child loves
enough to hold this power totally for the Divine and never for
himself or herself. Only the child is so much in love with love
that he or she only wants to do what love wants, and so can
be moved by love from miracle to miracle.

> Great tree of bliss! Your swaying braziers
> Musk each second with Eternity!
> I wade incessantly your sea of star-flowers,
> Your trunk soars blazing from my heart.
>
> I have shrunk beyond the smallest atom,
> Expanded further than the last star,
> All that is left of Rumi is only
> This garden, laughing with fruit.
>
> The law of Wonder rules my life at last,
> I burn each second of my life to love,
> Each second of my life burns out, in love,
> In each leaping second, love lives afresh.

As we face intolerable agony, and the intolerable amount
of work that is needed to heal the agony, we will need the freshness of the divine child. With it, we will face everything; we
will work for Love, tirelessly; we will give ourselves without
stint; we will love beyond all possible hope of return; and we
will become signs and flames of deathless and tender joy for
everyone.

Whatever you have said or heard is only a shell:
The kernel of Love is mystery that cannot be divulged.

And in the light-core of that kernel, the child is always dancing, always at play, lost and found in Love.

Chapter Ten

Death as Triumph

The divine essence, the divine light is like a pot of musk. This material world and its delights are the scent of the musk, so everything that you love and adore and delight in, everything that you see is the scent of the musk. This scent of the musk is transient, for it is only accident. And he who has sought of this scent, the musk itself, and has not been content with only the scent, that man is good, for goodness is to seek the essence and not the accident. But he who has been satisfied to possess the scent, that man is evil, for he has grasped after a thing that does not remain in his hand. For the scent is merely the attribute of the musk, so long as the musk is apparent in this world, its scent comes to the nostrils. When, however, it enters the veil and returns to the other world, all those who lived by its scent die.

THIS PASSAGE FROM Rumi's *Discourses* is a clue to the Sufi mystical understanding of what happens in death. The *Koran,* as many of you know, is full of severe and terrifying visions of what happens to the evil after death. The Sufis do not bother with those visions, but they make a distinction between those who have "died before they die," and those who die only for the first time in terror and ignorance at death, and so miss the whole experience.

> ... so long as the musk is apparent in this world, its
> scent comes to the nostrils. When, however, it enters the
> veil and returns to the other world, all those who lived
> by its scent die, for the scent is attached to the musk and
> departs whither the musk reveals itself. Happy then is
> he who reaches through the scent and becomes one with
> the musk.

For many years I used to imagine my life before I met Mother
Meera as if I were wandering through room after room of a
great, shambling, strange house. In each of these rooms, with
all the other noise and difficulty and strangeness that were also
there, was always the scent of perfume, a strange miraculous
mysterious sweetness. This perfume was something I looked
for in reading, in sex, in drinking, in walking through the park,
in meditating alone, in looking at Greek statues, or listening
to Beethoven—something that was present in all of those activities. Then one day, I walked into a room and there She was,
the one from whom emanated this scent. Our lives are full of
clues, each of the rooms of our lives has the scent of the essence.
As Rumi writes:

> Whatever gladdens the mind is of the scent of my
>   beloved,
> Whatever enraptures the heart is a ray from my Friend.

But the point of life is to follow that scent, that ray, right
to its source and to become one with that light-source of eternal fragrance.

> Happy then is he, who reaches the musk through the
> scent and becomes one with the musk. Therefore for
> him remains no passing away. He has become eternal
> in the very essence of the musk, and takes on the predica-
> ment of the musk. Thereafter he communicates its scent
> to the world, and the world is revived by him.
>   Only the name of what he was survives in him, as
> with a horse or any other animal that has turned to salt

in a salt pan. Only the name of "horse" remains to it, in effect and influence it is that ocean of salt. What harm does that name do to it? It will not bring it out of its saltiness, and if you give some other name to the salt mine, it will not lose its saltiness.

To die in life is to become one with the source, and to become life free from the ego. It is to become the entire experience, pain and rapture, joy and grief, even the joy and grief of the insects.

This is how Sheik Ibn-Ata-Allah describes the final state in all its mystery, a marriage of all opposites, as reflected in the perfect being, a being like Rumi:

He drinks, and increases in sobriety: he is absent, and increases in Presence: his union does not veil him from his separation, nor does his separation veil him from his union: his extinction does not divert him from his permanence, nor does his permanence divert him from his extinction.

"Happy then, is he who reaches the musk through the scent and becomes one with the musk," and at that moment, because the identification with the body and ego, with time and space, have ended forever, so death has died.

Death is an event only in the universe of time and space. In the eternal sun there is no shadow. In the eternal Light there is no darkness. In eternal life, there is no death. What people will call your death will simply be an event in the illusion, because you will remain always as the eternal "I," the one who cannot die because he has never been born.

When Ramana Maharshi was dying, his disciples begged him, "Please don't leave us." He said, "Where would I go?" "I" am the only reality.

Therefore for him remains no passing away. He has become eternal in the very essence of the musk.

When you have become one consciously with the source, you have become one with the eternity of the source, and the source has so impregnated you with its knowledge, with its vision and Light, that this knowledge, vision, and Light are always alive in you. The notion of death itself becomes irrelevant.

> He becomes eternal in the very essence of the musk, and takes on the predicament of the musk.

He takes on the entire nature of the musk that is endlessly emanating all the perfume that is the world. To be one with the source is to be one with all its emanations, and to know them as eternal manifestations of the eternal source, even though they seem to be passing away. Once your mind has absolutely been burned away and only the silence is present, there is no death, there is only this! Eternal awareness and eternal consciousness mean exactly what those words mean — awareness and consciousness of the unborn eternal in all things, in all moments *at* all moments. This is when the game is over, when the grieving is done, the sorrow is passed, and the world is revealed for what it is, an immense and fabulous *lila* of the Divine Light.

The man or woman who has become one with the musk in this life then communicates its scent to the world and the world is revived in him or her. He or she becomes like Rumi or Ramakrishna or Aurobindo, a vast force of perfume. It's a beautiful image of Rumi himself, for his poetry itself is perfume that is inebriating the world, making the world remember its divine origin.

> And only the name of what he was survives in him ...

The false self, the ego, the self addicted to time and space, is dissolved in the vision of the eternal knowing.

> And only the name remains, as with a horse or any other animal that has turned to salt in a salt pan. Only the

name of "horse" belongs to it, in effect and influence it
is that ocean of salt.

The process of the dissolution of the false "I," the false self,
is like being flung into a salt pan. It dissolves the flesh and
bones of the false self, but the outline of the horse flung into
the salt pit remains, just as Rumi or somebody who people
could identify as Rumi remained after his incineration by
Shams. Though the shape seems to be of a horse, the essence
is not the flesh and bones of the horse, but the soul itself. This
is what Rumi calls "the ocean of salt." Salt is white, like the
divine light.

> What harm does that name do to it? It will not bring it
> out of its saltiness, and if you give some other name to
> the salt mine, it will not lose its saltiness.

That's the first quotation I want to give to you, to sink into
your minds and dwell there. Why meditate on the death of
someone like Rumi? Because I think that in the deaths of the
great masters, such as Rumi, Ramana Maharshi, or Ramakrishna, the human race is given extraordinary signs, extraordinary hints of the complete consciousness, of what we
secretly all are. The deaths of the great masters are their final
masterpieces: their supreme poems, their final teaching. It is
the way in which they show to the world their secret laughter
in the face of everything that illusion tries to hurl against us.
As Rumi says:

> Heaven is made of the smoke of hearts who burn away,
> Blessed is the one who burns away like this.

The mystic "who burns away" actually reverses in every
way what the ordinary person considers life to be. The ordinary person considers life to be a brief, painful, tragic flight
between nothingness and nothingness. The mystic thinks of
life as a manifestation of the eternal, to be savored in all its
detail because it is inherently sacred and divine. While the ordi-

nary person, the unenlightened person, imagines death to be a disaster and deceit, loss and betrayal, the ultimate torment and grief, the one who has died to reality knows death to be what Rumi calls "our wedding day with eternity." He or she knows that death is the moment when we take off all our clothes and rush, naked, to the naked Beloved. He or she knows that death is not something to be feared, but the consummation of the reason for being here.

Aflaki relates that one day Rumi's servant told him: "Even the prophets have trembled with fear in front of death." The Master answered: "God preserve us from such a feeling! Do men know what death is? Death, for the mystics, is to see the Supreme Truth. Why would anyone run away from that view?"

In Sufi terms, death is the consummation of a lifetime's love-making between the lover and the Beloved. The mystic prepares all his or her life for that supreme opportunity, that supreme moment, that supreme ecstasy when all this created world, with all its beauties, illusions, and dangers, dissolves into the ultimate Light of the ultimate reality. In that moment, the fully awakened heart and mind meet the original Heart and original Mind in a deathless, ecstatic, eternal, and totally conscious embrace.

> When lovers die in their journey,
> The spirit's King runs out to meet them.
> When they die at the feet of that moon,
> They all light up like the Sun.

And to know that death is what we are here to live and to prepare for is why the great masters make of their dying an ultimate manifestation of power. What could console us more than watching a supreme master die in peace, bestowing grace as he dies? What could inspire us more than the light of ecstasy in their eyes as they come to that last amazing meeting, not with any trace of fear, but with rapture?

What do we really know about death? If you want to know about death, you have to go into the Divine Light here. You have to have already died to the false self, and undergone the whole process of dying into the Light here in a body. Then you will learn what all the mystics have learned from all the traditions—that death itself, physical death, merely repeats a process that can be understood in the body and can be lived through and prepared for in the body, so that when physical death comes, it is an opportunity of union with the Light that is creating all things.

Why don't we take our fear of death—the panic about dying that underlies nearly all of our actions, the fear that makes us grasp and crave and hunger so much—and use its force to propel us with immense passion and urgency into the mystic quest? That's what Rumi is urging us to do: to use our fear of death to propel us to die here, to die in a body into eternity, to die into Love.

Death for the mystic, for the one who has died here, is the vision of supreme truth. In all the traditions that describe dying, consciousness of those who die without having died already is described as bewilderment or panic. Whereas there is no panic for the one who has already died, there is simply a passing from one state into another, one room into another. Death for the mystic is to see the Supreme Truth. "Why would anyone run away from that view?"

But first let's listen with our whole being to what Rumi is trying to communicate to us about dying in one of his greatest odes, Number 833. In it is the clue to the whole of reality and to whole process of what we are living. If we could lessen our fear of death, we could begin to live in Love and begin to save the world around us. What makes us destructive, grasping, and violent is our fear of passing away. And only by knowing what does not pass away can this fear be lifted from us.

> Our death is our wedding with eternity.
> What is its secret? God is one.
> The sun divides itself
> Streaming through the different openings of the house,

But when these openings are closed, multiplicity
    vanishes.
Multiplicity exists in the separate grapes,
But cannot be found in the juice that springs from the
    grape.
For he who is alive in the Light of God,
The death of this carnal soul is grace.
About this don't say anything either good or bad,
Because this has passed beyond the good or bad.
Fix your gaze on God
And do not speak of what is invisible
So that into your gaze he can put another gaze.
It's only the vision of physical eyes
That construct that vision for which nothing invisible
    or secret exists.
Turn your gaze towards the Light of God,
For under such a searchlight, what thing could remain
    hidden?
Even though all Lights emanate from the Divine Light,
Do not call these Lights Light of God,
It is the eternal Light that is the Light of God.
The ephemeral light is only the attribute of the body
    and the flesh,
It is the infernal Light that glitters in the eyes of
    creatures,
Except for those for whom
God himself has anointed their eyes with kohl.
For His friend Abraham his fire became Light,
The eyes of intelligence are ignorant as the donkey's.
Oh Lord God, who graces the gift of vision,
This bird of vision is flying towards you
On the wings of passionate desire.

"Our death is our wedding with eternity," and Rumi's death-day, December 17, 1273, is celebrated by the Sufis as *Sheb-el-Arus*, "the night of the wedding," the night when Rumi merged with his beloved totally, finally, and forever.

During his last illness, Rumi said to a friend who had come to wish him prompt recovery: "When between the lover and the Beloved there is only a poor shirt left, wouldn't you want the Light to unite with the Light?"

So what, then, is the secret of the death Rumi is living out for us? It is in the phrase in a poem that Rumi takes from the *Koran,* "God is one." Rumi puts the quotation in there like a diamond shard, to wake you up. "God is one!" God is neither life nor death, God is neither pain nor joy. God is both pain and joy. Both life and death take place in the eternal flowering that is God. So the secret of death is to become one with the Mind and the Essence of God so that death takes place, as life does, as a passing event in that flowering mind, an event like any other.

Listen now to how a great Indian Master, Nisargaratta Maharaj, at the age of seventy-four, describes what it is to live in absolute consciousness.

> I am now seventy-four years old. And yet I feel that I am an infant. I feel clearly that in spite of all the changes I am a child. My guru tells me that child which is you even now is your real self. Go back to that state of pure being where the "I am" is still in its purity, before it was contaminated with "this I am" or "that I am." Your burden is of false self identifications: abandon them all. My guru told me "Trust me, I tell you you are divine, take it as the absolute truth. Your joy is divine, your suffering is divine, too. All comes from God. Remember it always you are God, your will alone is done." I did believe him and soon realized how wonderfully true and accurate were his words. I did not condition my mind by thinking "I am God, I am wonderful, I am beyond." I simply followed his instruction, which was to focus the mind on pure being, "I am," and "God is one," and stay in it. I used to sit for hours with nothing but the "I am" in my mind. Soon peace and joy and a deep all-embracing love became my normal state. In it, all dis-

appeared: my self, my guru, the life I lived, the world around me. Only peace remained and unfathomable silence.

To me, this is the clearest statement I know of what the absolute consciousness is like, feels like, from within the experience of someone who had realized it.

There is only this moment, always. Rumi and his poem are talking to you at this moment from within this moment, and to share it with him, you must also be within this moment.

> Our death is our wedding with Eternity.
> What is the secret? "God is one"
> The sun divides itself
> Streaming through the different openings of the house,
> But when these openings are closed, multiplicity
>   vanishes.

This is a very rich, very profound description of what life is. Remember that for Rumi, the sun is the Divine Essence, the Divine Light. And the openings are the five senses, and through the five senses, as the *Upanishads* also tell us, the Divine Light divides itself in streams, in all its different functions, playing in its different places. But when these five openings are closed by death, when eventually all the faculties dissolve and the openings are shut, then multiplicity vanishes, all these sensations and perceptions, all of them vanish. The sun that has been emanating all these things then reappears in its unmediated splendor. This is what is taught in the Tibetan tradition. This is what we derive from near-death experiences. This is what the Sufis know. This is what the Christians know. This is what mystics have always understood.

For life to be, the Sun "divides itself up," the Divine Self "streams through the different openings of the house." But when in death "these openings close," original unity reappears.

Multiplicity exists in the separate grapes,
It cannot be found in the juice that comes from the
    grape.

The mystic becomes, through passion, "the juice that comes from the grape," the wine. This wine is the bliss of Unity, the joy and rapture of Unity. And in that rapture, in that joy, in that bliss, all distinctions between life and death, this world and that world, vanish. What is seen and known is only the "I am" burning, the divine unity burning, the rapture of the *Kibriya*.

For he who is alive in the Light of God,
The death of this carnal soul is grace.
About this don't say anything either good or bad,
Because it has passed beyond the good or bad.

Then Rumi turns to us, having given us the secret, and tells us how to learn the secret. It is no good just knowing this poem. It is no good just reading the words of the mystics. What we have to do, all of us, individually, is learn this for ourselves:

Fix your gaze on God
And do not speak of what is invisible
So that into your gaze he can put another gaze.

There is a great mystic secret in that line. All of the senses that are put into the fire of gnosis are subtly and unmistakably transformed by that fire into another completely different set of senses. And when the mind is awakened to the presence of the Divine Light in all things, the eyes change, and into them comes the gaze that you see in Mother Meera, in Ramana Maharshi, in the great Tibetan masters—the gaze of those who know that what they are looking at is not separate from them, that they are looking at reality itself with infinite awareness, infinite compassion, infinite joy, infinite intelligence and understanding.

The moment when this enlightenment takes place is actually very subtle. It is not a grand moment. It is simply as if a

film between you and reality, a very subtle film, is peeled away
and there is no separation between what you're looking at and
what you are. You see all the things that people describe as
solid shimmering in the fire of the *shakti*. You see all living
creatures, from insects to presidents, as you, yourself. And the
fiction of death is over, because the "I" that is looking out cannot die. It is not the dying looking at the dying; it is the eternal looking at the eternal in infinite tender wit, hilarity, and
sweetness.

> It is only the vision of physical eyes
> That construct that vision for which nothing invisible
>   or secret exists.

So long as you're trapped within these eyes looking out,
you're going to be trapped in the universe that they to some
extent create in cahoots with the other senses. And you're going
to believe that nothing invisible or secret exists. But when you
turn the gaze towards the Light of God, and the eyes awaken
to the presence of the Divine Light, and the mind wakes up,
then, "under that searchlight, nothing can remain hidden."
You see into all the corners of the universe. What you know
then is knowledge itself, knowing itself. What you see is Yourself radiating to you in all things, eternally.

> Even though all Lights emanate from the Divine Light,
> Do not call these lights Light of God,
> It is the eternal Light that is the Light of God.

Rumi is making a distinction just as he made before, between
the musk and its perfume, between the eternal Light, the white
Light, the essential Light, the Light that comes up at the moment
of death, the Light that the mystics see every day of their lives
when they are awake, and the light of the world, the light of
desire, even the light of the sun. It is the eternal Light that you
must aim for, because that is where deathlessness lives.

The ephemeral light is only the attribute of the body
and the flesh,
It is the infernal light that glitters in the eyes of
creatures,
Except for those for whom
God himself has anointed their eyes with kohl.

Those "anointed with kohl" are the ones who have established a passionate relationship between lover and beloved, so God himself comes down and anoints them with vision and they can see the true nature of reality.

For the mystic, for the anointed one who is awake, the fire of death becomes a supreme experience of love and absorption, just as the fire into which Abraham was cast became a rose garden and smelled sweet to him. To the one who enters the true fire of mystic awareness, everything that before seemed terrible and horrible will be revealed to him as a rose garden, will show its face of love.

Oh Lord God, who graces the gift of vision,
This bird of vision is flying towards you
On the wings of passionate desire.

Rumi gives the truth at the beginning, then he tells you how to get to that truth. And then at the end he admits his own vulnerability, that he, too, is still searching for the vision that he knows is real, but which is not always stable in him. The poem ends with this invocation to the Giver of visions, that the vision may remain always stable, and a celebration of that mystical passion that is the core of true peace.

In an essential sense, then, all of Rumi's life was a dying, a preparation for the final death-into-life, in Shams, in God. Rumi knew this when he began the sixth book of the *Mathnawi*, his great epic poem cycle. He knew this would be the last part of the great work of his life. He was exhausted after a life in which he had reached the most ardent imaginable heights of spiritual love. After living the fiercest longing, the

deepest homelessness, and final spiritual union, and after pouring out more than 30,000 verses of lyric poetry, more than
26,000 verses of didactic poetry, talking to his friends as noted
down in the *Discourses,* composing numerous letters for the
benefit of his countrymen, Rumi felt tired.

There's another reason for the exhaustion of a great spirit
like Rumi's. It is difficult to imagine how painful and difficult
it is to remain absolutely unprotected, as you are in final awareness, in a world full of agony that devours you, in various
ways, at every moment. Rumi must have felt exhausted because
his entire life had been an invitation to a feast—the feast that
had been Rumi himself, his work, his presence, his being. This
incessant outpouring had exhausted him. I think he was not
only tired, but was longing to go home, to be one beyond all
separation, with the Beloved.

There must have been evenings when he prayed, "Let me
go now. Let me come back to you now, Shams. I have done
everything I could, I have given everything away that you gave
me, and I want to come home."

The political situation in Anatolia grew more disastrous
every year, the Mongols more and more violent and omnipotent. Rumi complains about the misbehavior of soldiers who
break into houses and about the triviality, hysteria, and fear
all around him. Despite everything he had done, despite the
wisdom he had poured out, despite the endless attempts at rec-
onciling everybody, despite all this the madness of the world
raged on.

In the autumnal days of 1273, Rumi started to fade away.
The physicians despaired of diagnosing his illness. One of the
most mysterious aspects of Rumi's last illness is that his physicians never knew what it was. They found water in his side,
but otherwise only an overall weakness. Friends, disciples, and
colleagues came to call upon him; he consoled them all, reciting poems about death as the door towards new life. When a
friend came to visit him in his last illness and said he was praying for his recovery, Rumi recited:

Why should I be unhappy,
Because each parcel of my being is in full bloom?
Why should I not leave this pit?
Haven't I got a solid rope?
I constructed a pigeon house for the pigeons of the soul.
Oh bird of my soul, fly away now,
For I possess a hundred fortified towers.

There were earthquakes as he lay dying. On December 17, 1273, at sunset, Rumi left his body and his soul flew at last into Shams' Sun.

The whole of his world, the whole of Konya mourned him as a saint, a prophet, a sign of love that transcended all religious dogma. Aflaki describes the extraordinary outpouring of universal grief and spiritual passion at Rumi's funeral:

> After they had brought the corpse on a stretcher, the totality of the people, rich and poor alike, uncovered their heads. Women, men, children, everyone was there. There was such an uproar you might imagine it was the day of the Great Resurrection. Everyone was crying and most of the men were walking and wailing, tearing their robes, their bodies bare. The members of all communities and cultures were present: Christians, Jews, Greeks, Arabs, Turks, etc. They were walking in front, each holding high their holy book. Each was reading the Psalms, the Pentateuch or the Gospels, according to their faith. So great was the jostling and lamenting that the Moslems could not restrain them with canes or swords. The wild thunderous tumult was soon heard by the Sultan and his Emir Pervane, who sent for the leaders of these denominations and asked them why they were so deeply moved when the one they were mourning was the *imam* of the Moslems. They answered: "When we saw Rumi, we understood the real nature of Christ, of Moses, and of all the Prophets. We have found, in him, the perfect conduct described in our books as being the conduct of the

perfect prophets. Just as you Moslems claim that Maulana was the Mohammed of our time, so we think that he is the Moses and Jesus of our time, and just as you are his faithful friends, so are we, and a thousand times more, his servants and disciples. Did he not say: "seventy-two sects will hear from us, their own mystery. We are like a flute, which, with a single mode, is tuned to 200 religions. Our master is the Sun of the Truth which has shone on all human beings and given them his favors. Everyone loves the Sun which lights everyone's house."

A Greek priest said, "Rumi is like the bread which everyone needs to eat. Has anyone seen a hungry man run away from bread? And you, how can you know who he was?" The Sultan, the Emir, and all the lords fell silent. The readers of the *Koran* were reciting gently its miraculous verses. It was a painful, somber moment: the muezzins, with their clear voices, chanted the Prayer of the Resurrection and twenty groups of master singers recited the funeral songs that our Master had written himself.

Since that day, Konya celebrates with solemn magnificence the anniversary of Rumi's "wedding night." A *sama* is held in the memory of the Sun who goes on lighting "everyone's house."

If you take seriously this account of the death of Rumi and realize that it extends dignity, glory, and beauty to us all, you'll take very seriously Al-Hallaj's statement, "Kill me, my faithful friends, for my slaughter is my life."

To meditate on death seriously is to understand just how acutely it is necessary to die now, that the moment will come for all of us when we will be faced with the fullness of reality. Unless we know what that reality is, we will be shaken and in terrible ignorance.

As long as we remain ourselves—the story, the biography, the vanity, the self-obsession, the addiction to the body—we will remain within the world of time and space, and death will terrify us, because death is the masterpiece of illusion. As long as we remain alive within the confines of the false self, we will be dead. "Kill me, my faithful friends, for in my slaughter is my life." Every time an illusion is taken from you, every time a vanity is stripped from you, every time humiliation brings you deeper into humility, every time the failure of passion brings you closer to true love, every time an insight into the emptiness of all things awakens beyond all your need to grasp onto experience, every time this happens you die. And every time you die in this way, you come closer to eternal life. "Kill me, my faithful friends, for in my slaughter is my life."

Remember Rumi's remarkable phrase: "Know that your life throws a veil over your path." Our life is constantly tempting us to identify ourselves with it. Every time we identify ourselves with it, we fall prey to the illusion of separateness from other people, we fall prey to the illusion of time and the illusion that we are dying. It's only by dying to that illusion that we can enter reality.

And now this poem of Rumi's, this information that is being given to us by someone who is "one now with the Sun, and lighting everyone's house."

> Look at me! I am your companion in the tomb.
> On that night you leave your shop and your house,
> You hear my salutation in the tomb,
> And you will know then that never ever
> Were you hidden from my eyes.
> I am that spark of intelligence and reason in your breast,
> At the moment of pleasure, at the moment of joy,
> At the moment of suffering, at the moment of misery.
> And on that strange night when you hear the voice of
>   the beloved,
> You will soar free of the bite of serpents or the terror
>   of ants.
> The drunkenness of love will carry into your tomb
>   these gifts:

Wine, the beloved, a candle, meat and delicacies, and
   incense.
In that instant, the lamp of true knowing is lit,
What a tumult rises from the dead in the tombs!
The earth of the cemetery is split open by their cries,
By the beating of the drum of resurrection,
By the glory of the rising of the dead.
They have torn their shrouds to stop their ears from fear.
What is the head, the ear before the shriek of that
   trumpet.
Be attentive to where you look, and don't let error in,
So that the one who sees and the one who is seen can
   become one.
Wherever you throw your gaze, you will see my face,
Whether you contemplate yourself or gaze at this
   tumult,
Give up all deformed vision,
Purify your eyes for the evil eye will then be far from
   my beauty.
Take care not to mistake my human form,
For the spirit is subtle and love is jealous.
What is form? Even with a hundred thicknesses of fur,
The rays of the mirror of the soul make the world
   manifest.
If men had looked for God instead of for gold and food,
You would not see one single blind man astride beside
   the ditch.
Since you have opened a shop in our town
And are showering us with carnations, do not talk,
Shoot out to all of us your lover's glances.
I keep silent and hide the secret from those who are
   not worthy.
Only you are worthy, for me the mystery is hidden.
Come, come, to the east, like the sun of Tabriz.
Gaze at the splendors of victory and the standard of
   triumph.

Rumi's power in his poetry so often comes from changing the pronouns whenever he feels like it and being completely different things. In one line he is the eternal sun, in another he is Rumi, in another he is Shams' disciple, in another he may be anything he chooses. He is continually altering the perspective by changing the pronoun from which he is speaking, so that you are continually shaken from one vision to another in the course of the poem. "I am not just Rumi dancing about here, I will be with you in the tomb, I am your companion in everything, and when you leave your shop and your house, you will hear my greeting in the tomb. You think that I am here and you are there, but one day you will know that you were never hidden from my eyes because I am the eternal I am." It is the eternal consciousness speaking through Rumi, saying look at me, become me. It defines itself, because Rumi always wants to unveil further. See, I am the "spark of intelligence" and the reason in your breast; at the moments of pleasure and joy, I am that which witnesses pleasure and joy, which savors pleasure and joy. I am that consciousness on which all the images are projected. I am "the white screen," as Ramana Maharshi says, "on which all the film is projected." At the moment of suffering and misery, "I am that spark of intelligence and reason in your breast." That's where you'll find the deathless. Then Rumi says, as if already beyond the grave, reporting simply what happens—the whole poem arrives from the "I am" beyond "life" or "death"—

> And on that strange night when you hear the voice of
> the beloved,
> You will soar free of the bite of serpents or the terror
> of ants.

Free of all the nightmare of this world, the ghastly cruelty and calumny, the bitchiness and stupidity, the terror of ants inside your own psyche, the small petrified creatures that run from everything.

> The drunkenness of love will carry into your tomb
>   these gifts:
> Wine, the beloved, a candle, meat and delicacies, and
>   incense.

In an earlier poem he told us that death was the marriage
with eternity, but the drunkenness of God's love for us carries
with it gifts. Wine means divine bliss. The beloved is the presence of the divine lover. A candle, an awake consciousness of
"I am," the eternal consciousness. "Meat and delicacies, and
incense," are everything that the consciousness might need in
which to delight itself, because although the body is being
dropped, Consciousness remains, and the feast of the Absolute
will be even more astonishing when the body is no longer there
to limit the senses. Each development in the poem enchants
you further and further into the rapture of death.

> In that instant, the lamp of true knowing is lit,
> What a tumult rises from the dead in the tombs!
> The earth of the cemetery is split open by their cries,
> By the beating of the drum of resurrection,
> By the glory of the rising of the dead.
> They have torn their shrouds to stop their ears from
>   fear.
> What is the head, what is the ear before the shriek of
>   that trumpet.

In Islam there is the myth of the last day and the last resurrection, but I think Rumi is talking about a much more
important resurrection here, the resurrection of total knowledge, the entry into glory. And then, Rumi goes back to telling
us how to get this awareness.

> Be attentive to where you look, and don't let error in,
> so that the one who sees and the one who is seen can
> become one.

The mirror of the heart can be cleaned through prayer,
through discipline, through deep mystic passion. So that the

whole of reality can tremble and shine without interference, and that you can know beyond any shadow of doubt the innermost meaning of the words, "I am that. I am one with the One."

> Wherever you throw your gaze, you will see my face,
> Whether you contemplate yourself or gaze at this
>   tumult,
> Give up all deformed vision,

Do you want to die in rapture? Do you want to hear the beloved whisper your name as you go into that dazzling light? Then really assume the meaning of this life, the responsibility for this life. Transfigure this life into a slaughterhouse of the ego. Burn away the false self and radiate that love, knowledge, bliss, and joy to everyone. When you *are*, you will never die, because there is only Being.

> Take care not to mistake my human form ...

And Rumi helps you even further, saying don't get obsessed with the master's form, don't be obsessed with Rumi, don't be obsessed with Mother Meera, don't be obsessed with the Dalai Lama—go beyond! The true divine experience is beyond all forms:

> For the spirit is subtle and love is jealous.
> What is form?
> Even with a hundred thicknesses of fur,
> The rays of the mirror of the soul make the world
>   manifest.

Even though there are hundreds of layers of illusions, still the Divine Light streams through them and manifests the world.

> If men had looked for God instead of for gold and food,
> You would not see one single blind man astride beside
>   the ditch.

We're all like blind people, sitting beside the ditch of death, frightened, gazing into it, unable to see what is there. And if

you really had been sincere in your life, if you really wanted
to find out, the divine Light would have helped you, the divine
mercy would have opened your eyes and you would have been
led to a Master. If you really had practiced serious spiritual
meditation, your eyes, your inner eyes would have been open
and you would see the glory of the Light everywhere. Because
it is your birthright and inheritance. But you've done no work!
You have not burned enough, you've not loved enough, you've
not ached enough, not hungered enough, not cried enough.
You have not opened and opened so that the vastness of this
consciousness could arise and become you and you become it.
There is immense pain in the poem, the pain of the enlightened ones who report back from this astonishing country, and
they see that nobody else seems to want to take the journey.
Rumi is not satisfied with simply sending us a report, he is
telling us how to get there. He is *begging* us to get there, because
he knows out of his compassion how miserable our lives will
be and how baffled and ignorant our deaths if this journey is
not taken.

> If men had looked for God instead of for gold and food,
> You would not see one single blind man astride beside
>   the ditch.
> Since you have opened a shop in our town
> And are showering us with carnations, do not talk,
> Shoot out to all of us your lover's glances.

After all this dazzling mystical information, Rumi is still
saying that the true experience is beyond words. You have to
get beyond all this discussion about death, all these poems
about death, you have to get into a sacred and mystical relationship with the divine Master, because that is where you will
find this consciousness. That is where you will awaken to the
divine Self inside you.

> I keep silent and hide the secret from those who are
>   not worthy.
> Only you are worthy, for me the mystery is hidden.

Rumi has just revealed, in a way, the mystery. But he is also saying the mystery is even further than any words, concepts, or ideas can possibly reach. It is too beautiful to be expressed and it can only live finally in a completely realized being, which is Shams. He is still some distance from that complete realization. But the poem ends with a cry, a passionate exhortation:

> Come, come, to the East, like the sun of Tabriz.
> Gaze at the splendors of victory and see the standard
>   of triumph.

If you want to see the "splendors of victory," die now. But to see the "splendors of victory" and to see the "standard of triumph," you have to "come to the East," and you have to die into the sun.

There is a divine order, a divine law, and a divine sacrifice that has to be made to enter that order and to understand that law. There is a divine death that must be undergone before the divine life can be unveiled. As Rumi wrote:

> People shun death,
> But dying before Him is to me like sugar,
> Life without him is my death,
> Glory without him my dishonor.

The reward for that death is to die as Rumi did, and to be able, as you die, to imagine yourself saying this poem:

> When on the day of my death you carry my bier,
> Do not imagine my heart has remained in this world.
> Do not weep over me, do not say, "O how sad, how
>   sad!"
> That would be tumbling into the trap of the devil,
>   and that would be sad.
> When you see my corpse laid out, don't cry out,
> "He has gone, he has gone!"
> For union and meeting will be mine then forever.
> And as you lower me into my tomb, do not say,
>   "Farewell, farewell."

For the tomb veils from us the union of paradise.
My decline you have seen, now discover my soaring
    ascent.
Would setting cause any harm to the sun or moon?
To you, my death seems a setting, but really it is
    dawn.
Does the tomb seem a prison to you? It is the
    liberation of the soul.
Has any seed been sown in the earth that has not one
    day flowered?
Why doubt? Man also is a buried seed.
What bucket would go down empty without being filled?
The spirit is like Joseph, would he complain of the well?
Keep your mouth closed over here, to open it over there.
So that beyond space may thrill your song of victory.

The breath of liberation, the ecstasy of "soaring free" is in that poem. My heart hasn't stayed behind, it isn't attached to anything, it isn't mourning for anything, everything has been accomplished, the work has been done, the love has been given, it has all been given, all of it, all of it, all of it. There is nothing left undone, nothing left to weep for.

Do not weep over me, do not say, "how sad, how sad!"

If you do, you will be the ignorant ones. It isn't sad to die in glory, it isn't sad to die in the consciousness of the Divine Light. If you say it is sad, you will have fallen into the trap of this whole monstrous illusion, and *that* indeed will be sad. When a great Master passes away there should be great celebration and glory, because that being becomes one with the immortal One and radiates throughout all experience.

I was sitting on a cliff overlooking the sea in Big Sur when I heard the news that Bede Griffiths had died. It was the most glorious day, and suddenly I realized that I was being given a message and the message was that the sun, which was rising, had absorbed Bede's spirit and Light into it, and that Bede was shining from the center of that sun to all beings forever. Bede

is one with the Source of Light, while remaining Bede, and that
eternal Bede was smiling at me out of the sun, toward all beings.
I felt him, I saw him, I knew him to be there, one with the One;
himself and yet one with the eternal, like the flames in Dante's
Paradise, like the flames that are St. Bonaventura or St. Francis
or St. Bernard, all flames of one Fire, yet all uniquely themselves. I understood for the first time, really completely, beyond
all words, what Rumi meant when he said:

> When you see my corpse laid out, don't cry out,
> "He has gone, he has gone!"
> For union and meeting will be mine then forever.

Forever.

> And as you lower me into my tomb, do not say,
> "Farewell, farewell."

Don't go through this mournful, boring liturgy of the ego
that doesn't know who it is, that doesn't know what I am, that
doesn't know what life is. Concentrate on glory.

> And as you lower me into my tomb, do not say,
> "Farewell, farewell."
> For the tomb veils from us the union of paradise.

He is one with the One, why are you saying "Farewell,
farewell"? Rumi is in everything around us, he's in that bed,
that tree, this hand—Rumi has become one with every atom
of the universe, consciously, in ecstatic love. And you're saying, "How sad" and "Farewell"? Where do you think he has
gone? Rumi is here! Rumi is here in a way none of us are yet!

Rumi is trying to tell us the most outrageous, liberating
possible truth in this poem.

> My decline you have seen, now discover my soaring
> ascent.
> Would setting cause any harm to the sun or moon?
> To you, my death seems a setting, but really it is
> dawn.

> Does the tomb seem a prison to you?
> It is the liberation of the soul.
> Has any seed been sown in the earth that has not one
>   day flowered?

Again, the simplest images. You see all around you that nature is death and life, dancing together, creating. How could you possibly imagine in this universe, in which seeds that are buried in the earth flower, that you, too, won't flower in some other dimension?

> Keep your mouth closed over here, to open it over there.
> So that beyond space may thrill your song of victory.

What he has done, our beloved master Rumi, has been to die in this life, to tell us of the glory of that death, and then in his own death shows us the beauty of the fearlessness that is born from that death into eternal bliss, eternal life, and eternal consciousness.

> I have died, time and time again, and your breath has
>   revived me.
> If I should die in you a hundred times more,
> Again I will die in the same way.
> I was scattered like dust, and then became gathered up,
> And how can I die in dispersion before your
>   gatheredness?
> Like the child that dies at its mother's breast,
> I will die at the breast
> Of the mercy and the bounty of the all-merciful.
> What talk is this? How could the lover ever die?

How could the lover ever die? If you love the Divine, you love the eternal. And if you love the eternal, then eternal love is awakened in you. And if eternal love is awakened in you, from eternal love springs eternal life, eternal knowledge. And if eternal love and life and knowledge are awakened in you, you become one with the Divine Beloved. And so how can the lover ever die?

What the mystic accepts is death, again and again, a thousand times a day. You never protect yourself from breaking, heartbreak, desolation, despair, the pain of the world, or the terror of the apocalypse. "How could the lover ever die?"

Once your heart has awakened to the glory of this experience, you've awakened to the divine glory which cannot die in you. The glory of your love is the presence of God in your heart and that presence of God will never die. "How could the lover ever die?" That would really be absurd, to die in the water of life.

Rumi wasn't just a very great mystic poet—he lived everything out with this supreme beauty, including his dying. Everything in his life was transformed into a supreme poem. The great poets are those like Christ, like Rumi, who make of their lives and their deaths the supreme poem. Rumi has achieved everything that a man can achieve, on every conceivable level. He was a lover, a father, a poet, and he was a universal being whose enlightenment has perfumed the whole world.

Wasn't it wonderful that Rumi died at sunset. The sun goes down, to rise again. The divine Master leaves his body in the sun, and the sun sets over Konya. So his Beloved was blazing in fire, in red, as he left. That's why when they dance in Konya on Rumi's wedding day, they dance on a carpet the color of the setting sun, the color of blood. If you're a Sufi, you dance in your own blood. Blood becomes sunset, becomes glory, becomes union.

The least sad place in the world is Rumi's tomb, in Konya. These are some of the last words that we have from him:

> When we are dead, seek not our tomb in the earth.
> But find it in the hearts of man.

That's where you find Rumi, he's alive at the core of the heart, because he is love itself, eternal love. And the lover never dies.

Chapter Eleven

In Love, As Love, For Love

I BELIEVE WE ARE all in the last moments of a civilization, and facing a tremendous, indeed, an absolute challenge. It is up to us, up to you and me, to sacrifice our every moment and thought to the Divine so the Divine can act through us at this moment to allow its will to be done. Its will is that this sublime experiment should be saved, that this theater of enlightenment should be saved, and that we, as a human race, should go into a different spiral of evolution. We are free either to turn away from this challenge, or go forward with gratitude, wonder, and humility into what is being offered us. So I come to you with Rumi in my hand and heart because I want to share with you the work of a supreme witness of the heart. I want to share with you the work of someone who really understands what has to be done for the heart to become divine and the will to become focused in the Light. I want to share Rumi's work because I consider him to be one of the most sublime mystic poets and masters who has ever been here. This is the work of someone who is not dead, whose vast heart is now poised over the hearts of the human race in a great outspread of Light, trying to guide us all into that Light. He and all the other Bodhisattvas and enlightened beings are waiting to greet us into that Light.

We are here, on this earth, to learn who we essentially are: children of the divine love and power. We are here not merely to learn that, but to embrace it and begin to act out of the heart of this knowledge. It has never been so important to embrace

that identity and act out of its passion. We are here to learn
who we are, and learning who we are, what could we do but
praise, adore, love, and serve? The meaning of existence is in
praising, in loving, in adoring, and in serving.

This a poem that Rilke, at the end of his life, wrote about
Orpheus, but it is about Rumi as well. It is about all of us, and
our secret reason for being here. This is the Seventh Sonnet of
The Sonnets to Orpheus, from the first section:

> Praising is what matters.
> He was summoned for that,
> And came to us like the ore from a stone's silence,
> His mortal heart presses out a deathless, inexhaustible
>   wine.
> Whenever he feels the gods' paradigm grip his throat,
> The voice does not die in his mouth,
> All becomes vineyard, all becomes grape,
> Ripened on the hills of his sensuous self.
> Neither decay in the sepulchre of kings,
> Nor any shadow that has fallen from the gods,
> Can ever detract from his glorious praising.
> For he is a herald who is with us always,
> Holding far into the doors of the dead
> A bowl with ripe fruit worthy of praise.

When Rilke, Rumi, and all the great mystics tell us with
one overwhelming voice that praising is what matters, it is
because they know that the ultimate relationship on this earth
is one of ecstatic love and gratitude to the earth, cosmos, and
everything that is, despite all pain, and also because of the
glory, challenge, and difficulty of all pain. They know that we
are incomplete and callous, self-absorbed and narcissistic, use-
less to ourselves and to each other, until that moment when
suddenly we understand that we are one with everything that
is, that everything is one with us, and that we are singing always
the song of the one.

Praising is what matters.
He was summoned for that . . .

We have all been summoned for that.

And came to us like the ore from a stone's silence . . .

Until we are awake, ignorance in us is like a stone and life
has this dreadful silence, which only the mystical imagination
can awaken to true speech. When that true speech is awakened, then:

His mortal heart presses out a deathless, inexhaustible
wine.

This refers to Rilke's own life-work, it refers to Rumi, but
it also refers to what we are called upon to do. We are called
upon to dance in our own blood, to burn away in time for
eternity. We are called upon to press out from this mortal, infinitely vulnerable heart a deathless and inexhaustible wine. And
we can only press out that "deathless, inexhaustible wine" if
we are in love, absolutely, with the deathless, with what can
never be exhausted, the Source itself.

Whenever he feels the gods' paradigm grip his throat,
The voice does not die in his mouth . . .

Those lines don't refer just to Rilke, they don't refer just to
Rumi, they refer to *us*. May we all have the courage to let the
Divine find us and when it has "gripped our throat," may we
not let the "voice die in our mouth," but may we testify in our
lives, in our private and public lives, in all the different lives
we lead, to the presence of that paradigm within us. Then the
great mystics promise us that:

All becomes vineyard, all becomes grape,
Ripened on the hills of his sensuous self.

If you can really find in yourself the courage to testify to
the power of the divine Presence at every moment, whether in
happiness or grief, if you can find in yourself the courage to

praise whatever is happening in your life, "pressing out the deathless, inexhaustible wine" of praise; if you can do that, then, by the power and love of the Divine, "all will become vineyard and all will become grape," just as all became vineyard when Lily helped the children die in the concentration camps. We have within us the power to make of our lives a complete offering of praise to God. And we are given in return the power to transform all that surrounds us into vineyard and grape, into living and vibrant fields of grace.

> Neither decay in the sepulchre of kings,
> Nor any shadow that has fallen from the gods,
> Can ever detract from his glorious praising.

Once you have come by courage and passion, by the love of the deathless, and by the extreme experience of the Light in all things to that awareness, then your life is praise itself. There is no power on earth, in heaven or hell that can diminish one note of the song that is your life, because you—in your mortal body and with your mortal heart—are singing the song of the eternal. You are singing God's own song back to God. Singing and being, praising and being, loving and being, have become one. Orpheus' and Rumi's praise belong to the order of eternity. The praise that Rumi invites us to, the praise that is always fighting to arise in us, despite all our misery, self-absorption, and hysteria, despite all our fear of what is going on in the world, that praise springs from the heart of the divine magnificence itself. To be that magnificence, to serve that glory in the spirit of that endless praise, is why we are here.

> For he is a herald who is with us always,
> Holding far into the doors of the dead
> A bowl with ripe fruit worthy of praise.

Our destiny is for all of us to become heralds, companions of heaven and earth, here always. It is up to each of us now to take the call of this divine poet and become divine heralds ourselves to a world desperately in need of our witness.

Rilke also wrote in Sonnet Eight of the first section of *The Sonnets to Orpheus*:

> Only in the realm of praising should lament walk,
> The naiad of the wept-for fountain,
> Watching over the stream of our complaint,
> That it be clear upon the very stone
> That bears the arch of triumph and the altar.
> Look, around her shoulders dawns the bright sense
> That she may be the youngest sister among the deities
> Hidden in our heart.
> Joy knows, and Longing has accepted,
> Only Lament still learns upon her beads night after night,
> She counts the ancient curse.
> Yet awkward as she is,
> She suddenly lifts a constellation of our voice,
> Glittering into the pure nocturnal sky.

Everything around us tempts us to lament. The facts are unspeakable, the situation is terrifying, the people that rule us are mad, the education system is bankrupt, the media is absurd. However, we have the sacrificial passion of the mystics to remind us of something absolutely essential which we must now place at the center of our will and of our heart. This is that "only in the realm of praising should lament walk." Laments that do not end in praise are not worth our time. We are called to a far more difficult and far nobler work.

"Joy knows," Rilke tells us, because when real joy springs deep from the source of joy within our hearts, then we know that it is the only finally real emotion. Nothing else at that moment exists. We soar like birds in its essence, as if suddenly a vast amount of oxygen were released in all the imprisoned cells of our being. We *know.* "And longing has accepted" that there is something that isn't present. Lament still learns, because lament is a preliminary stage to the great act of praising. We cannot avoid lament. Tears must flow to wash away the forces that make the tears. We must mourn so as never to mourn again, we must use the power of lament to wing us to a place beyond lament.

> Only Lament still learns upon her beads night after night,
> She counts the ancient curse.
> Yet awkward as she is,
> She suddenly lifts a constellation of our voice,
> Glittering into the pure nocturnal sky.

From the lament in us that begins so awkwardly and self-absorbedly "counting the ancient curse"—endlessly absorbed in our biography, in the personal miseries we cling to—we suddenly arrive, as if by a mysterious logic, at an inner power that lifts in us a "constellation of our voice." And the pain that we thought would defeat us becomes the energy for a praise that takes us straight into the heart of the heart of God.

Now listen to a translation of Rumi's "Ode 323." This poem is something we all need to etch on our souls and to remember every moment of every day. The poet who is giving this poem to us is someone who knows all the temptations of narcissism, all the temptations of the ego. Be fearless as you listen, and fearlessly offer up everything that prevents praising. To praise is to be awake to what is deathless, and you can only be awake to what is deathless when you no longer identify with what is dying, when you are no longer concerned with the petty hysterical concerns of the dying false self.

> In that moment you are drunk on yourself,
> The friend seems a thorn,
> In that moment you leap free of yourself, what use is
>   the friend?
> In that moment you are drunk on yourself,
> You are the prey of a mosquito,
> And the moment you leap free of yourself, you go
>   elephant hunting.
> In that moment you are drunk on yourself,
> You lock yourself away in cloud after cloud of grief,

And in that moment you leap free of yourself,
The moon catches you and hugs you in its arms.
That moment you are drunk on yourself, the friend
abandons you.
That moment you leap free of yourself, the wine of
the friend,
In all its brilliance and dazzle, is held out to you.
That moment you are drunk on yourself,
You are withered, withered like autumn leaves.
That moment you leap free of yourself,
Winter to you appears in the dazzling robes of spring.
All disquiet springs from the search for quiet.
Look for disquiet and you will come suddenly on a
field of quiet.
All illnesses spring from the scavenging for delicacies.
Renounce delicacies and poison itself will seem
delicious to you.
All disappointments spring from your hunting for
satisfactions.
If only you could stop, all imaginable joys
Would be rolled like pearls to your feet.
Be passionate for the friend's tyranny, not his tenderness,
So the arrogant beauty in you can become a lover that
weeps.
When the king of the feast, Shams-ud-Din, arrives
from Tabriz,
God knows you'll be ashamed then of the moon and
stars.

This poem is written directly to our moment, as spiritual mystical activists at the ending of a world. It flames with the intelligence and passion that we will need to fight to save the world. The poem tells us we cannot at this moment afford narcissism, any drunkenness on ourselves, nor pampering of our individual fantasies and individual lives. What is at stake is the whole human experiment.

We really must keep in mind what Rumi is telling us, "When you are drunk on yourself, you are the prey of a mosquito." You are prey to all your private anxieties, to all the fears that arise out of the situation. But when "you leap free of yourself," you have the Divine power and you can then go "elephant hunting." We must all go elephant hunting. There were times when I first began to talk of Mother Meera to the world. Just as I entered a room to talk about her, I would feel so frightened that I could not imagine how I would get the words out. I was scared because I imagined what people would think of me, this crazy man, talking about an Indian woman who he knew to be the Divine Mother. And only her grace got me through. Before I began I would to say to her, "Empower me now! Give me the Light now, infuse my cells with your courage, your love, your compassion, your power, because I am nothing without you, and with you I don't mind if the room itself is a gas chamber, because I will be dying into you." And it was *this* that saved my life, that gave me the passion to testify to her power, so that now thousands of people can experience what I have experienced with her. That—and always having in my mind the unspoken challenge her presence on the earth is: to give and risk everything. We must, all of us, take up that challenge now and testify in our lives to that glory of God. If we do, if we call upon the divine Light to empower us, we will be given the strength to go "elephant hunting," and we will be given the holy power to transform elephants into the hawks of God; hawks that arise out of fallen grey skin, fly into the sky, and land on the wrist of the emperor.

> In that moment you are drunk on yourself,
> You lock yourself away in cloud after cloud of grief...

The great enemies of this time are apathy and depression, the dreadful, dreary, self-absorbed, narcissistic, endless gloating over all the suffering in the world as an excuse for doing nothing. There are many reasons for this, and we know all of them. But these are luxuries we can no longer afford, because every hour you waste in depression, you are not serving a burning humanity. When that idiotic journalist asked Mother Teresa, "Don't you ever cry?," she said: "I don't have time." She has seen that a true mystical life is one that burns out in passionate, inexhaustible, deathless, pure action, whether in prayer or in loving service. There is no other life worthy of our true birthright, no other life worth living at this excruciating moment. We are given this promise, and you can feel this promise when you read Rumi alone in your room and suddenly the entire room becomes radiant with divine Light or with the Presence of a love that has no name and no end. You can feel the truth of what Rumi says when he says:

> In that moment you leap free of yourself,
> The moon catches you and hugs you in its arms.

The moon catches you, not a star, not a cloud, but the moon itself, the Divine beloved catches you and holds you in its arms. When you have escaped from your private concerns and your narcissistic fears, what opens up is the knowledge that the entire universe is shining with your own shining, with the shining of your own ecstasy and love. At that moment, you are in the Beloved's arms, embracing the Beloved, and being held by the Beloved to its Heart. This moment is one we must all learn to repeat again and again in every hour of every day. It is only from that embrace that the courage will come to embrace the fire of God, and to live in this time as signs of the presence of the fire of God, so that those who wish our destruction may be amazed and awakened into working for the salvation of the planet. It is an extreme time and it requires extreme lives, and extreme love.

When Rumi says, "All disquiet springs from the search for quiet ..." isn't he talking about us, our endless desire to be free from the cares of the world? That won't work. We have to embrace the world, we have to take upon us its suffering, and if we do so with a completely broken heart, that broken heart will be filled with the peace of the Divine.

As you burn out in love and become ash, then the peace that passes all understanding will come, the peace of continually burning away to ash, the peace of being no one, because you have given so much, so deeply, so passionately, that there is no one left. Into that no one, the great winds of silence and love will come. All other kinds of peace are provisional. The only peace that will stay with you is the peace that remains when you have burned out in love.

> All illnesses spring from the scavenging for delicacies.
> Renounce delicacies and poison itself will seem
>   delicious to you.

This really is a call to arms in this time. Renounce the private search for pleasure, renounce the private search for goods and status, renounce them. If you do, then the poison of living now, in a dying world, in a potentially destroyed world, will seem delicious to you, because you will realize that this time is giving you an extraordinary gift. It is stripping you of every illusion and demanding that you decide at the bottom of your spirit whether you are for God or against God.

> All disappointments spring from your hunting
>   for satisfactions.
> If only you could stop, all imaginable joys
> Would be rolled like pearls to your feet.

Give up what you want and what will be given to you are peace, joy, and bliss far beyond anything that you could ever have wanted. When the small ego has gone, then the Divine can appear and give you its epiphanies and astounding graces. And when they come, they give you far more than anyone, even Rumi, could ever express.

Then this fierce and very important phrase. It is a fierce injunction, but a truthful one.

> Be passionate for the friend's tyranny, not his
>   tenderness . . .

Anybody can love God for his tenderness. Anybody can love God for the sweetness of a summer morning or a lover's kiss. It takes a real lover of God to love God in disaster, to love God in 1993, when the world is on the brink of extinction. It takes a real lover of God to go cheerfully into the night of the future. It takes a real lover of God to say, "I bless this terrifying series of choices that you're making me face. I bless these absolutely stripping and scouring sights that you are presenting to me every day: each of them brings me closer to the authenticity of absolute love."

Now Rumi is calling us to immense bravery. The only bravery that matters now is not something that only mystics need, it is the essential form of spiritual action now. Courage like this fueled Gandhi; courage like this fueled Martin Luther King, Jr.; courage like this fuels steadily the inexhaustible passion of the Dalai Lama for peace. Unless we have this courage, unless we have this love, we are not going to be able to awaken the cynical and lost who are destroying the planet, or allowing it to be destroyed. They'll just look to us and say, you can be bought, you can be dismayed, you can be scared. We are not going to be bought, dismayed, or scared. We will be standing in the center of divine love, radiating divine love, and we're not going to care even if we are killed, because we know death is only a moment that passes. It is going to require a passion for spiritual action of which the world has no knowledge yet, if the world is going to be saved. We will need what Rumi has shown us. We will need to really root ourselves in divine passion and divine courage and in adoration—otherwise our entire being will tremble in the whirlwinds and tempests that are about to come.

> Be passionate for the friend's tyranny, not his
> tenderness,
> So the arrogant beauty in you can become a lover that
> weeps.

If you really learn to embrace tragedy and apocalypse, to hold them to your heart until your heart breaks into a million pieces, then you become the "lover that weeps" for the Presence at every moment. You become humble enough to beg in each moment to be filled with Divine Light, its passion and its courage. The more you ask, the more you will be given. The more you implore with your entire being, the more will be given to you. We have all come to this appalling time to really learn, from the depths of our hearts, how to beg the Divine to use us to help this planet live.

> When the king of the feast, Shams-ud-Din, arrives
>   from Tabriz,
> God knows you'll be ashamed then of the moon and
>   stars.

At the end of this heroic effort that we are all called to make, there will be, if we prevail, the most extraordinary transformation of humankind. We know that it is possible because it is beating in all of our hearts. We know it is possible because our lives are full of yearning for it. We know it is possible because nothing else could possibly save our world now. So we also know the truth that when, finally, the dawn of our true humanity comes, when Shams' and the Mother's and Christ's and the Buddha's Sun comes up in all of our minds and hearts and lives, when at last we are at the feast with the King and Queen, we'll be ashamed of the "moon and stars"— all the old ideas, concepts, and fantasies. We will be finally what we are: divine children living a divine life on earth.

> Each moment from all sides rushes to us the call to love.
> We are running to contemplate its vast green field.
> Do you want to come with us?
> This is not the time to stay at home,
> But to go out and give yourself to the garden.
> The dawn of joy has arisen,
> And this is the moment of union, of vision.

> O king, master of this time, awaken from your
>   drugged sleep.
> Straddle the horse of joy, it is here, the moment of our
>   reunion.
> The drum of the coming true of promises is beating,
>   beating,
> The pathway of heaven is being swept, your joy is now.
> What remains for tomorrow is ash.
> The horses of day have put to flight the armies of the
>   night,
> And heaven and earth are full of the purity of Light.
> What joy arrives to the one
> Who has sprung free of this world of perfumes and
>   colors,
> For beyond these colors, these perfumes,
> There are in the heart and soul other colors.
> What joy arrives in that soul, that heart,
> That has fled this world of water and clay,
> Although this water and this clay
> Hide the cradle of the philosopher's stone.

It is 1993 and only Love and action springing from Love can help us now.

> This is not the time to stay at home,
> But to go out and give yourself to the garden.

This is not the time to stay trapped in neurosis and absorption in our private lives. Now is the time to go out and give ourselves to the garden. The garden is the world and other people, the garden is the rose garden of mystery and divine beauty. One garden: one fire: one diamond: one love: one, one, one.

> The dawn of joy has arisen,
> And this is the moment of union, of vision.

Before there can be union, before there can be true vision, there has to be darkness, night, passionate longing, and tremendous grief. And surely the human race has come to the moment, after so much darkness, after so much cruelty and grief, when it really can leap toward the Sun. The joy of the Sun can rise. The secrets of our identity can no longer be known only by a few mystics; they are a feast we can all share, a passion we can all enact. Rumi says:

> The dawn of joy has arisen,
> And this is the moment of union, of vision.

He is saying that as well as catastrophe, there is also this extraordinary possibility now. If you even glimpse it, you have no other choice but to dedicate your whole life to making it happen. This is the possibility of "the moment of union" that the whole evolution of humanity has been so painfully spiraling toward.

> What joy arrives to the one
> Who has sprung free of this world of perfumes and
> colors ...

Leaping free of this world of perfumes and colors, you will come to the source; leaping into the source, you will be infused with the joy of eternity.

> It is the time, it is the time, it is the time, it is the time
> of union,
> It is the time, it is the time, it is the time of vision,
> It is the time, it is the time, it is the time of resurrection,
> It is the time, it is the time, it is the time of eternity,
> It is the time of grace, it is the time of generosity,
> All this, all this is the ocean of infinite purity.
> The treasure of gifts has arrived.
> The brilliance of the sea has flashed forth.
> The dawn of blessing has arisen.
> No, not the dawn, but the Light, the Light of God.
> Whose is this figure? Whose is this face?
> Who is this monarch, this prince?

Whose is this ancient wisdom,
These are all veils and to heal these veils
There are ecstasies of equal power.
The source of these living waters is in your head and
in your eyes.
Busy yourself with your head,
But really this head of clay comes from earth and
That pure head comes from heaven.
O how many pure heads have rolled in the dust
So that you can know that it is on the other head
That this one depends.
The original head is hidden,
This derived one is manifest.
Behold, behind this world there is the infinite universe.
O water carrier, shut your vessel, take wine from our jar.
In this limited world the range of perceptions is narrow,
Take wine from our jar and dance
And dance in the new world.

Dance, become active and passionate divine servants of peace. Active servants of peace are what I am begging you, all of you, to become. We need servant-lawyers, servant-performance artists, servant-politicians, servant-doctors and economists, servant-teachers and scientists, servant-technicians and engineers, servants everywhere, working consciously as channels of divine love and wisdom at every level and in every situation of society. Work tirelessly, in the certain knowledge of the support of Rumi, Shams, and the enlightened beings of all traditions, for the preservation of our world, and for a more merciful future. As Teilhard de Chardin said, "Someday after we have mastered the winds, the waves, the tides, and gravity, we shall harness the energies of love. And then for the second time in the history of the world, man will have discovered fire." And in Rumi's wonderful prayer:

O love, O pure, deep love, be here, be now, be all.
Worlds dissolve into your stainless, endless radiance.

Frail living leaves burn with you brighter than cold stars.
Make me your servant, your breath, your core.

May we never give up hope, whatever the terrors, difficulties, and obstacles that rise up against us. May those obstacles
only inspire us to even deeper determination. May we have
faith in the undying love and power of all the enlightened
beings that have blessed and still bless the earth with their
presence. May the visions of so many mystic masters of all traditions of a future world free of cruelty and horror, where humanity can live on earth in the ultimate joy of union, be realized
through all our efforts.

It is the time of union,
It is the time of vision,
It is the time of resurrection,
It is the time of grace,
It is the time of generosity,
The treasure of gifts has arrived.
The brilliance of the sea has flashed forth.
The dawn of blessing has arisen
What is this ancient wisdom?
The source of these living waters is in your head
    and in your eyes.

I beg you all to look for it there. You will find it very quickly,
if you really ask for it. And when you have found the source
of the living water, bathe in it. Change your life, act in Love in
every dimension: economic, political, and spiritual—in Love,
as Love, for Love—to transform this time of Apocalypse into
the time of Resurrection.

The whole world could be choked with thorns:
A lover's heart will stay a rose garden.
The wheel of heaven could wind to a halt:
The world of lovers will go on turning.
Even if every being grew sad, a lover's soul
Will still stay fresh, vibrant, light.

Are all the candles out? Hand them to a lover—
A lover shoots out a hundred thousand fires.
A lover may be solitary, but he is never alone:
For companion he has always the hidden Beloved.
The drunkenness of lovers comes from the soul
And Love's companion stays hidden in secret.
Love cannot be deceived by a hundred promises:
It knows how innumerable the ploys of seducers are.
Wherever you find a lover on a bed of pain—
You find the Beloved right by his bedside.
Mount the stallion of love and do not fear the path—
Love's stallion knows the way exactly.
With one leap, Love's horse will carry you home
However black with obstacles the way may be.
The soul of a real lover spurns all animal fodder,
Only in the wine of bliss can his soul find peace.
Through the Grace of Shams-ud-Din of Tabriz,
    you will possess
A heart at once drunk and supremely lucid.